LDAP:

Programming Directory-Enabled Applications with Lightweight Directory Access Protocol

Timothy A. Howes

Mark C. Smith

Macmillan Technical Publishing, Indianapolis, Indiana

LDAP: Programming Directory-Enabled Applications with Lightweight Directory Access Protocol

By Timothy A. Howes and Mark C. Smith

Published by:
Macmillan Technical Publishing
201 West 103rd Street
Indianapolis, IN 46290 USA

Copyright © 1997 by Macmillan Technical Publishing

Printed in the United States of America   3 4 5 6 7 8 9 0

Library of Congress Catalog Card Number: 96-78510

ISBN: 1-57870-000-0

Warning and Disclaimer

This book is designed to provide information about the LDAP computer program. Every effort has been made to make this book as complete and as accurate as possible, but no warranty or fitness is implied.

The information is provided on an "as is" basis. The author(s) and Macmillan Technical Publishing shall have neither liability nor responsibility to any person or entity with respect to any loss or damages arising from the information contained in this book or from the use of the disks or programs that may accompany it.

Publisher	*Don Fowley*
Publisher's Assistant	*Rosemary Lewis*
Publishing Manager	*Jim LeValley*
Marketing Manager	*Kourtnaye Sturgeon*
Managing Editor	*Carla Hall*

Acquisitions Editor
Jim LeValley

Senior Editors
Sarah Kearns
Suzanne Snyder

Development Editor
Tim Huddleston

Project/Copy Editor
Mitzi Foster

Acquisitions Coordinator
Amy Lewis

Cover Designer
Sandra Schroeder

Cover Production
Aren Howell

Book Designer
Sandra Schroeder

Manufacturing Coordinator
Brook Farling

Production Manager
Kelly Dobbs

Production Team Supervisors
Laurie Casey, Joe Millay

Graphics Image Specialists
Dan Harris
Laura Robbins
Dennis Sheehan

Production Analyst
Erich J. Richter

Production Team
Trina Brown, Tricia Flodder, Christopher Morris, Megan Wade

Indexer
Eric Brinkman

About the Authors

Timothy A. Howes received his Ph.D. and M.S.E. degrees in Computer Science and Engineering from the University of Michigan. He also holds
a B.S.E. in Aerospace Engineering. He co-authored the Lightweight Directory Access Protocol (LDAP) specification, LDAP Application Program Interface specification, and numerous other Internet RFCs and papers. He also led the team of programmers responsible for the most widely used implementation of LDAP, from the University of Michigan. As Project Director and Principal Investigator for the National Science Foundation-sponsored WINX grant, and Project Leader of the team providing the U-M campus directory, one of the largest and most successful LDAP directory services in the world, Tim gained broad experience as a directory protocol designer, developer, implementor, administrator, and researcher. He remains an active member of the IETF, chairing the Access and Searching of Internet Directories (ASID) working group, continuing the evolution of the LDAP protocol. He is currently Directory Server Architect for Netscape Communications Corp., where he leads Netscape's directory implementation.

Mark C. Smith received his B.S.E. degree in Computer Engineering from the University of Michigan. He has broad experience as a directory services researcher, designer, developer, and administrator. He co-authored the Lightweight Directory Access Protocol (LDAP) Application Program Interface specification and several other Internet RFCs and papers. While at the University of Michigan, he was a key member of the development team that produced the most widely used implementation of LDAP, and he was co-project leader of the team that deployed and maintained one of the world's largest and most widely used LDAP directory services. Mark developed maX.500, one of the first and most popular LDAP directory clients, and he has implemented many enhancements for the LDAP client access library. Mark is active in the Internet Engineering Task Force (IETF), where he participates in the continuing evolution of LDAP. He is currently employed as a member of the Directory Server engineering team at Netscape Communications Corp., Mountain View, California.

munications Corp., Mountain View, California.

Trademark Acknowledgments

All terms mentioned in this book that are known to be trademarks or service marks have been appropriately capitalized. Macmillan Technical Publishing cannot attest to the accuracy of this information. Use of a term in this book should not be regarded as affecting the validity of any trademark or service mark.

Dedication

For my parents, who taught me well. —Mark Smith

For my family, who support me even when they don't know what I am doing. —Tim Howes

Acknowledgments

We would like to thank our management at Netscape for believing in LDAP, and also for their support in writing this book.

Thanks goes to the University of Michigan for supporting our initial LDAP work, and also to the many Internet LDAP users who have provided us with such useful feedback.

Contents at a Glance

Table of Contents

C Lightweight Directory Access Protocol 387

1

Introduction

Everyone is familiar with some kind of directory. From the white and yellow pages in your local phone book to your local library's card catalog, from the Sears catalog to *TV Guide*, these everyday directories provide the means by which people find what they are looking for. In most computing environments users have similar, but often vastly expanded, needs. A directory service allows people to locate other users, resources, services, and information. It allows e-mail to be addressed in a user-friendly way, and resources and services to be accessed with location-independence and selected with ease.

In a widely distributed computing environment such as the Internet, the directory service has an even more vital role: linking people, applications, and resources across machines, networks, and geographic boundaries. The directory provides the means by which users can access their environment from wherever they are, not just from a single machine. If the computing environment is not homogeneous, but diverse in terms of protocol, implementation, and administrative control (as is the Internet) the problems are even more challenging.

Directories provide powerful enabling technology that has the potential to make your life as an application developer and the lives of the people who use your applications easier. System administrators and network managers also benefit from directories, as they make the task of managing users, groups, configuration, and other information easier.

The goal of this book is to provide you with the tools and expertise you need to write Internet directory or directory-enabled applications. The Internet directory protocol is called LDAP for Lightweight Directory Access Protocol. Though other directory protocols exist (as do other e-mail protocols in addition to SMTP, other information access protocols in addition to HTTP, and so on), we will restrict our attention to LDAP, the directory protocol of choice on the Internet. We also mainly restrict our attention to the C/C++ programming languages, though the LDAP API is callable from other languages. We focus on version 2 of the LDAP protocol, but we also include some information on what's likely to be coming up in LDAP version 3.

Organization

The rest of this chapter describes the concepts behind and uses of a directory in more detail, providing some examples of what directory-enabled means in the context of your application. It goes on to explain in general terms what LDAP is and what it can do for you. The next chapter dives right in with a couple of simple yet complete LDAP programming examples designed to get you up and running quickly with something that produces visible results. Chapter 3 steps back and describes the models behind LDAP in more formal detail, and Chapter 4 covers what you'll need to know on the three major platforms (Windows, Macintosh, and UNIX) and most popular development environments to begin writing LDAP programs of your own.

The next 10 chapters present various aspects of the LDAP API in detail. Our treatment is example-driven, with plenty of sample code for you to try out. Each chapter is written to stand on its own as much as possible, so once you understand the basics of LDAP you should be able to skip to the chapter you're interested in without confusion. Chapter 15 explains the basic concepts behind the API and gives a more detailed road map of the entire LDAP API and how our coverage is organized in the subsequent chapters. Chapter 16 presents a larger complete example that pulls together as many parts of the API as possible, showing how they fit together in a fairly complicated sample directory application.

Following the description of the API are Chapters 17 and 18 describing a set of command line tools for accessing and modifying LDAP directories. The tools are complete programs that you can run to learn about LDAP or to perform even relatively complicated LDAP tasks, from searching to adding to modifying information in an LDAP directory. These tools are especially useful for system administrators and others writing quick-and-dirty shell or Perl scripts intended as one-off prototype directory applications. Chapter 17 describes the tools. Chapter 18 presents several complete annotated example applications.

Finally, following the last chapter describing future LDAP directions are two appendices. These appendices include pointers to sources for more information and a reference for the complete C/C++ API.

How to Use This Book

Beginning and intermediate programmers, or those who have the time to spend and want a complete treatment of every corner of LDAP, would do well to start at the beginning and read through to the end, trying out as many examples as possible along the way. More advanced programmers who have experience with other Internet protocols but not LDAP can read Chapter 3 describing the LDAP models, and then pick and choose from the remaining chapters, depending on what sort of directory-enabled application they are writing. Programmers already familiar with LDAP and the LDAP API will certainly find the reference appendix useful, along with sections throughout the API chapters that describe the differences between various versions of the API.

Programmers, system administrators, and even ordinary users of LDAP may find the LDAP models chapter interesting, and will no doubt have fun playing with the command line tools described in Chapters 17 and 18.

What Is a Directory?

The short and not-very-satisfying answer to this question is: It depends. Directories mean different things to different people in different contexts. We'll give a more complete and formal definition of what an LDAP directory is in Chapter 3, but first we briefly take a general look at directories as you may be used to experiencing them.

While directories come in all shapes and sizes, most examples share some common elements that bind them together. Directories are special purpose databases, usually containing typed information. Read access to the directory is typically much more frequent than update access. Some directories do not allow updates at all, although LDAP does. Directory services are distinguished from name services by their ability to search for, as well as retrieve, named information. They are distinguished from general databases by their higher access/update ratio, their lack of transaction semantics, and their limited ability to separate search from retrieval. The concept of "result set," so useful in a general database system, is not often found in a directory service.

Directories may be replicated for improved reliability and performance, with either strong or weak consistency requirements. Directories may include authentication and access control capabilities, or they may only provide world-readable information that does not require such protection.

Many directories, including LDAP-based ones, essentially provide a way to name, manage, and access collections of attribute-value pairs. Where directories differ from one another is in the way in which this information is represented and accessed, the flexibility with which the information can be searched, whether the kinds of information in the directory may be extended, and whether and how the information can be updated.

The preceding paragraphs provide a description of a directory service, not a formal definition. It is intentionally broad, though we will narrow our definition later when we focus in on LDAP directory service, the subject of this book.

What a Directory Service Is Not

Having a directory service capable of storing arbitrary attribute-value pairs is an attractive thing. So attractive, in fact, that you may be tempted to put some things in it that you should not, or to use the directory for purposes for which it is not well suited. So the question naturally arises, "What should you *not* do with a directory service?"

The first thing you should not do is treat the directory like a general database. It's not designed with that kind of use in mind, and you'll likely be disappointed with the results. This means the directory is not suited to provide transaction-based service, cannot generally handle huge numbers of updates, and usually would make a bad engine for an SQL application.

Second, a directory is not a file system. Storing all the files on your system in the directory is probably a bad idea. In fact, any time you are thinking of storing very large objects in the directory, you should ask yourself whether it might not be more appropriate to store only a pointer to the object in the directory, and the object itself in a service more suited to storing and retrieving large objects (for example, on an FTP server or in a file system).

Finally, a directory should not be used unless it's providing your application some benefit. Does the information you want to store in the directory need to be accessed by others? By you or your application from different locations? If it is only to be accessed by one application on a specific host, then there is little benefit derived from storing it in the directory, yet there could be overhead, added complexity, and other factors that argue for a local solution.

Directory-Enabled Applications

For a few applications—those that read, write, or manage directory information as their primary purpose—the benefit of directory-enabling is clear. The applications could not exist without it, after all. But for the vast majority of applications, directory support is ancillary to the application's main purpose, which might be browsing the World Wide Web; sending, receiving, and processing e-mail; organizing information on your intranet; or just about anything else you can think of. It is this latter category of applications that represents the vast majority of potential directory client applications that might benefit from being *directory-enabled*.

A directory-enabled application is one that uses directory service to make its main function more efficient, faster, more convenient, easier to use, and so on. In most cases the application could exist without the directory support, though perhaps at some reduced level of functionality or convenience.

An example of a common directory-enabled application is just about any modern e-mail client. Netscape Communicator, Qualcomm's Eudora, Pine, and most other popular clients provide some kind of address book capability that allows you to maintain a simple directory of names and e-mail addresses. You type in a name or part of a name and the application looks it up in the directory to extract the corresponding e-mail address. Usually the "directory" is a simple file or small database on the same machine as the client, or even more common, part of the application itself, not accessible by any other application or users. Such a directory is called *application-specific.*

If you as a user or system administrator must maintain information about yourself or your users in multiple application-specific directories, numerous opportunities for inconsistency and error arise. With the advent and wide acceptance of LDAP, directories enter the Internet's client server paradigm for the first time in an accessible, open, cross-platform, and easy-to-use way. The Internet model for directory service enables users to exist in a single logical place, accessible from any application. The advantage this gives to your application is substantial, especially when run in an Internet or intranet environment with many users and machines.

For our example e-mail application, the Internet LDAP model opens up a whole new world of additional possibilities. Leveraging the global connectivity provided by the Internet, you could look up someone's address in Australia as easily as you could on your own corporate intranet. As LDAP becomes ubiquitous, so will this kind of directory look up.

But directories can do more than provide simple address books, even on a global level, or logically centralized user management. Directories can provide the means by which people are unchained from their desktops, free to access their computing environment from wherever they choose.

For example, most applications are customizable at some level, allowing people to tailor the application to their personal preferences. These preferences are typically stored in a file on the user's machine. If the user accesses the application from a different machine (for example, from home or a colleague's office), their often painstakingly construct-ed environment is not available. A directory provides the answer. By storing user preferences in an LDAP directory that is accessible from anywhere on the network, users can access their computing environ-ment from anywhere on the network.

Of course, those among you with a more practical mind may recognize that introducing a network transaction to retrieve user preferences every time your application starts up may lead to some new problems. Reading preferences over the network is almost certainly more time-consuming than reading them from a local file. What if the directory server is down or partitioned from your application on the network? What if the directory server is busy and unable to answer your request right away? What if the application being run is disconnected from the network altogether? All of these concerns must be kept in mind when accessing any kind of network service, and directory service is no excep-tion.

Luckily, with careful programming and foresight most of these poten-tial problems can be mitigated or eliminated entirely. For example, to guard against the directory being down or unavailable, a good technique is to cache locally the preferences the application last read for this user from the directory. If the application starts up again and cannot access the direc-tory server, it can simply read the old preferences from its local cache. Changes in the preferences made after the cached copy was read from the directory won't be available, but that is a small price to pay. For disconnect-ed operation, the application can skip the direc-tory step entirely, going instead straight to the cached preferences. These trade-offs are typical with any kind of networked application.

Why LDAP?

As we mentioned earlier, there are other directory protocols out there. Some even run on the Internet. So what is it that LDAP offers that makes LDAP superior? Why is it that LDAP has emerged as the Internet standard directory service protocol? A detailed comparison of LDAP with other directory services is beyond the scope of this book, and largely a moot point anyway as far as the Internet is concerned. The answers come down to four basic areas in which LDAP excels: features, standards, implementations, and APIs.

LDAP is reasonably simple, but provides a wealth of features capable of supporting any kind of application. LDAP offers both access and update capabilities, allowing directory information to be managed as well as queried. LDAP has a rich set of searching capabilities, permitting complex searches to be performed on portions of the directory. LDAP includes an authentication mechanism, enabling the security of information in the directory via access controls. And finally, LDAP is based on a well-thought-out and extensible information model that allows the type of information stored in the directory to be extended dynamically. Many other directory services fail to provide one or more of these features.

LDAP is an open Internet standard, produced by the Internet Engineering Task Force (IETF), the same body that gave the world TCP/IP, DNS, SMTP, NNTP, SNMP, HTTP, and other highly successful protocols. The importance of open standards, especially those produced by a body with a proven track record like the IETF, is hard to overstate, though it may not be readily apparent. After all, if any protocol works, can be implemented, and provides the required functionality, isn't that good enough? In a word, no. Without an open protocol, you, your application, and everyone using it is at the mercy of the company that controls the protocol. Aside from the inevitable competitive advantage this gives the controlling company, it is unfair to the rest of the world as well. What if the company goes out of business? What if they decide to make an incompatible change in the protocol? What if the protocol does not get the rigorous review it deserves and ends up lacking? What if the protocol itself does not work in your environment, simply because it's not one the company supports?

In short, competition is a good thing because it reduces or eliminates concerns such as these, and open standards lead to competition. The IETF standards process is superior to many others because it is based on standardization with implementation. Early in the process, multiple implementations of the proposed standard are developed, and the experience from these implementations is aggressively fed back into the standards process so that the standard can be revised and improved.

There are many implementations of LDAP available, from commercial products to freely available packages you can FTP off the Internet. In this book, we try to assume as little as possible about the implementation you're using, though sometimes we assume features found only in the Netscape or University of Michigan implementations. These are the two most widely used and available versions of the LDAP API. The LDAP API was originally developed at the University of Michigan, and its evolution now continues at Netscape.

There are literally dozens of other LDAP products available, with more in development. This plethora of availability is a result of LDAP itself being simple enough to be implemented easily. Ease of implementation is an important reason for LDAP's success. And it's a nice feature for you and the users of your applications, since it provides more choice.

Finally, LDAP is one of the very few protocols that has become associated with a well-documented, well-known, and easy-to-use API. This makes it almost unique among Internet protocols, which typically do not have associated APIs (except perhaps for DNS, which has gethostbyname() and friends, and TCP/IP, which has the sockets API).

It's important to understand that the API is separate from the protocol. The LDAP protocol is defined in RFCs 1777 and 1778, which are currently Draft Internet Standards. Even though the LDAP API is documented in RFC 1823, it is not an Internet standard. RFC 1823 is *informational*, and the standard status the LDAP API has is de facto. There's no reason another API could not be devised that also gave you access to the same LDAP protocol, just in a different way. However, the existence of the LDAP API, its easy availability, and its de facto standard status have been major reasons for LDAP's success.

LDAP itself and the LDAP API are not without their warts, many of which we will point out to you in this book. But LDAP the protocol and LDAP the API have gotten some basic things right, following some fundamental principles that have served the Internet well in other areas. The LDAP API makes simple things simple, keeping the startup overhead low. This makes entering the LDAP programming game easy, and means that adding simple directory-enabled support to an existing application can be done with low overhead. Yet, the LDAP API is very flexible and the information it conveys is easily extensible. This makes the API also work well when more complicated directory tasks must be carried out.

Getting Down to Business

Armed with this wealth of general information about directories, it's now time to dive in and start programming. If you'd rather learn more about LDAP and the models behind it first, skip ahead to Chapter 3, "The LDAP Models." Otherwise, the next chapter will get you started with some examples that should give you a feel for what LDAP programming is like.

2

A Quick-Start Guide to LDAP Programming

This chapter presents three simple but complete LDAP programming examples geared to get you started right away with some useful, working code, even if you don't fully understand what the code does yet. As you will see, programming with LDAP is pretty easy. The LDAP API was designed to make simple things simple, while still providing enough flexibility and power to accomplish more complicated directory programming tasks with ease. This chapter is designed to give you some real examples that you can get up and running quickly. We won't go into great detail about what's happening under the covers, but as you'll see, it's pretty easy to figure out. Later chapters explain in more detail the calls you'll see here.

Setting Up Your Environment

Before diving into the examples, you'll need to set up your programming environment so you can create LDAP programs. What's required depends on what platform you're working on and what tools you're using, but the basics should be the same. For the Netscape LDAP SDK there is one include file you'll need to install and one library or DLL. For the University of Michigan LDAP SDK, you'll need to install two include files and two libraries, but still only one DLL. Depending on your compiler and where you decide to install things, you may need to tell the compiler where to find the include file and tell the linker where to find the library. The next sections give the basics for three of the most widely used platforms and development environments. In this chapter, we assume you are using the Netscape LDAP SDK. See Chapter 4 for more details and an explanation of how to use the University of Michigan SDK as well.

Microsoft Windows

On Windows 3.1 or Windows 95/NT you need to tell your compiler or development environment where to find the include files and the LDAP DLL. Using Microsoft Visual C++ version 4.2, you can do this by choosing Options from the Tools menu and clicking the Directories tab to set up the include files. On Windows 3.1, add the NSLDAP.LIB import library to your project or Makefile. On Windows 95/NT, add NSLDAP32.LIB. Static libraries are also provided, but you probably want to use the DLLs.

See Chapter 4 for a more complete discussion of setting up your environment to develop LDAP programs.

Macintosh

On the Macintosh, you will need to tell your compiler or development environment where to find the LDAP include files and library. If you are using Metrowerks CodeWarrior version 10, these settings can be changed through the Project/Access Paths dialog box that is accessed by choosing Project Settings from the Edit menu. You will also need to add the appropriate LDAP library to your project. If you are on a 68K family Macintosh, use either `NSLDAP (2i).68k.Lib` or `NSLDAP (4i).68k.Lib`, depending on whether you are using 2 or 4 byte integers. On a PowerPC Macintosh, use `NSLDAPLib`.

See Chapter 4 for a more complete discussion of setting up your environment to develop LDAP programs.

UNIX

On most UNIX systems you can install the `ldap.h` include file in the `/usr/include` directory, or sometimes `/usr/local/include` to have it found by the compiler automatically. Alternatively, you can install it wherever you want and just give your compiler the appropriate `-Idirectory` flag, where `directory` is the directory in which you've installed `ldap.h`.

You can usually install the library, `libldap.a`, in `/usr/lib`, or sometimes `/usr/local/lib`, to have the linker find it automatically. Or, you can install it in the directory of your choice and then use the `-Ldirectory` flag, where `directory` is the directory in which you've installed `libldap.a`.

If you choose to install things in a non-standard place, say `/usr/local/ldap`, you might compile the first example with a command like this:

```
cc -I/usr/local/ldap/include example1.c -L/usr/local/ldap/lib -lldap
```

See Chapter 4 for a more complete discussion of setting up your environment to develop LDAP programs.

A Simple Search Example

Example 2.1: For our first programming example, we chose to write a program that searches for all the entries containing a surname of "Jensen" at Ace Industries, a hypothetical company somewhere in the United States. The program gets all the entries and then prints them out, one at a time. Each entry consists of a name and some attributes. Each attribute consists of a type and one or more values. (More about this in Chapter 3, "The LDAP Models.") Here's the program, with line numbers included for reference purposes only:

```
1. #include <stdio.h>
2. #include <ldap.h>

3. main()
4. {
5.      LDAP                *ld;
6.      LDAPMessage*result,  *e;
7.      BerElement *ber;
8.      char                *a, *dn;
9.      char                **vals;
10.     int       i;

11.     /* get a handle to an LDAP connection */
12.     if ( (ld = ldap_init( "ldap.netscape.com", LDAP_PORT ))
13.      == NULL ) {
14.         perror( "ldap_init" );
15.         return( 1 );
16.     }
17.     /* authenticate to the directory as nobody */
18.     if ( ldap_simple_bind_s( ld, NULL, NULL )
19.        != LDAP_SUCCESS ) {
20.         ldap_perror( ld, "ldap_simple_bind_s" );
21.         return( 1 );
22.     }
23.     /* search for all entries with surname of Jensen */
24.     if ( ldap_search_s( ld, "o=Ace Industry, c=US",
25.        LDAP_SCOPE_SUBTREE, "(sn=Jensen)", NULL, 0, &result )
26.        != LDAP_SUCCESS ) {
27.         ldap_perror( ld, "ldap_search_s" );
28.         return( 1 );
29.     }
30.     /* for each entry print out name + all attrs and values */
31.     for ( e = ldap_first_entry( ld, result ); e != NULL;
32.       e = ldap_next_entry( ld, e ) ) {
33.             if ( (dn = ldap_get_dn( ld, e )) != NULL ) {
34.                     printf( "dn: %s\n", dn );
35.                     ldap_memfree( dn );
36.             }
37.             for ( a = ldap_first_attribute( ld, e, &ber );
38.               a != NULL; a = ldap_next_attribute( ld, e, ber
                ➡) ) {
39.                 if ((vals = ldap_get_values( ld, e, a)) !=
                    ➡NULL ) {
```

```
40.                          for ( i = 0; vals[i] != NULL; i++ ) {
41.                                  printf( "%s: %s\n", a,
                                 ↪vals[i] );
42.                          }
43.                          ldap_value_free( vals );
44.                  }
45.                          ldap_memfree( a );
46.                  }
47.                  if ( ber != NULL ) {
48.                          ber_free( ber, 0 );
49.                  }
50.                  printf( "\n" );
51.      }
52.      ldap_msgfree( result );
53.      ldap_unbind( ld );
54.      return( 0 );
55. }
```

This program does a lot, but it's pretty short—just over 50 lines of code. And it even includes some comments and error checking! You can type it in, or you can get it already typed in for you from the LDAP Web site at http://www.mcp.com/MOREInfo/15787/1578700000. All the examples in this book are available there. Compiling and running the program should produce output similar to the following for each entry in the Jensen family.

```
dn: cn=Barbara Jensen, o=Ace Industry, c=US
cn: Barbara Jensen
cn: Babs Jensen
sn: Jensen
mail: babs@aceindustry.com
objectclass: person
objectclass: top
objectclass: inetorgperson
```

As you will see later, our little 50-line program has produced output very similar to the LDIF (LDAP Data Interchange Format) described in detail in Chapter 17.

The intention of this chapter is not to go into the details of the LDAP API, but it's worth taking a moment to go over the major pieces of this example to let you know what's going on at a high level. The program starts by including <ldap.h>, the LDAP header file. Any program you write that uses LDAP should include this file. It contains prototypes for the LDAP functions and various definitions you'll need.

Next come some variable declarations on lines 5 through 10. These variables are used to reference the LDAP session, receive the results of the LDAP search, and to step through and parse these results.

Lines 11 through 16 initialize and return a handle to our LDAP session, setting it up to contact the LDAP server running on the host ldap.netscape.com at the standard LDAP port of 389. Note that this call does not actually connect to the LDAP server. The fact that ldap_init() does not connect right away allows you to set options on the session before connecting.

Lines 17 through 22 connect to the server and authenticate as the anonymous user. This step is necessary for all LDAP applications.

Lines 23 through 29 actually search the LDAP server for the entries we want. As you can see, the ldap_search_s() routine takes quite a few parameters, the explanation of most of which we will leave until later. For now, just notice the following parameters. The first parameter is the handle identifying the LDAP session. The second parameter specifies the base object of the search, or where in the LDAP directory tree to start our search. Because we want to search Ace Industry, we set this parameter to "o=Ace Industry, c=US". If you have a local LDAP directory, you could set this parameter to the root of your local tree and the hostname in the ldap_init() call to the host running your local LDAP server. The fourth parameter is the search filter. It specifies which entries we want to retrieve, in this case any entries with a surname of Jensen (sn is LDAP shorthand for surname). The last parameter will receive any entries that match our query, assuming all goes well.

Lines 30 through 51 actually step through the entries the LDAP server returns, printing out their names and contents (attributes and values). Finally, the last few lines free up the LDAP entries returned from the search and disposes of the LDAP session handle, closing the connection that was made to the LDAP server.

A Simpler Search Example

Example 2.2: The previous example illustrated how to retrieve and parse information in bulk from an LDAP server. This example shows how you can be a little more selective, retrieving only the e-mail address of one of the entries we retrieved previously.

```
1. #include <stdio.h>
2. #include <ldap.h>

3. main()
4. {
5.      LDAP            *ld;
6.      LDAPMessage*result, *e;
7.      char            **vals;
8.      char            *attrs[2];
9.      int         i;

10.     /* get a handle to an LDAP connection */
11.     if ( (ld = ldap_init( "ldap.netscape.com", LDAP_PORT ))
12.     == NULL ) {
13.       perror( "ldap_init" );
14.       return( 1 );
15.     }
16.     /* authenticate to the directory as nobody */
17.     if ( ldap_simple_bind_s( ld, NULL, NULL )
18.     != LDAP_SUCCESS ) {
19.         ldap_perror( ld, "ldap_simple_bind_s" );
20.         return( 1 );
21.     }
22.     /* retrieve Babs' email address */
23.     attrs[0] = "mail";
24.     attrs[1] = NULL;
25.     if ( ldap_search_s( ld, "cn=Babs Jensen, o=Ace Industry,
     ➥c=US",
26.         LDAP_SCOPE_BASE, "(objectclass=*)", attrs, 0, &result )
27.         != LDAP_SUCCESS ) {
28.             ldap_perror( ld, "ldap_search_s" );
29.             return( 1 );
30.     }
31.     /* print it out */
32.     if ( (e = ldap_first_entry( ld, result )) != NULL ) {
33.             if ( (vals = ldap_get_values( ld, e, "mail" )) !=
            ➥NULL ) {
```

```
34.                          for ( i = 0; vals[i] != NULL; i++ ) {
35.                              printf( "%s\n", vals[i] );
36.                          }
37.                          ldap_value_free( vals );
38.                      }
39.                  }
40.          ldap_msgfree( result );
41.          ldap_unbind( ld );
42.          return( 0 );
43. }
```

This program is even shorter, and is probably more like what you would need to do if you were integrating a bit of LDAP code into a larger application. The basic parts are the same as those shown in Example 1 (declarations, initialization, search, parse), but the differences worth noting start at line 22. The search has a different starting point and scope. Whereas our first example started searching at the Ace Industry entry and covered the entire subtree below it, this one starts at Babs's entry and searches it alone. This is accomplished by setting the third argument of ldap_search_s() to the constant LDAP_SCOPE_BASE.

The filter is also different. Our earlier example was looking only for entries with the surname Jensen. In this example we are not so much searching for information in entries we can't yet name, as we are reading information from a single named entry. The (objectclass=*) filter is designed to always match any entry it's applied to. All entries in LDAP must have an object class attribute.

Lines 31 through 39 parse the result we got back and print out the value(s) of the mail attribute. Note that we didn't have to step through the attributes this time, because we knew which one we wanted. Instead, we called ldap_get_values() directly with the name of the mail attribute. Note also that we are expecting to get only one entry back from the search, a reasonable assumption given that the scope of our search is only one entry.

An Update Example

Example 2.3: Our final example demonstrates LDAP's capability to update information. Much more on this will be said later in

Chapter 14. This example replaces Babs's e-mail address with a new value. In doing this, we introduce the concept of authentication via the `ldap_simple_bind_s()` routine as well as updates using the `ldap_modify_s()` routine.

```
1. #include <stdio.h>
2. #include <ldap.h>

3. #define ENTRYDN "cn=Babs Jensen, o=Ace Industry, c=US"
4. #define ENTRYPW "secret"

5. main()
6. {
7.      LDAP            *ld;
8.      LDAPMod         mod;
9.      LDAPMod         *mods[2];
10.     char            *vals[2];

11.     /* get a handle to an LDAP connection */
12.     if ( (ld = ldap_init( "ldap.netscape.com", LDAP_PORT )
13.         == NULL ) {
14.                 perror( "ldap_init" );
15.                 return( 1 );
16.     }
17.     /* authenticate */
18.     if ( ldap_simple_bind_s( ld, ENTRYDN, ENTRYPW ))
19.         != LDAP_SUCCESS ) {
20.                 ldap_perror( ld, "ldap_simple_bind_s" );
21.                 return( 1 );
22.     }
23.     /* construct the list of modifications to make */
24.     mod.mod_op = LDAP_MOD_REPLACE;
25.     mod.mod_type = "mail";
26.     vals[0] = "babs@ace.com";
27.     vals[1] = NULL;
28.     mod.mod_values = vals;
29.     mods[0] = &mod;
30.     mods[1] = NULL;
31.     /* make the change */
32.     if ( ldap_modify_s( ld, "cn=Babs Jensen, o=Ace Industry,
        ➥c=US",
33.     mods ) != LDAP_SUCCESS ) {
34.         ldap_perror( ld, "ldap_modify_s" );
```

```
35.          return( 1 );
36.      }
37.      ldap_unbind( ld );
38.      return( 0 );
39. }
```

Two new steps have been added in this example. First, lines 17 through 22 perform real authentication, allowing you to prove that you are in fact Babs Jensen, and therefore have the right to change your entry. (If you're not Babs Jensen, don't worry—we give you permission to pretend for the purposes of this example—or substitute your own DN and password if you have one.) Authentication is performed by specifying the entry to authenticate as and the password for that entry. In this case, the password is "secret", though hopefully if it were your entry, you'd choose something a little harder to guess.

Next, lines 23 through 30 set up the modification to make to Babs' entry. We could have specified a whole list of modifications to make by adding extra elements to the mods array, but we are only interested in replacing the e-mail address, which can be done by a single modification. Note that vals, which holds the new value of Babs' e-mail address, is an array. We could have replaced the existing address(es) with several new addresses in one modification.

Lines 31 through 36 actually make the change, reporting an error if anything bad happens. Finally, line 37 closes the LDAP connection and frees up any session resources.

Looking Ahead

So, now that you've had a taste of LDAP programming you know that it is pretty easy to do useful things without writing a lot of complicated code. Most of the remaining chapters show you how to do more complicated LDAP programming tasks, usually with a similar sweet simplicity. But first, it's time to back up and explain the information, naming, and operation models on which LDAP is based. The next chapter does this.

3

The LDAP Models

N ow that you have had a taste of LDAP and some idea of its
capabilities, it's time to take a step back and give a more formal definition of LDAP and the models on which it is based.
We begin with a short discussion of the history of LDAP and then
move on to describe the LDAP information, naming, functional, and
security models. Throughout our discussion of these models, we will tie
the concepts introduced to the appropriate parts of the LDAP API.

The goal of this chapter is to give you a general understanding of
LDAP from a perspective independent of the API. Armed with this
broader knowledge, the concepts expressed in the LDAP API and described in detail in later chapters will be easier to understand.

A Brief History of LDAP

LDAP is the Lightweight Directory Access Protocol. As the name suggests, LDAP was originally developed as a lightweight front end to the X.500 Directory Access Protocol. Born out of earlier work with two protocols called DIXIE (defined in RFC 1249) and DAS (defined in RFC 1202), LDAP was developed first by the IETF OSI-DS working group, and later by the IETF ASID working group as a standard replacement for these lightweight X.500 access protocols. The early developers of the LDAP specification were Wengyik Yeong, Steve Kille, Colin Robbins, and one of the authors (Tim), though many other working group participants have also made important contributions.

X.500 is the OSI directory service. Like many other parts of OSI, X.500 incorporates many fine ideas. Unfortunately, X.500 has proven to be not well-suited to implementation and deployment on the Internet. X.500's complexity and heavyweight nature led to implementations that were hard to use and required more computing horsepower than most users have on their desktops.

Enter LDAP, which was designed to provide access to 90 percent of the functionality of full X.500, at 10 percent of the cost. LDAP was remarkably effective at achieving this goal. LDAP accomplished this remarkable feat by making four simplifications to the X.500 approach in the following areas.

- **Transport.** LDAP runs directly over TCP, bypassing much of the upper-layer overhead of the OSI multi-layer communications stack.

- **Functionality.** LDAP simplifies the functionality provided by X.500, leaving out little-used features and redundant operations.

- **Data representation.** LDAP represents most data elements using simple string formats, which are easier to process than X.500's more complicated and highly structured representation.

- **Encoding.** LDAP encodes data for transport over networks using a simplified version of the same encoding rules used by X.500.

When used in the LDAP environment, a client's interaction with X.500 is typically achieved through the use of an intermediate LDAP server functioning as a gateway. This configuration is shown in Figure 3.1.

Figure 3.1

LDAP front end to X.500 client/server interaction.

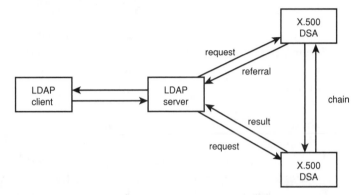

This approach did a lot to spur LDAP (and thus X.500) client development, but server development was still handicapped by the heavyweight X.500 protocols. This situation led to the desire to divorce the LDAP models from X.500 and provide a stand-alone LDAP server that presents a complete LDAP directory without requiring the use of X.500. This configuration is shown in Figure 3.2.

Figure 3.2

Stand-alone LDAP client/server inter-action.

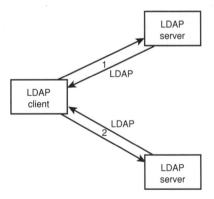

It is this approach that has catapulted LDAP to the forefront of the Internet directory debate. In this configuration, LDAP servers function just like other Internet servers, with similar low overhead and full integration with the Internet environment.

In this book, we focus primarily on version 2 of the LDAP protocol, which is currently a Draft Internet Standard (one step away from Full Standard). LDAPv2 is not without its shortcomings, of course, and work is already well underway on the next version.

So, the history of LDAP is still being written. The IETF is hard at work defining version 3 of the LDAP protocol, designed to address the shortcomings of version 2. Joining the usual team of suspects working on this version of the protocol is Mark Wahl and an even more impressive array of contributors from across the Internet. We'll say more about LDAPv3 later in this chapter and throughout the book whenever it's appropriate. LDAPv3 has not been finalized yet, so unfortunately we can't tell you exactly what features it will include. But when there are features likely to be in LDAPv3 that address some deficiency we've pointed out with LDAPv2, we'll be sure to point them out.

Overview of the LDAP Models

LDAP defines four basic models that fully describe its operation, what can be stored in LDAP directories, and what can be done with it. These models include:

- An information model, defining what kind of information can be stored in an LDAP directory.

- A naming model, defining how information in an LDAP directory can be organized and referenced.

- A functional model, defining what can be done with the information in an LDAP directory, and how it can be accessed and updated.

- A security model, defining how the information in an LDAP directory can be protected from unauthorized access or modification.

The next sections describe each of these models in detail, along with sections on the format of LDAP names and the use of referrals in LDAP.

Information Model

The LDAP information model is centered around the *entry*. While there is no requirement for it, entries often are created in the directory to hold information about some object or concept in the real world (for example, a person, an organization, or a printer). Entries are composed of *attributes* that contain the information to be recorded about the object. Each attribute has a *type* and one or more *values*. The relationship between an entry and its attributes and values is depicted in Figure 3.3.

Figure 3.3

Entries, attributes, types, and values.

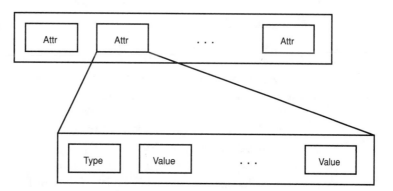

The type of an attribute has an associated *syntax* that defines what kind of information is allowed to be stored in the attribute's values and how those values behave during searches and other directory operations. For example, the attribute cn (short for common name in LDAP parlance) has a syntax called caseIgnoreString that implies lexicographic ordering, that case is ignored during comparisons, and that values must be character strings. The attribute telephoneNumber has a syntax identical to caseIgnoreString syntax, except that spaces and dashes are ignored during comparisons. This allows values such as "555-1212" and "5551212" to be considered equivalent.

Attribute types can also have various constraints associated with them, limiting the number of values that can be stored in the attribute to one or many and the size of those values. For example, an attribute to hold a person's social security number might be single-valued. An attribute to hold a photo might be constrained to a size of no more than 10 Kb, to prevent people from using unreasonable amounts of storage space.

Which attributes are required and allowed in an entry are controlled by *content rules* defined on a per-server basis, or by a special attribute in every entry called objectClass. The values of this attribute identify the type of entry (person, organization, and so on) and determine which attributes are required and which are optional. For example, the object class person requires the sn (for surname) and cn (for common name) attributes, and allows description, seeAlso, and other attributes. This is the LDAP equivalent of what traditional databases call *schema*.

In LDAP, the schema in force in a particular entry may be changed by adding new object classes to the entry. One of the entry's object classes—the one that determines what kind of entry it is—is called the *structural* object class and cannot be changed. Other object classes are called *auxiliary* and may be added to or deleted from the entry, subject to any access control that may be in effect.

LDAPv3 Feature: Sometimes it is more convenient to do away with schema enforcement altogether and add any attribute one chooses to an entry. This is useful in environments where the overhead of defining new schema elements and making both clients and servers aware of the new elements is prohibitive. In version 3 of the LDAP protocol, a special object class called extensibleObject has been proposed to fill this need. If an entry's objectClass attribute contains the value extensibleObject, any other attribute is allowed in the entry, regardless of the schema rules in place.

Naming Model

Though not a protocol requirement, entries are usually arranged in a tree structure that follows a geographical and organizational distribution. Entries are named according to their position in this hierarchy by a distinguished name (DN). Each component of the DN is called a relative distinguished name (RDN) and is composed of one or more attributes from the entry.

To anyone familiar with a hierarchical file system such as those provided by Windows or UNIX, this concept is easy to understand. The RDN is analogous to the name of the file, and the DN is analogous to the absolute path name to the file. As with a file system, sibling entries (entries with the same parent) must have different RDNs. Unlike a file system, both leaf nodes and nonleaf nodes may contain content, or attributes in the case of the LDAP directory.

One difference between the LDAP namespace and a file system namespace is that LDAP names are "little endian" while file system names are typically "big endian." This means that in LDAP, names start with the least significant component (that naming the entry itself) and proceed to the most significant (that just below the root). File system names usually start at the root and proceed down to a file or directory. This difference is syntactic only, not semantic.

Another syntactic difference is in the separators used between components of the name. Your file system may use a forward '/' or backward '\' slash to separate components of a name. In LDAP, name components are separated by commas ','. For example, you might have a file named "/usr/local/ldap/include/ldap.h". Your LDAP entry might be named "cn=Joe User, o=Ace Industry, c=US". The next section describes the format of distinguished names in more detail.

Alias entries, which point to other entries, are allowed, circumventing the hierarchy. Figure 3.4 depicts the relationship among entries, attributes, and values, and shows how entries are arranged into a tree. In this example, the expanded entry has RDN "o=XYZ" and DN "o=XYZ, c=US".

It's important to realize that a hierarchy is supported, but not required, by the LDAP protocol. In many applications, the ability to organize information hierarchically is a useful tool. But in other applications, such a requirement may be an inconvenience. The LDAP model is general enough to handle both kinds of applications, because in the degenerate case, a one-level hierarchy can be used as a flat namespace.

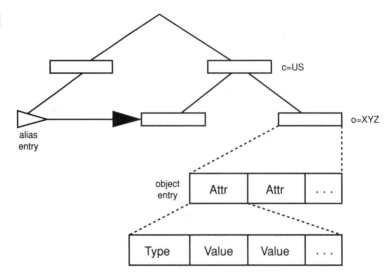

LDAP namespace and information model. The LDAP model is centered around entries composed of attributes that have a type and one or more values. Entries are organized in a tree structure. Alias entries can be used to build non-hierarchical relationships.

Distinguished Names

As described previously, distinguished names are used to name LDAP entries. The formal definition of the format a distinguished name must follow is given in RFC 1779. In this section, we cover the basics of distinguished name format more formally than the casual description previously given.

A distinguished name is a sequence of RDN components, separated by commas ',' or semicolons ';'. Each RDN component is a set of attribute-value assertions, separated by plus signs '+'. The following grammar covers the basic format.

```
<dn> ::= <rdn> | <rdn> <dnsep> <dn>
<dnsep> ::= ',' | ';'
<rdn> ::= <rdncomp> | <rdncomp> <rdnsep> <rdn>
<rdnsep> ::= '+'
<rdncomp> ::= <attr> '=' <value>
<attr> ::= an LDAP attribute type (e.g., cn, sn, mail, …)
<value> ::= an LDAP attribute value of the attribute type
```

If <value> contains one of the separator characters (',', ';', or '+'), the value must be enclosed in double quotes, or the offensive character must be escaped by preceding it with a backslash character '\'. If the value contains a double quote or backslash character, the character must be escaped by preceding it with a backslash.

Examples of some valid distinguished names are given in the following table.

Example DN	Notes

`c=US`
`o=Ace Industry, c=US`
`o="Ace Industry, Inc.", c=US`
	The value of o must be double quoted because it contains a comma.

`cn=\"Quotes\" 'r' US, c=GB`	The value of cn contains double quote characters, so they must be escaped using backslashes.

`cn=http:\\\\company.com,`
`o="Wrong Web Addresses, Inc.",`
`c=US`
	The value of cn (`http:\\`
	`company.com`) contains backslash characters, so they must be escaped using backslashes. The value of o contains a comma, so it must be quoted.

`cn=Babs Jensen + l=Cayman Islands,` `o=Bankers Unlimited, c=US`	Babs's RDN has two components, so a plus sign '+' is used to combine them.
`cn="Babs + Gern",` `o=Jensen Co., c=AU`	The RDN contains a plus sign, and so it must be quoted.

Tip

As you can see, the DN format is actually relatively complicated, especially when you consider all the possible combinations of quoting and separator combinations. Recognizing this needless complexity, the next version of LDAP will likely try to reduce it. You would do well to stick to things that are as simple as possible. Staying away from multi-valued RDNs is a good start, as is settling on commas as the separator of choice for DN components.

There is more to the distinguished name format than is shown here. The complete definition in RFC 1779 includes a facility for representing binary attributes in a DN using a hexadecimal notation, for example. This feature is seldom used.

Functional Model

Now that you know what kind of information can be stored in an LDAP directory and how that information is named and organized, it's time to find out what you can do with the information. Functionally, LDAP defines nine operations in three areas:

- **Interrogation: Search, Compare.** These operations are used to interrogate the directory and retrieve information.

- **Update: Add, Delete, Modify, Modify RDN.** These operations are used to update information in the directory.

- **Authentication: Bind, Unbind, Abandon.** The Bind and Unbind operations lay the groundwork for securing information in the directory. The Abandon operation allows you to cancel an operation in progress.

In the first category, the search operation is used to select entries from a defined area of the tree based on some selection criteria known as a *search filter*. For each matching entry a requested set of attributes (with or without values) can be returned. The searched entries can span a single entry, an entry's children, or an entire subtree. Alias entries can be followed automatically during a search, even if they cross server boundaries. The client can specify size and time limits on the search, restricting the number of entries returned, and how long the client is willing to wait for the search to complete.

LDAPv3 Feature: Normally a server returns all entries resulting from a search to the client. They come back one at a time, but the client has no ability to regulate this flow. With one of the proposed features in LDAP version 3, search results can be retrieved a page at a time, allowing the client to window around in a search result. This kind of interaction is important in environments supporting the popular "type-down" interface found in many e-mail packages, where a user types the first few letters of a name and a scrolling list is presented containing matching results. At the time of this writing, this feature was "on the cusp" of the LDAPv3 feature list, likely to be dropped, because it is more of a bell or whistle.

In the second category, LDAP defines four operations for updating the contents of the directory. The modify operation is used to change the attributes and values contained within an existing entry. It allows attributes and values to be added and deleted. The add operation is used to insert a new entry in the directory. The delete operation is used to remove an existing entry from the directory. The modify RDN operation is used to change the name of an entry.

LDAPv3 Feature: The modify RDN operation can only be used to change the RDN of an entry, making it impossible to move an entry to a new parent. Version 3 of the LDAP protocol proposes a more general modify DN operation, allowing entries to be moved arbitrarily. Entries still cannot be moved across servers.

The final category defines a bind operation, allowing a client to prove its identity to the directory. The client supplies a DN identifying itself and a simple clear-text password. The server does not prove its identity to the client. If no authentication is required, the client can specify a NULL DN and password. The unbind operation is used to terminate a directory session. An abandon operation is also defined, allowing an operation in progress to be canceled. The abandon operation is most useful in canceling a lengthy search operation before it completes.

LDAPv3 Feature: In version 3 of the LDAP protocol, stronger and more extensible authentication mechanisms have been proposed and will almost certainly be included. The weak security provided in LDAPv2 is one of its most serious shortcomings. In the current LDAPv3 proposal authentication can also be two-way, both client to server and server to client.

Security Model

The LDAP security model is built around knowing the identity of clients requesting access to the directory. This information is provided by the bind operation, described in the previous section. Once a requesting client is identified, access control information can be consulted to determine whether the client has access to do what it is requesting.

LDAP does not specify the format or capabilities of access control information. This is an advantage in that implementations are free to design the system most suitable for their needs. It is a disadvantage in that if implementations do not agree on access control, it makes it difficult or impossible to replicate information between the implementations and harder to develop applications that deal with directory access control information that work with multiple implementations.

The Netscape and University of Michigan LDAP server implementations define different ACL mechanisms. The Netscape model allows entries and attributes to be protected. Clients granted or denied access can be specified by distinguished name, IP address, or domain name. The University of Michigan model provides similar capabilities, but in a different way.

Referrals in LDAP

In its original use as a front end to the X.500 directory, LDAP counted on the X.500 directory to be able to resolve all queries and return only the final result or error to the client. This method of operation, where the server you contact either answers a question directly or contacts other servers and asks them the question on your behalf, is called *chaining*. This is the mode of operation supported by LDAPv2.

As LDAP broadened its influence, taking on a life of its own as the Internet directory service, it began to cover directories beyond X.500. In this environment the universally connected global X.500 directory cannot be counted on to provide the chaining service described previously. In addition, the chaining model proved to be too restrictive in the Internet environment. The chaining model implies a well-connected, rigidly controlled infrastructure of upper-level servers, which does not fit well with the grass-roots Internet philosophy that has proven so successful in the explosive deployment of World Wide Web and other services. A new model that encourages grass-roots deployment of LDAP was called for.

Enter the referral model. Unlike the chaining model, the referral model allows a client to ask an LDAP server a question and be told to contact another server. This is called a *referral*. Referrals make it easier to deploy LDAP servers in a highly distributed and administratively diverse environment like the Internet. They also make it possible to construct alternate directory hierarchies, opening a whole new world of possibilities.

As we stated, LDAPv2 does not support referrals. However, both the Netscape and University of Michigan LDAP implementations have worked around this limitation by including referrals within an error message field in the LDAPv2 protocol. The referrals do not bother clients who don't know about them, but open the door to an exciting range of new capabilities to clients that understand them.

One can argue about whether this inclusion of referrals in LDAPv2 is an elegant solution or a bit of a kludge, but there is no question as to the usefulness of this feature. You should be aware, though, that because this is an extension to LDAPv2 and not part of the standard protocol, some implementations may not support it.

LDAPv3 Feature: As we said, there is little argument about the usefulness of referrals. Because of the success the LDAPv2 referral extension has had, referrals are a safe bet to be included in LDAPv3. The LDAPv3 referral support will likely be more formal, though, and not tucked away in a corner of the protocol that should really be used for something else.

From Theory to Practice

Now that the LDAP models have been presented to you in some detail, it's time to focus our attention once again on the specifics of the API that is the main subject of this book. The next chapter dives into the details of the API.

But before we dive into that, a word or two to help you bridge the gap between theory and practice, and to help you better understand what the LDAP models mean to you when writing programs.

The LDAP information model requires you to know something about what can be stored in an entry of a particular type (object class). This is especially important if you are adding or modifying information via LDAP. Without an understanding of the schema rules involved, you are likely to be frustrated in your attempts. Likewise, if you are writing an application to retrieve an e-mail address, you need to know the name of the attribute that contains the information you want (in this case, it's called `mail`), so schema is even important when searching the directory.

The LDAP namespace model means that you typically have to know where in the namespace you want to do anything. This applies whether you are starting a search (you need to know the base object), modifying an entry (you need to know the entry's distinguished name), or adding an entry (you need to know the DN of the entry's parent). This information is key to getting started doing useful work.

Finally, because LDAP is an Internet client-server protocol, you naturally need to know the IP address of an LDAP server to contact. Like HTTP and most other Internet protocols, LDAP has a default port number assigned to it (it's 389), but you may need to contact LDAP servers on other ports. In this case, you'll need to know the port number as well.

Looking Ahead

Armed with the understanding of LDAP you gained in this chapter and the three bits of information about schema, namespace, and IP address, you are ready to enter the world of LDAP programming described in the following chapters.

4

Preparing to Program with LDAP

n this chapter we tell you how to obtain a software development kit for LDAP and how to set up your development tools so the LDAP header files and libraries can be located. We also cover the basics of compiling and linking an application that uses LDAP. Some of the information in this chapter is specific to particular computing platforms, operating systems, and development tools. While we can't possibly cover every possible environment, you should be able to take the information in this chapter and apply it to your own environment without too much trouble.

LDAP Software Development Kits (SDKs)

We use the term *software development kit* (SDK) to describe the set of header files and libraries that are needed to develop applications that use the LDAP protocol. A good SDK typically includes documentation and sample code as well. We refer to the set of function calls provided by the LDAP SDK as the LDAP API.

In this book we discuss two LDAP SDKs: one that is freely available from the University of Michigan and one that is distributed commercially by Netscape Communications Corporation. Because the Netscape LDAP SDK is based on the University of Michigan (U-M) one, these two SDKs share an almost identical API. As we discuss the LDAP API in this book, any important differences between the U-M and the Netscape SDKs are noted.

Both of the LDAP SDKs contain a small set of header files and several libraries. The libraries are available in dynamic form, static form, or both depending on the SDK and operating system used for development. Dynamic or shared libraries can be shared between applications, thus reducing disk and memory use. They also have the important advantage that the LDAP library itself can be upgraded independently of the applications that use LDAP.

You will probably want to install the LDAP header files and libraries in a central place on your system so you can use them for a variety of development projects, but it doesn't really matter where you put them. You'll just have to tell your compiler or development environment where they are.

Appendix A provides information on how to obtain the University of Michigan and Netscape LDAP SDKs. The U-M SDK is free and can be downloaded from the Internet anonymously, but does not include good documentation or sample code. It is also distributed in source code form, so you will need to follow the instructions for building the U-M LDAP software before you can begin developing your own LDAP applications. The Netscape LDAP SDK is currently available to anybody through the Netscape DevEdge web site (you don't have to be a member to get it) and will be bundled with the Netscape Directory

Server. It comes with complete documentation and some sample code. The Netscape SDK features an updated LDAP API that, among other enhancements, allows you to use LDAP from within threaded applications.

Using the LDAP SDK in a Microsoft Windows Environment

The U-M and Netscape LDAP SDKs can be used with Microsoft Windows 3.1, Windows 95, and Windows NT. Each SDK actually contains two sets of libraries: a 16-bit flavor to be used with Windows 3.1 and a 32-bit flavor that is compatible with Windows 95 and NT. The LDAP libraries should be compatible with all standard Windows C/C++ development tools. Our testing for this book was done using Microsoft Visual C++ version 4.2.

When you create a project (or makefile) for an application that will use LDAP, you need to tell your compiler or development environment where to find the LDAP SDK header files and libraries. If you are using Microsoft Visual C++, the list of directories the compiler will look in can be changed from within Developer Studio by choosing Options from the Tools menu and clicking on the Directories tab. (See Figure 4.1.) You will also need to add the appropriate library to your project. Table 4.1 shows the available import and dynamic libraries. Note that the Netscape SDK also includes static LDAP libraries, but these are rarely used on Windows.

Figure 4.1

Configuring Microsoft Visual C++ to find the LDAP SDK.

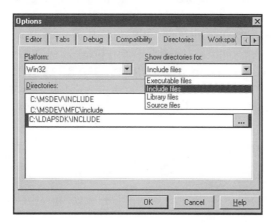

Table 4.1

LDAP Libraries for Microsoft Windows

SDK	Operating System	Import Library	Dynamic Library
Netscape	Windows 3.1	NSLDAP.LIB	NSLDAP.DLL
Netscape	Windows 95/NT	NSLDAP32.LIB	NSLDAP32.DLL
Univ. of Michigan	Windows 3.1	LIBLDAP.LIB	LIBLDAP.DLL
Univ. of Michigan	Windows 95/NT	LDAP32.LIB	LDAP32.DLL

To execute LDAP applications that are dynamically linked, you will need to copy the appropriate LDAP DLL into the directory where the application is installed or into your Windows system directory (usually C:\WINDOWS\SYSTEM on Windows 3.1 and 95 and C:\WINDOWS\SYSTEM32 on Windows NT).

Using the LDAP SDK in a Macintosh Environment

The LDAP SDKs can be used with Motorola 680x0-based Macintoshes and on PowerPC-based Macintoshes. The LDAP libraries should be compatible with most standard Macintosh C/C++ development tools. Our testing was done using Metrowerks CodeWarrior version 10.

When you create the project file for an application that will use LDAP, you need to tell your development environment where to find the LDAP SDK include files and libraries. If you are using CodeWarrior, these settings can be changed through the Project/Access Paths dialog box that is accessed by choosing Project Settings from the Edit menu. (See Figure 4.2.) You will also need to add the appropriate LDAP library to your project. Table 4.2 shows the available Macintosh libraries.

Figure 4.2

Configuring
CodeWarrior to
find the LDAP
SDK.

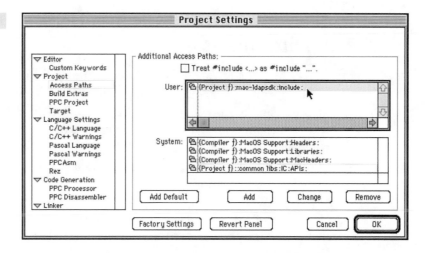

Table 4.2

LDAP Libraries for the Apple Macintosh

SDK	Library Name	Type
Netscape	NSLDAP (2i).68k.Lib	680x0 static (2-byte integers)
Netscape	NSLDAP (4i).68K.Lib	680x0 static (4-byte integers)
Netscape	NSLDAPLib	PowerPC shared
Univ. of Michigan	ldap68k.lib	680x0 static (2 or 4-byte integers*)
Univ. of Michigan	ldapPPC.lib	PowerPC static

*This depends on how you compile the library.

To execute applications that are dynamically linked to the Netscape
shared LDAP library, you will need to copy the NSLDAPLib file into the
directory where the application is installed or drop it into your MacOS
system folder.

Using the LDAP SDK in a UNIX Environment

The U-M and Netscape LDAP SDKs can be used with a variety of UNIX operating systems, including Sun's Solaris, Hewlett-Packard's HP/UX, and Silicon Graphics' IRIX. The LDAP libraries should be compatible with most compilers (our testing was done using the native compiler for a system, for example, the SunPro C compiler on Solaris). For most systems, the libraries come in static versions (`libldap.a`) and shared versions (`libldap.so` or `libldap.sl`).

When compiling your LDAP application, you need to include a `-I` flag that points to the directory that contains the LDAP SDK include files. For example:

```
cc -c -I/usr/ldap/include myldapapp.c
```

When linking your application, include a `-L` flag that points to the directory that contains the LDAP SDK libraries and a `-l` flag for the LDAP library itself. For example:

```
cc -o myldapapp myldapapp.o -L/usr/ldap/lib -lldap
```

If you are using the University of Michigan SDK, you also need to link with the LBER library, which is also part of the LDAP SDK. This library must appear after the LDAP library in the link line. It is not required by the Netscape SDK (the lber routines have been folded into the LDAP library itself). For example:

```
cc -o myldapapp myldapapp.o -L/usr/ldap/lib -lldap -llber
```

If you are working on a Sun Solaris 2.x (SunOS 5.x) system, you will also need to include `-lsocket` and `-lnsl` when you link. Additional flags and libraries may be required on other UNIX operating systems.

To execute LDAP applications that are linked with a shared LDAP library, you will need to install the library into the standard system library directory (usually, `/usr/lib`) or set the LD_LIBRARY_PATH variable (or its equivalent) to point to the directory where the LDAP shared library is installed. If you want to statically link to the LDAP library, you will want to consult your compiler documentation for the appropriate flag to use. You can force the linker to use the static library by deleting the shared LDAP library or moving it out of the way before you link your program.

A Word About LDAP Directory Servers

To test any of the sample code included in this book or to test and debug your own LDAP-enabled applications, you will need to have access to an LDAP directory server. If your organization is already running an LDAP directory server, you are in luck. If not, you will want to obtain and install one yourself.

A number of different LDAP servers are available, including a completely free version from the University of Michigan that runs on a variety of UNIX systems. Netscape sells an LDAP Directory Server that runs on Windows NT as well as many UNIX systems. There are other vendors who sell directory servers that respond to the LDAP protocol as well, including many vendors of X.500 software. Appendix A includes some pointers to help you locate directory server software.

Looking Ahead

Now that you have obtained an LDAP SDK and learned how to configure your development tools to use it, you should be ready to learn about the LDAP API itself. The next chapter begins this journey by providing an overview of the API. Subsequent chapters explore in detail the function calls that make up the various parts of the API.

CHAPTER 5

Overview of the LDAP API

T he LDAP programmer's API includes more than 50 distinct functions. While this is not a great many compared to the APIs provided by operating systems such as UNIX, MacOS, and Microsoft Windows, understanding and using a programming API is easier if it is broken down into manageable pieces. In this book, we use an example and task-driven approach to explain how to use the LDAP API. In this chapter the API is introduced along with some concepts that aid in understanding the API.

The Core LDAP Functions

One way to categorize the LDAP API is by separating the functions that are used to initiate LDAP protocol operations and receive results over the network from those that do other things. It may surprise you to learn that relatively few of the LDAP API calls actually send or receive data over the network. Those functions that do include the following:

Function	Description
ldap_search()	Searches for directory entries
ldap_compare()	Sees if an entry contains a given attribute value
ldap_bind()	Authenticates (prove your identity) to a directory server
ldap_unbind()	Terminates an LDAP session
ldap_modify()	Makes changes to an existing directory entry
ldap_add()	Adds a new directory entry
ldap_delete()	Deletes an existing directory entry
ldap_modrdn()	Renames an existing directory entry
ldap_result()	Retrieves the result(s) of one of the previous operations

These functions map almost one-to-one onto the operations supported in the Lightweight Directory Access Protocol itself, and are therefore the heart of the LDAP API. However, you will need to surround calls to these functions with a variety of other calls that are used to interpret errors, pull information out of the entries returned from a search, prepare lists of changes to be performed during a modify operation, and other essential tasks. It is safe to say, though, that nearly all source code that makes use of LDAP will call one or more of the above functions.

Typical Use of the LDAP Library

If you read Chapter 2, "A Quick-Start Guide to LDAP Programming," then you already have an idea what a typical block of code that uses LDAP looks like. The general sequence is as follows:

```
Step 1. Initialize the library and obtain an LDAP session handle.
Step 2. Initiate an LDAP operation, and wait for any result(s).
Step 3. Process the result(s).
Step 4. Dispose of the LDAP session handle obtained in step 1.
```

Note that steps 1 and 4 are required by nearly all applications that use the LDAP library. Typically, these steps consist of one LDAP API call each: `ldap_init()` and `ldap_unbind()`, respectively. Some programmers may want to obtain a single LDAP session handle once when their application starts up and use it throughout their application, finally disposing of it just before exiting. Other programmers will use a different strategy to manage their use of the LDAP library. For example, you could obtain a new session handle each time you need to use LDAP and dispose of it as soon as you are done.

Remember that when you dispose of the LDAP session handle you are closing your connection to the directory server, and re-opening the connection can be costly if done too often. Sometimes the structure of the application itself may dictate the right strategy (for example, it may be convenient in a multi-threaded application to obtain one LDAP session handle per thread). The important point to remember is that every time you obtain an LDAP session handle you must dispose of it. That is, for every call to `ldap_init()` there should be a matching call to `ldap_unbind()`.

Step 1: Initialize the Library and Obtain a Session Handle

The LDAP session handle is of type `LDAP *` and is the first parameter passed to nearly all of the LDAP API functions. Roughly speaking, an LDAP library session corresponds to a single connection to an LDAP directory server (in reality, multiple connections may be opened underneath the covers to handle LDAP URLs and referrals). When you use the `ldap_init()` call to obtain a session handle, you pass the hostname and port of the server to be used. The TCP connection itself is not opened until needed (that is, when some LDAP operation call is made). The LDAP library hides most of the connection-related details from you.

Step 2: Initiate an LDAP Operation and Wait for Results

This is where the network action occurs. First, any work needed to construct the parameters for the LDAP operation to be performed is done. (For example, construct a filter to use for a search operation or a list of changes for a modify operation.) Next, one of the core LDAP functions mentioned earlier is called to send an LDAP request to the directory server. The application then waits for an LDAP result to be returned by the server.

The result includes a result code (typically, LDAP_SUCCESS if all went well) and may include other error-related information. For an LDAP search operation, one or more entries may also be returned by the server before the LDAP result.

This process of initiating the LDAP operation and receiving entries and the result may be done *synchronously* (in which case a single LDAP API function is called) or it may done *asynchronously* (in which case several simple functions are called). This is explained in more detail in the section "Synchronous versus Asynchronous Use of the LDAP API" later in this chapter.

As part of this step, the LDAP result code returned by the server is checked for errors and appropriate action is taken. For most operations, a result code of LDAP_SUCCESS means the operation completed successfully. For the modify, add, delete, and modify RDN operations any other result code indicates that the library or LDAP server failed to perform the requested directory modification. The compare operation uses two special codes to indicate the result of the comparison. The LDAP search operation may return one or more entries even though an error result is returned. This essentially means that only some of the available entries were examined during the search, and your application must decide whether this should be treated as an error or not.

Step 3: Process the Result(s)

Step 3 is where your application makes use of the data that was returned. For all operations except search, there is probably very little work to do here. Because the search operation returns directory entries, your application will want to parse the entries to pull out information returned from the directory server.

For example, if the purpose of the LDAP search operation was to obtain a person's e-mail address, you will want to call ldap_get_values() to obtain the e-mail address attribute value from the entry. If the purpose of the search operation was to obtain and print the names of a list of entries, you will want to call ldap_first_entry() and ldap_next_entry() to step through the entries, calling ldap_get_dn() on each entry to retrieve its name.

Step 4: Dispose of the LDAP Session Handle

This is done when you are completely finished with an LDAP session, and is accomplished by calling ldap_unbind() as discussed earlier. It is an error to reference an LDAP session handle after it has been disposed of by a call to ldap_unbind().

Synchronous versus Asynchronous Use of the LDAP API

The LDAP protocol is completely asynchronous in that multiple operations can be underway at the same time and the directory server can perform the operations and return results in any order. Each message that is passed in the protocol is tagged with a number, called the "message ID," that is unique for a given session. This feature of LDAP supports complex applications that want to initiate several operations at once, without opening multiple connections to the server.

After an asynchronous operation is initiated, the application must call ldap_result() to check on the status of the operation and retrieve the result(s) sent by the LDAP server. This interaction is shown in Figure 5.1.

Figure 5.1

Asynchronous LDAP API interaction.

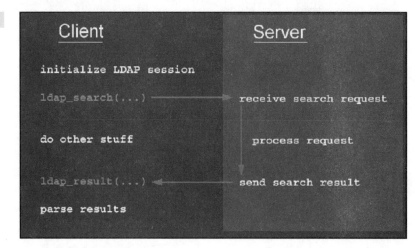

The LDAP API supports this asynchronous paradigm with the core API functions, but also provides a simpler set of synchronous functions. These functions are named so they end in "_s", for example, ldap_search_s() instead of ldap_search(). The synchronous functions combine initiating a request and waiting for the server's response and eliminate any need to worry about message IDs and other details. This interaction is shown in Figure 5.2.

Use of the synchronous LDAP operation functions has the disadvantage that the application will block (wait) until the server completes the request and returns all entries and the final result message to the application.

Figure 5.2

Synchronous
LDAP API interaction.

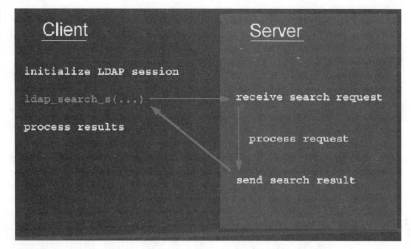

By using the asynchronous API functions, you can ensure that your
application (and users of it) will not be locked out of the opportunity
to do other work while the directory server is handling a request. On
the other hand, for simple applications, you will find it much easier to
use the synchronous calls.

Looking Ahead

The next 11 chapters use an example-driven approach to explain how
to use the LDAP API. Each chapter begins with an overview of the
functions that are presented in the chapter. Then, one or more examples are presented that show how to perform the tasks explained in the
chapter. Next, we include a detailed description of the functions that
are being discussed. Finally, we include a summary at the end of each
chapter that lists the API calls covered in that chapter.

Chapter 6, "Initialization and Configuration," lays the groundwork for
any LDAP application, showing how to get started. Chapter 7, "LDAP
Programming with Threads," lays more groundwork, discussing the use
of the LDAP SDK in a threaded environment. Chapter 8, "Handling
Errors," tells you how to interpret and deal with errors returned by the
LDAP API.

Chapters 9 and 10, "Search" and "Search Filters" respectively, dive into
perhaps the most interesting and useful aspect of LDAP: its ability to

search for, retrieve, and parse information. Chapter 11, "Distinguished Names and Sorting," completes the coverage of search with details on functions to deal with LDAP distinguished names and to sort entries returned from a search. Coverage of LDAP's interrogation functions concludes with Chapter 12, "Compare."

Authentication (usually a prerequisite to changing directory information) is explained in Chapter 13, "Authentication." Chapter 14, "Update," is all about modifying the directory, including adding, deleting, changing, and renaming entries.

Routines for dealing with LDAP URLs are discussed in Chapter 15, "LDAP URLs." Finally, our LDAP API coverage is rounded out in Chapter 16, "Using the LDAP API to Build an Application," where we put together many of the API calls and techniques we've covered in the previous chapters and present a complete, annotated example application.

Chapter 17, "The LDAP Command Line Tools," describes a set of shell- or scripting language-callable tools that let you access LDAP without writing a line of C/C++ code. Chapter 18, "Using the Command Line Tools to Build Applications," provides several complete examples showing how to use the tools.

Finally, we conclude our coverage of LDAP with Chapter 19, "Future Directions," which talks about the future of LDAP and directories on the Internet in general. Seven appendices at the end of the book list many useful LDAP resources you can find on the Internet, and a complete function reference for the entire LDAP API.

The general progression of these chapters is from searching and reading of directory information to the more complex task of adding new entries and changing existing ones. The assumption is that more applications will need to read information from a directory server than will need to change its contents. However, each chapter is designed to stand on its own, so you can skip directly to the chapter that interests you the most without penalty.

6

Initialization and Configuration

As you saw in the quick-start examples that were presented in Chapter 2, the LDAP API minimizes application overhead by limiting the initialization and configuration calls that must be made to use LDAP. In most directory-enabled applications, only a few lines of code will precede the calls that interact with the actual directory server(s). The story on LDAP configuration is similar—because the LDAP library chooses good default options, very few calls to set session options will find their way into most applications. Initialization and configuration are common to nearly all LDAP applications, however, and so these topics are covered before we move on.

All applications that access an LDAP directory server will need to call one of two initialization functions. These functions return an LDAP session handle, which must be passed as the first argument to most of the other LDAP API calls. The basic LDAP bind (authentication) call is covered next because it too is used by most applications. Directory servers usually require a successful bind before other operations (such as search) can be performed. When you are done using LDAP, a single "unbind" call must be made to dispose of the LDAP session. Some of the options that can be changed to alter the behavior of an LDAP session are also described in this chapter.

Like most chapters in this book, this one uses an example-driven approach to present these LDAP API calls. A detailed description of each call is presented after it is introduced, and a summary of all routines covered appears at the end of the chapter. If you are impatient and want to get started right away doing interesting things with LDAP, it is probably safe to skip this chapter and come back to it after reading Chapter 9 on search.

Creating and Disposing of an LDAP Session

Example 6.1: This first example creates an LDAP session, binds to the directory server, and disposes of the session. This example doesn't do anything very useful by itself, but it does show the initialization and cleanup steps that are required by nearly all LDAP applications. It binds to the LDAP directory server running on the host ldap.netscape.com using the default TCP port of 389.

```
1. #include <stdio.h>
2. #include <ldap.h>

3. main()
4. {
5.      LDAP *ld;

6.      if ( (ld = ldap_init( "ldap.netscape.com", LDAP_PORT ))
7.          == NULL ) {
8.              perror( "ldap_init" );
9.              return( 1 );
10.         }

11.         if ( ldap_simple_bind_s( ld, NULL, NULL ) !=
           ➥LDAP_SUCCESS ) {
12.             ldap_perror( ld, "bind" );
13.             ldap_unbind( ld );
14.             return( 1 );
15.         }

16.         /* do some real work here: LDAP search, modify, etc. */
17.         ldap_unbind( ld );
18.         return( 0 );
19.     }
```

The ldap_init() call on line 6 is used to specify the TCP/IP host name and port that will be used to connect to an LDAP directory server. Note that the `ldap_init()` call itself does not actually open a network connection to the server—this will be done by the LDAP library when the first call is made that actually needs to communicate with the server. The `ldap_init()` call allocates a data structure called the LDAP session handle and returns a pointer to it to the caller. LDAP session handles are used internally by the LDAP library to maintain state about open connections, outstanding requests, optional settings, and other information. Generally, you need to obtain one LDAP session handle for each separate directory server you want to talk to, although LDAP referrals and LDAP URLs can cause the LDAP library to open connections to other servers on the caller's behalf.

The first argument to `ldap_init()` is a string that names the host or IP address of the directory server, and the second argument is an integer that indicates which server TCP port to connect to. `LDAP_PORT` is defined as `389` in the `ldap.h` header file. This is the standard port to use for LDAP.

The call to `ldap_simple_bind_s()` on line 11 is used to bind, or authenticate, to the LDAP directory server. This is a synchronous call, which is covered in more detail in Chapter 13. The general differences between synchronous and asynchronous API calls are covered in more detail in Chapter 5. Because no connection has yet been opened to the server, this call will make one before issuing the LDAP bind request itself. The bind operation is used to identify the person or application that is accessing information over LDAP. In this example, two NULL parameters are passed to `ldap_simple_bind_s()` to cause an unauthenticated bind to occur. Because no name or password was provided, the server will not grant any special privileges to our LDAP connection. In effect, we are binding as "nobody," the anonymous user.

Note that in version 2 of the LDAP protocol, a bind step is always required even if only anonymous access is needed. Some servers such as the Netscape Directory Server and the University of Michigan *slapd* server do not require the bind call, but you should always include the bind step to ensure compatibility with stricter LDAP server implementations.

Tip

Most directory servers will allow searching of non-confidential information when you are bound as the anonymous user, but they will probably disallow access to sensitive information and will almost certainly not allow changes to be made to directory information unless you identify yourself.

As you have probably guessed by now, the calls to `ldap_unbind()` on lines 13 and 17 are used to dispose of an LDAP session handle. This call frees any memory associated with the session handle and also closes any TCP/IP connections that have been opened to LDAP directory servers during the session.

The `ldap_perror()` call on line 12 is used in case of error. It is described in detail in Chapter 8 on error handling.

The next section examines the parameters to `ldap_init()`, `ldap_simple_bind_s()`, and `ldap_unbind()` calls in more detail.

Synopsis:

```
LDAP *ldap_init( char *defhost, int defport );
```

Initializes the LDAP library and returns a session handle for use in subsequent calls.

Return Value:

Type: `LDAP *`

If successful, a handle to an LDAP session is returned. If an error occurs, `NULL` is returned and your operating system global error mechanism should be used to determine what error occurred. In the Netscape SDK, the session handle is an opaque data type. In the University of Michigan SDK, the handle is a pointer to a structure that is exposed to your application.

Parameters:

char *defhost*: This parameter specifies the default LDAP server. This server is used for all subsequent LDAP operations except when the LDAP URL calls are used (see Chapter 15) or when referrals are being handled. If this parameter is NULL, the host that the calling application is running on is used. Otherwise, this parameter must be the name or IP address of a TCP/IP host. If *defhost* contains blanks, it is taken as a list of hosts or IP addresses to use (if a directory server on the first host cannot be contacted, the next one will be used).

int *defport*: This parameter specifies the TCP port of the default LDAP server. If this parameter is zero or LDAP_PORT, the standard LDAP port of 389 is used. If you are using the Netscape SDK, you can pass LDAPS_PORT for this parameter to indicate that port 636 should be used. This is the standard port when using LDAP over the Secure Session Layer (SSL); see Chapter 13 for more information on LDAP and SSL.

Tip

Most LDAP servers will listen on port 389 for connections, but for maximum flexibility you should be sure to make the port number configurable by the users of your application.

Synopsis:

```
int ldap_simple_bind_s( LDAP *ld, char *dn, char *passwd );
```

Synchronously authenticates to the directory server using a DN and password.

Return Value:

Type: int

An LDAP error code (equal to LDAP_SUCCESS if the operation succeeds). Error handling and the possible values of an LDAP error code are discussed in more detail in Chapter 8.

Parameters:

> `LDAP *ld`: A handle to an LDAP session as returned by
> `ldap_init()` or `ldap_open()`.
>
> `char *dn`: The Distinguished Name of the entry that is binding to
> the directory. If this parameter is `NULL` or a zero-length string, an
> unauthenticated bind is performed.
>
> `char *passwd`: The password associated with `dn`. If this is `NULL` or
> a zero-length string, an unauthenticated bind is performed.

Tip

> The `ldap_simple_bind_s()` call is just one function within a whole
> family of calls your application can use to identify itself to the directory server. See Chapter 13 for more information.

Synopsis:

> `int ldap_unbind( LDAP *ld );`
>
> Disposes of an LDAP session, freeing all associated resources.

Return Value:

> Type: `int`
>
> An LDAP error code (equal to `LDAP_SUCCESS` if the operation
> succeeds). Error handling is discussed in more detail in Chapter 8.

Parameters:

> `LDAP *ld`: A handle to an LDAP session as returned by
> `ldap_init()` or `ldap_open()`.

Creating an LDAP Session and Opening a Server Connection

Example 6.2: This second example checks to see if a directory server is up and running. It shows how to use the `ldap_open()` call, which is an alternate way to obtain an LDAP session handle.

```
1.  #include <stdio.h>
2.  #include <ldap.h>

3.  #define LDHOST    "ds.internic.net"

4.  main()
5.  {
6.          LDAP      *ld;

7.          if ( (ld = ldap_open( LDHOST, LDAP_PORT )) != NULL ) {
8.                  printf( "The directory server on %s is up!\n",
                    ➥LDHOST );
9.                  ldap_unbind( ld );
10.                 exit( 0 );
11.         } else {
12.                 printf( "The directory server on %s can't be
                    ➥contacted.",
13.                         LDHOST );
14.                 perror( LDHOST );
15.                 exit( 1 );
16.         }
17. }
```

The key thing to notice in this example is that all of the action takes place on line 7. Here we call `ldap_open()` and use a non-`NULL` result to tell us that the directory server on the host `ds.internic.net` is up and was contacted by us. `ldap_open()` allocates and returns an LDAP session handle just like `ldap_init()` does, but it also opens a connection to the directory server.

Using `ldap_open()` does not allow you to change any LDAP session settings before the connection to the directory server is made. Using `ldap_init()` does allow this, because it defers the opening of the connection until the first LDAP operation is carried out. Older versions of the University of Michigan LDAP SDK did not include the `ldap_init()` call at all, but it was added to provide more flexibility to the writers of LDAP-enabled applications in the face of referrals, SSL, and other features.

Tip

> Although in this trivial example `ldap_open()` is the better call to use, the preferred method of obtaining an LDAP session handle is to use the `ldap_init()` call.

The next section describes the `ldap_open()` call in greater detail.

Synopsis:

```
int ldap_open( char *host, int port );
```

Initializes the LDAP library, connect to a directory server, and returns a session handle for use in subsequent calls.

Return Value:

Type: `LDAP *`

If successful, a handle to an LDAP session is returned. If an error occurs, `NULL` is returned and your operating system global error mechanism should be used to determine what error occurred. In the Netscape SDK, the session handle is an opaque data type. In the University of Michigan SDK, the handle is a pointer to a structure that is exposed to your application.

Parameters:

`char *host`: This parameter specifies the LDAP server to connect to. This server is also used for all LDAP subsequent operations except when the LDAP URL calls are used (see Chapter 15) or when referrals are being handled. If this parameter is NULL, the host that the calling application is running on is used. Otherwise, this parameter must be the DNS name or IP address of a host on which an LDAP server is running. If *host* contains blanks, it is taken as a list of hosts or IP addresses to use (if directory server on the first host cannot be contacted, the next one will be used).

int *port*: This parameter specifies the TCP port of the LDAP server. If this parameter is zero or LDAP_PORT, the standard LDAP port of 389 is used. If you are using the Netscape SDK, you can pass LDAPS_PORT for this parameter to indicate that port 636 should be used. This is the standard port when using LDAP over the Secure Session Layer (SSL). See Chapter 13 for more information on LDAP and SSL.

Tip

Most LDAP servers will listen on port 389 for connections, but for maximum flexibility you should be sure to make the port number configurable by the users of your application.

Setting Options That Affect an LDAP Session

The behavior of an LDAP session can be altered by setting a number of options. In the Netscape SDK, the LDAP session handle is an opaque data pointer and therefore you must use the ldap_set_option() API function to set options. In the University of Michigan SDK, the LDAP session handle is a pointer to a structure in which various fields can be directly manipulated to set session options.

Example 6.3: In this example you will turn off the automatic following of LDAP referrals.

```
1. #include <stdio.h>
2. #include <ldap.h>

3. main()
4. {
5.      LDAP      *ld;
```

```
6.          if ( (ld = ldap_init( "ldap.netscape.com", LDAP_PORT ))
7.              == NULL ) {
8.                  perror( "ldap_init" );
9.                  exit( 1 );
10.         }

11. #ifdef LDAP_OPT_ON  /* Netscape SDK:  use ldap_set_option() */
12.         if ( ldap_set_option( ld, LDAP_OPT_REFERRALS, LDAP_OPT_OFF)
13.             != 0 ) {
14.                 ldap_perror( ld, "ldap_set_option" );
15.         }
16. #else                          /* U-M SDK:  directly access LDAP
    ↪handle */
17.         ld->ld_options &= ~LDAP_OPT_REFERRALS;
18. #endif

19.         /* do some real work here: LDAP search, modify, etc. */

20.         ldap_unbind( ld );
21.         exit( 0 );
22. }
```

The symbols LDAP_OPT_ON and LDAP_OPT_OFF are defined by the
Netscape LDAP SDK but not by the U-M SDK. Line 11 in this example tests for the presence of LDAP_OPT_ON to determine if the Netscape
SDK's ldap_set_option() API call should be used or not. If it is not
available, the ld_options field within the LDAP session handle is manipulated directly to clear the referrals option.

Table 6.1 lists all of the LDAP session options. The first column shows
the option name used in the Netscape SDK. The second column shows
the name of the field within the LDAP session handle that is used to set
the same option in the University of Michigan SDK.

Table 6.1

Session Options

Netscape SDK Option Name	U-M SDK Equivalent	Type	Description
LDAP_OPT_DEREF	ld_deref	integer	search alias control (see Chapter 9)
LDAP_OPT_ SIZELIMIT	ld_sizelimit	integer	search size limit (see Chapter 9)
LDAP_OPT_ TIMELIMIT	ld_timelimit	integer	search time limit (see Chapter 9)
LDAP_OPT_DESC	ld_sb.sb_sd	*	network I/O socket
LDAP_OPT_ REFERRALS	ld_option	Boolean	chase referrals
LDAP_OPT_ REBIND_FN	ldap_set_ rebind proc()	function pointer	authentication callback function (see Chapter 13)
LDAP_OPT_ REBIND_ARG	not available	void *	authentication callback argument (see Chapter 13)
LDAP_OPT_ THREAD_FN_PTRS	not available	structure	threading functions (see Chapter 7)
LDAP_OPT _IO_FN_PTRS	not available	structure	I/O functions (see Chapter 7)

* The type of this option is operating-system dependent.

The next section describes the ldap_set_option() call in greater detail.

Synopsis:

```
int ldap_set_option( LDAP *ld, unsigned long option, void
*in );
```

Configures an LDAP session by changing session options. This call is only available in the Netscape SDK.

Return Value:

Type: `int`

If successful, zero is returned. If an option is unrecognized or cannot be set for some other reason, a non-zero value is returned and a specific error code is set within the LDAP session handle. Error handling is discussed in detail in Chapter 8.

Parameters:

`LDAP *ld`: A handle to an LDAP session as returned by `ldap_init()` or `ldap_open()`.

`unsigned long option`: This parameter specifies which option to set. The available options are defined in the `ldap.h` header file and are also shown in the first column of Table 6.1.

`void *in`: The new value for the option. This is declared as type `void *` because the appropriate type to pass depends on what option is being set. For some of the more complex options, you must pass a pointer to a structure that is defined in `ldap.h`. For integer options, pass a pointer to an `int`. For Boolean options, pass `LDAP_OPT_ON` to enable the option and `LDAP_OPT_OFF` to disable it.

Retrieving Current Settings of LDAP Session Options

In the Netscape API, the `ldap_get_option()` call can be used to retrieve the current setting of an LDAP session option. In the University of Michigan SDK, the fields of the LDAP session handle can be examined directly to retrieve current settings.

Example 6.4: In this example a function takes an LDAP session handle and doubles the current search size limit (see Chapter 9 for more information about this option).

```
1. int
2. double_sizelimit( LDAP *ld )
3. {
4. #ifdef LDAP_OPT_ON
5. /* Netscape SDK:  use ldap_get/set_option() */
6.                  int             szlimit;

7.                  if ( ldap_get_option( ld, LDAP_OPT_SIZELIMIT,
                     ⮕&szlimit ) != 0 ) {
8.                          return( -1 );
9.                  }
10.                 szlimit = szlimit * 2;
11.                 if ( ldap_set_option( ld, LDAP_OPT_SIZELIMIT,
                     ⮕&szlimit ) != 0 ) {
12.                         return( -1 );
13.                 }
14. #else
15. /* U-M SDK:  directly access sizelimit field within the LDAP
    ⮕structure */
16.                 ld->ld_sizelimit = ld->ld_sizelimit * 2;
17. #endif

18. return( 0 );              /* success */
19. }
```

The next section describes the ldap_get_option() call in greater detail.

Synopsis:

```
int ldap_get_option( LDAP *ld, unsigned long option, void
*out );
```

Retrieves the current setting of an LDAP session option. This call is only available in the Netscape SDK.

Return Value:

Type: `int`

If successful, zero is returned. If an option is unrecognized or cannot be retrieved for some other reason, a non-zero value is returned and a specific error code is set within the LDAP session handle. Error handling is discussed in detail in Chapter 8. In case of error, the setting of the *out* parameter is undefined.

Parameters:

`LDAP *ld`: A handle to an LDAP session as returned by `ldap_init()` or `ldap_open()`.

`unsigned long option`: This parameter specifies which option to retrieve. The available options are defined in the `ldap.h` header file and are also shown in the first column of Table 6.1.

`void *out`: A pointer to the place to store the value of the retrieved option. This is declared as type `void *` because the appropriate type to pass depends on what option is being retrieved. For some of the more complex options, you must pass a pointer to a structure that is defined in `ldap.h`. For integer and Boolean options, pass a pointer to an `int` (a non-zero value means that a Boolean option is enabled).

Summary

The following table summarizes the routines described in this chapter.

Name	Description
`ldap_init()`	Initializes the LDAP library and returns a session handle for use in subsequent calls.
`ldap_simple_bind_s()`	Synchronously authenticates to the directory server using a DN and password.
`ldap_unbind()`	Disposes of an LDAP session, freeing all associated resources.

Name	Description
`ldap_open()`	Initializes the LDAP library, connects to a directory server, and returns a session handle for use in subsequent calls.
`ldap_set_option()`	Changes the behavior of various aspects of an LDAP session.
`ldap_get_option()`	Retrieves the current value of an LDAP session option.

Looking Ahead

Now that you know how to obtain an LDAP session handle, set options, and dispose of the session, we can move on to more interesting topics. Searching is arguably the most useful feature of LDAP, and you may want to skip ahead to Chapter 9 at this point. The next two chapters lay more groundwork for using LDAP in threaded environments (Chapter 7), and for dealing with errors (Chapter 8).

LDAP Programming with Threads

Until now, all of our examples have assumed a single-threaded access model for the LDAP API. In the University of Michigan SDK, this is the only approach possible without providing a layer on top of LDAP to ensure single-threaded access to the library. This is necessary because the LDAP library is not thread-safe by default. In the University of Michigan SDK separate threads can open and use separate LDAP sessions, but multiple threads accessing the same LDAP session will cause problems without careful synchronization. Even if multiple threads access different LDAP session handles, they must use the University of Michigan SDK carefully, since it is not even thread operative and may make calls to unthread-safe system calls. One of the improvements provided in the Netscape SDK is to make the LDAP SDK thread-safe.

When using the Netscape SDK, multiple threads may safely access a single LDAP session without any special synchronization by you. The use of the LDAP SDK in a threaded environment requires some extra setup by your program, but once this set up is complete, use of the library is no different from non-threaded use.

The next section examines the issues involved in writing threaded programs that use the LDAP library, how the library interacts with your program, and the approach taken to make the Netscape SDK thread-safe in virtually any threading environment. You can safely skip this chapter if you are using LDAP in a single-threaded environment, or if your strategy calls for no more than one thread accessing a single LDAP session handle.

General Threading Issues

There are a number of issues that must be addressed by a threaded library. First, the library must have some way of protecting critical data that must not be accessed or updated by more than one thread at a time. Typically this is done, as in your code, by calling functions to lock and unlock a mutual exclusion device such as a mutex or semaphore.

Given that the LDAP library must work in many threading environments, including yours, this presents an interesting challenge. The library can either implement its own mutual exclusion functions, or it can require the calling application to provide call-back routines for this purpose. The Netscape LDAP SDK uses the latter approach.

The second issue faced by a thread-safe library is the definition of global state variables, such as errno. In a non-threaded program, errno is global to the entire process. In a threaded program, errno is often either redefined to be a function returning per-thread data, or it is replaced by functions that get and set per-thread data.

Because the redefinition of errno is typically dependent on the type of threading model used, this approach is not possible if multiple threading models are to be supported. Instead, the Netscape SDK uses the second option, again having the calling program provide call-back routines to get and set the value of errno.

Third, to be thread-safe or even thread-operative (able to work in a threaded environment even if only one thread is allowed in the library at a time), the LDAP library must be careful to call only thread-safe system and library calls. If it were not, two threads in your program could get in the unsafe code at the same time, even if they were excluded from being in the LDAP library at the same time. The Netscape SDK calls only thread-safe system and library routines.

Finally, the LDAP SDK itself keeps some state that describes the error of the last LDAP operation. There are three pieces of information containing this information. In the University of Michigan SDK the information is kept in the following fields in the LDAP structure.

```
int     ld_errno;
char    *ld_matched;
char    *ld_error;
```

In the Netscape SDK, the information is accessed by calling the ldap_lderrno() routine, described in Chapter 8 on LDAP error handling. This information is similar to errno, except that it is global to a single LDAP session, rather than the process as a whole.

Like errno, these data items need to become per-thread data in a threaded program with multiple threads sharing the same LDAP session. Again, in an effort to assume as little as possible about the caller's environment (and therefore to support as wide a variety of environments as possible) the Netscape LDAP SDK tackles this problem through the use of call-back functions.

LDAP Thread Call-Backs

The call-back functions your program needs to provide to the LDAP library are all contained in the following structure.

```
struct ldap_thread_fns {
  void *(*ltf_mutex_alloc)( void );
  void (*ltf_mutex_free)( void * );
  int  (*ltf_mutex_lock( void * );
  int  (*ltf_mutex_unlock)( void * );
  void (*ltf_set_errno)( int );
  int  (*ltf_get_errno)( void );
  void (*ltf_set_lderrno)( int, char *, char * );
  int  (*ltf_get_lderrno)( char **, char ** );
};
```

The fields in this structure have the following meanings.

`void *(*ltf_mutex_alloc)( void )`: This field is a pointer to a function the LDAP library will call to allocate, initialize, and return a mutex. The LDAP library does not interpret the return value of this function in any way. It simply passes it to the other `ltf_mutex_*()` routines.

`void (*ltf_mutex_free)( void * )`: This field is a pointer to a function that frees a mutex. The `void *` argument will be the result of a previous call to the `ltf_mutex_alloc()` function. The LDAP library will call this function when it no longer needs to use the mutex (for example, when you call `ldap_unbind()`).

`void (*ltf_mutex_lock)( void * )`: This field is a pointer to a function that locks a mutex. The `void *` argument will be the result of a previous call to the `ltf_mutex_alloc()` function. The LDAP library will call this function before it enters a section of critical code. The function should not return until the mutex is locked.

`void (*ltf_mutex_unlock)( void * )`: This field is a pointer to a function that unlocks a mutex. The `void *` argument will be the result of a previous call to the `ltf_mutex_alloc()` function. The LDAP library will call this function before it leaves a section of critical code.

`void (*ltf_set_errno)( int )`: This field is a pointer to a function that the LDAP library will call when it needs to set the value of `errno`. The integer parameter is the value of `errno` to set.

`int  (*ltf_get_errno)( void )`: This field is a pointer to a function that the LDAP library will call when it needs to access the value of `errno`. The integer return value should be the value of `errno`.

`void (*ltf_set_lderrno)( int, char *, char * )`: This field is a pointer to a function that the LDAP library will call when it needs to set the value of the last LDAP error. The three parameters correspond to the three LDAP error-related fields. They are `ld_errno`, `ld_matched`, and `ld_error`, respectively.

`int  (*ltf_get_lderrno)( char **, char ** )`: This field is a pointer to a function that the LDAP library will call when it needs to access the value of the last LDAP error. The return value should be the value of the ld_errno field, and the two parameters, if non-NULL should be filled in with the value of the ld_matched and ld_error fields, respectively.

Threads Programming Example

An example should help clear things up. For our example, we've chosen an application that creates two threads, one that repeatedly searches the LDAP directory, and one that repeatedly modifies an entry in the directory. Not the most realistic application, perhaps, but it should suffice to illustrate multithreaded programming with the LDAP library.

For our threading model, we've chosen POSIX threads. Similar concepts exist in all threading models. Our example consists of four parts. First, there is the main program that initializes things, creates the two threads, and waits for them to finish. Second, there is the function implementing the search thread. Third, there is the function implementing the modify thread. Fourth, there is the collection of call-back thread support routines that are passed to the LDAP library. Each part is presented and explained in the following sections. We've broken up this program for readability, but keep in mind that it is meant to live together in one .c file.

Main Program

```
1.    #include <stdio.h>
2.    #include <errno.h>
3.    #include <pthread.h>
4.    #include <ldap.h>

5.    #define BASEDN   "o=Ace Industry, c=US"
6.    #define MODDN    "cn=Babs Jensen, o=Acd Industry, c=US"

7.    static void thread_specific_setup( void );
8.    void *search_thread( void * );
9.    void *mod_thread( void * );
10.   void *my_mutex_alloc( void );
11.   void my_mutex_free( void *mutex );
12.   int my_mutex_lock( void *mutex );
13.   int my_mutex_unlock( void *mutex );
```

```
14.   void my_set_errno( int err );
15.   int my_get_errno( void );
16.   void my_set_lderrno( int err, char *matched, char *errmsg, void
      ➥*dummy );
17.   int my_get_lderrno( char **matched, char **errmsg, void *dummy );
18.   void *search_thread( void * );
19.   void *mod_thread( void * );

20.   struct ldap_error {
21.           int          le_errno;
22.           char         *le_matched;
23.           char         *le_errmsg;
24.   };
25.   pthread_key_t        key;        /* for per-thread data */
26.   LDAP                         *ld;    /* shared LDAP session
      ➥handle */

27.   main( int argc, char **argv )
28.   {
29.           struct ldap_thread_fns   tfns;
30.           pthread_t                search_tid, mod_tid;
31.           void                         *status;

32.           if ( (ld = ldap_init( "ldap.netscape.com", LDAP_PORT ))
33.              == NULL ) {
34.                   perror( "ldap_init" );
35.                   exit( 1 );
36.           }
37.           if ( pthread_key_create( &key, NULL ) != 0 ) {
38.                   perror( "pthread_key_create" );
39.                   exit( 1 );
40.           }
41.           thread_specific_setup();
42.           tfns.ltf_mutex_alloc = my_mutex_alloc;
43.           tfns.ltf_mutex_free = my_mutex_free;
44.           tfns.ltf_mutex_lock = my_mutex_lock;
45.           tfns.ltf_mutex_unlock = my_mutex_unlock;
46.           tfns.ltf_set_errno = my_set_errno;
47.           tfns.ltf_get_errno = my_get_errno;
48.           tfns.ltf_set_lderrno = my_set_lderrno;
49.           tfns.ltf_get_lderrno = my_get_lderrno;
50.           if ( ldap_set_option( ld, LDAP_OPT_THREAD_FN_PTRS, &tfns )
51.              != 0 ) {
```

```
52.                     ldap_perror( ld, "ldap_set_option" );
53.                     exit( 1 );
54.             }
55.             if ( ldap_simple_bind_s( ld, NULL, NULL ) != LDAP_SUCCESS
        ➡) {
56.                     ldap_perror( ld, "ldap_simple_bind_s" );
57.                     exit( 1 );
58.             }

59.             if ( pthread_create( &search_tid, NULL, search_thread,
        ➡NULL )
60.                 != 0 || pthread_create( &mod_tid, NULL, mod_thread,
        ➡NULL )
61.                 != 0 ) {
62.                 perror( "pthread_create" );
63.                 exit( 1 );
64.             }
65.             pthread_join( search_tid, &status );
66.             pthread_join( mod_tid, &status );
67.             ldap_unbind( ld );
68.             return( 0 );
69.     }

70.     static void
71.     thread_specific_setup( void )
72.     {
73.             void        *tsd;

74.             tsd = (void *) calloc( 1, sizeof(struct ldap_error) );
75.             pthread_setspecific( key, tsd );
76.     }
```

The program starts off with the usual LDAP initialization call at line
32. Notice, however, that before any actual LDAP operations are performed (for example, the call to ldap_simple_bind_s() on line 55), we
set up the thread-specific data area for the main thread and we initialize
the LDAP library for threaded use by setting the thread call-back functions via a call to ldap_set_option(). This setup is on lines 42–54.

The call to pthread_key_create() on line 37 and subsequent call to
thread_specific_setup() on line 41 are used to initialize a thread-
specific data area that will be used by each thread to keep thread-specific

copies of the LDAP error fields. This call is specific to the POSIX threading environment, though similar calls exist in all thread environments.

The two threads are created on lines 59 and 60, and the main thread just waits for them both to terminate (lines 65 and 66) before freeing up the LDAP session with the call to ldap_unbind() on line 67.

Search Thread

In our example, the search thread is not very useful. In a real application, the thread might traverse the entries returned, doing something with each one. See Chapter 9, "Search," for more ideas on this.

```
1.    void *
2.    search_thread( void *arg )
3.    {
4.            int         i;
5.            LDAPMessage     *result;

6.            thread_specific_setup();
7.            for ( i = 0; i < 100; i++ ) {
8.                if ( ldap_search_s( ld, BASEDN,LDAP_SCOPE_SUBTREE,
9.                    "(sn=Jensen)", NULL, 0, &result ) !=
                    ➡LDAP_SUCCESS ) {
10.                        ldap_perror( ld, "ldap_search_s" );
11.                        exit( 1 );
12.                }
13.                /* ...do something with the results... */
14.                ldap_msgfree( result );
15.            }
16.            return( NULL );
17.    }
```

The search thread is pretty simple. It does the same search 100 times before returning. The interesting thing to note is the call to thread_specific_setup() on line 6. This call allocates storage specific to this thread that is accessed later by the call-back routines defined below.

The search thread itself interacts with the LDAP library just like an unthreaded function would. After setup is complete, LDAP programming proceeds as usual.

Modify Thread

Like the search thread, the modify thread is not the most useful piece of code in the world. In fact, it's not even complete, since it leaves out the important step of creating the modifications to make to the directory entry. See Chapter 14, "Update," for detailed information on how to do this.

```
1.   void *
2.   mod_thread( void *arg )
3.   {
4.           int        i;
5.           LDAPMod    **mods;

6.           thread_specific_setup();

7.           /* … fill in mods … */
8.           for ( i = 0; i < 100; i++ ) {
9.                   if ( ldap_modify_s( ld, MODDN, mods ) !=
                     ➥LDAP_SUCCESS ) {
10.                          ldap_perror( ld, "ldap_modify_s" );
11.                          exit( 1 );
12.                  }
13.          }
14.          return( NULL );
15.  }
```

The modify thread is also pretty simple. It does the same modification 100 times before returning. Again, the interesting thing to note is the call to thread_specific_setup() on line 6. This call allocates storage specific to this thread that is accessed later by the call-back routines defined below.

Once this thread-specific setup is accomplished, the modify thread accesses the LDAP API just like an unthreaded function would.

Support Routines

There are three sets of support routines defined in this section. First are routines to deal with mutual exclusion. Second are routines to get and set the global per-thread value of errno. Third are routines to get and set the LDAP-specific error information. Each set of routines is defined and explained in the following paragraphs.

```
1.    void *
2.    my_mutex_alloc( void )
3.    {
4.            pthread_mutex_t       *mutex;

5.            mutex = (pthread_mutex_t *) malloc(
              ➥sizeof(pthread_mutex_t) );
6.            pthread_mutex_init( mutex, NULL );
7.            return( (void *) mutex );
8.    }

9.    void
10.   my_mutex_free( void *mutex )
11.   {
12.           pthread_mutex_destroy( (pthread_mutex_t *) mutex );
13.           free( mutex );
14.   }

15.   int
16.   my_mutex_lock( void *mutex )
17.   {
18.           return( pthread_mutex_lock( (pthread_mutex_t *)mutex ) );
19.   }

20.   int
21.   my_mutex_unlock( void *mutex )
22.   {
23.           return( pthread_mutex_unlock( (pthread_mutex_t *)mutex ) );
24.   }
```

Pointers to the above routines are passed to the LDAP library to be called when the library needs to protect critical data that should only be accessed by a single thread at a time. The my_mutex_lock() and my_mutex_unlock() functions are simple pass-through functions that call the underlying POSIX thread mutex lock and unlock routines.

The other two routines allocate and free individual mutexes. Note that you should not assume anything about the number of mutexes the

LDAP library will allocate. It will likely be a small number, but there is no guarantee that this number will not change in future versions of the LDAP SDK.

The next set of functions deal with errno.

```
1.   void
2.   my_set_errno( int err )
3.   {
4.          errno = err;
5.   }

6.   int
7.   my_get_errno( void )
8.   {
9.          return( errno );
10.  }
```

The my_set_errno() and my_get_errno() routines are used to get and set the per-thread copy of errno. As you can see, these functions are very simple. They are required, though, because the LDAP library may have been compiled with one idea of what errno is while your program may have been compiled with another. In a threaded environment, the definition of errno is specific to the thread implementation.

The next set of routines deals with setting and getting the LDAP-specific error indications.

```
1.   void
2.   my_set_lderrno( int err, char *matched, char *errmsg, void
     ➥*dummy )
3.   {
4.          struct ldap_error      *le;

5.          le = pthread_getspecific( key );
6.          le->le_errno = err;
7.          if ( le->le_matched != NULL ) {
8.                 ldap_memfree( le->le_matched );
9.          }
10.         le->le_matched = matched;
11.         if ( le->le_errmsg != NULL ) {
12.                ldap_memfree( le->le_errmsg );
```

```
13.          }
14.          le->le_errmsg = errmsg;
15.    }

16.    int
17.    my_get_lderrno( char **matched, char **errmsg, void *dummy )
18.    {
19.          struct ldap_error      *le;

20.          le = pthread_getspecific( key );
21.          if ( matched != NULL ) {
22.                *matched = le->le_matched;
23.          }
24.          if ( errmsg != NULL ) {
25.                *errmsg = le->le_errmsg;
26.          }
27.          return( le->le_errno );
28.    }
```

The final two functions are my_set_lderrno() and my_get_lderrno().
These functions manage the per-thread error information specific
to an LDAP connection. Each routine begins by calling the
pthread_getspecific() routine to retrieve its own thread-specific copy
of the LDAP error structure that we defined above. This thread-specific
area was set up by each thread in a call to thread_specific_setup().

Tip

Notice that the my_get_lderrno() routine is careful to allow the
LDAP library to pass NULL for the matched and errmsg parameters,
which it will often do.

Summary

As you can see, it's a bit of a pain to set up multi-threaded access to
LDAP. The advantage to the approached used, though, is that once
you've done the setup (code you might write once in your life), accessing LDAP proceeds just like in an unthreaded environment. Another
advantage is that the same LDAP library can be used in many different
threading environments. All you have to do is change the call-back
routines.

The following table summarizes the routines and structures defined in this chapter.

Name	Description
`struct ldap_thread_fns`	Structure used to pass thread-specific call-back routines to the LDAP library.

Looking Ahead

The next chapter lays more important groundwork for writing robust LDAP applications. It talks about error handling in the LDAP API. After that, Chapter 9 dives into the heart of LDAP by explaining the various search facilities provided by the API.

8

Handling Errors

Properly handling errors is a lost art within the software development community (some would argue that it never established itself as an art at all). We have all been tempted to omit an error check once in a while. The justification for this usually goes something like this: "That function call almost never fails, so I won't bother to check the return value right now. I'll come back and fix it later of course, but right now I'd rather focus on other things." The hard lesson is that such omissions always catch up with you eventually. Incorrect or missing error checking is often behind the really difficult-to-explain crashes and other hard-to-find bugs that haunt you and your customers.

Like all programming interfaces, the LDAP API places some of the responsibility for handling errors in the programmer's hands. If you are tempted to skip past the information in this chapter, don't. Life will be much better if you adopt a "catch all the errors before they catch up with me" attitude.

Now that we've gained the moral high ground as far as LDAP error handling is concerned, it's worth noting that another familiar error-check-omission excuse is "This is just sample code for a book. Of *course* our readers will insert the proper error checking when they actually write real code!" In other words, just because we don't always follow our own advice doesn't mean you shouldn't!

Functions That Return an LDAP Error Code

Many of the LDAP API functions return an LDAP error code directly. Examples of such functions include all of the synchronous LDAP operation routines (`ldap_search_s()`, `ldap_simple_bind_s()`, and so on). Most of the error codes returned come directly from the LDAP directory server, but some are generated locally by the LDAP client library. Table 8.1, near the end of this chapter, lists all of the possible LDAP error codes. Error handling for functions that return an LDAP error code is straightforward: check the return value of the function and take appropriate action.

Example 8.1: A function that checks to see if the manager password provided is correct by opening a connection to an LDAP server, trying a bind operation, and checking the error code returned. One of three values is returned by this function: 0 if the password is correct, 1 if it is incorrect, and 2 if it could not be checked for some reason.

```
1.      #define PASSWD_OK                          0
2.      #define PASSWD_BAD                         1
3.      #define PASSWD_COULD_NOT_CHECK             2

4.      #define MANAGERDN      "cn=Directory Manager, o=Ace Industry,
        ➥c=US"

5.      int
6.      password_is_ok( char *passwd )
7.      {
8.              LDAP  *ld;
9.              int  lderr, rc;

10.             if ( (ld = ldap_init( "ldap.netscape.com", LDAP_PORT ))
11.                  == NULL ) {
12.                     perror( "ldap_init" );
13.                     return( PASSWD_COULD_NOT_CHECK );
14.             }

15.             lderr = ldap_simple_bind_s( ld, MANAGERDN, passwd );

16.             switch( lderr ) {
17.             case LDAP_SUCCESS:
```

```
18.                              rc = PASSWD_OK;
19.                              break;

20.          case LDAP_INVALID_CREDENTIALS:
21.          case LDAP_INAPPROPRIATE_AUTH:
22.                              rc = PASSWD_BAD;
23.                              break;

24.          default:                     /* an unexpected error occurred */
25.                              rc = PASSWD_COULD_NOT_CHECK;
26.                              ldap_perror( ld, "ldap_simple_bind_s" );
27.          }

28.          ldap_unbind( ld );

29.          return( rc );
30.    }
```

Let's take a closer look at error handling within this function. If the
ldap_init() call fails (line 10), it returns NULL and we use the perror()
function to print the system error message.

The ldap_simple_bind_s() call on line 15 is an example of a function
that returns an LDAP error code directly. We test the error code in the
switch statement that follows, with special cases included for
LDAP_SUCCESS (the bind succeeded so the password must be correct),
LDAP_INVALID_CREDENTIALS (returned if the password was incorrect),
and LDAP_INAPPROPRIATE_AUTH (returned if the entry specified has no
password to check). If any other error occurs, we call on the
ldap_perror() function to print an error message. The ldap_perror()
function retrieves the last error that occurred from the LDAP session
handle and prints a message to standard error, preceding the message
with the string argument that is passed by the caller.

The next section provides a summary of the ldap_perror() function,
which is designed to work a lot like the standard perror() function.

Synopsis:

```
void ldap_perror( LDAP *ld, char *s );
```

Prints a message that corresponds to the most recent LDAP error that occurred.

Return Value:

NONE

Parameters:

LDAP *ld: A handle to an LDAP session, as returned by ldap_init() or ldap_open().

char *s: A message that is printed before the LDAP error message itself. Usually, this is used to provide some context for the error (for example, the name of the function that failed or an indication of where the error occurred within your application).

Converting Error Codes into Error Messages

The ldap_perror() writes to standard error, which means that unless you are writing an application that has a completely text-based interface you will probably not want to use it. The ldap_err2string() function can be used to retrieve the error message string that corresponds to an LDAP error code.

Synopsis:

```
char *ldap_err2string( int err);
```

Retrieves the error message string that corresponds to an LDAP error code.

Return Value:

Type: char *

A pointer to an LDAP error string. You do not have to worry about freeing this string pointer, because it points to a static string (you should not try to modify it either).

Parameters:

> int *err*: An LDAP error code, as returned by one of the many LDAP API functions that return these codes, such as ldap_search_s() or ldap_result2error().

Checking Errors Contained Within an LDAP Result

If you are using the asynchronous LDAP operation routines, you must call the ldap_result() function to retrieve the result. Because ldap_result() does not return an LDAP error code (instead, it returns the type of the result retrieved), you should use the ldap_result2error() function to retrieve the error that is present within the LDAP result message.

Example 8.2: Search for entries with a surname of "Jensen", printing entry names as they come in from the server.

```
1.    #include <stdio.h>
2.    #include <ldap.h>

3.    #define SEARCHBASE    "o=Ace Industry, c=US"
4.    #define HOST                  "ldap.netscape.com"

5.    #ifdef LDAP_OPT_SIZELIMIT                      /* only defined in
      ➥Netscape SDK */
6.    #define GET_LDERROR( ld )          ldap_get_lderrno ( (ld),
      ➥NULL, NULL )
7.    #else   /* UMICH SDK */
8.    #define GET_LDERROR( ld )          (ld)->ld_errno
9.    #endif

10.   void
11.   report_ldap_error( char *s, int err )
12.   {
13.           char    *msg;
```

```
14.              msg = ldap_err2string( err );
15.              fprintf( stderr, "The following LDAP error occurred
                 ↪while %s\n(%s)\n", s, msg );
16.    }

17.    main()
18.    {
19.              LDAP    *ld;
20.              LDAPMessage   *result, *e;
21.              char    *dn;
                 int   rc, msgid, lderr;

22.              if ( (ld = ldap_init( HOST, LDAP_PORT ))
23.                   == NULL ) {
24.                       perror( HOST );
25.                       exit( 1 );
26.              }

27.              if ( ldap_simple_bind_s( ld, NULL, NULL ) !=
                 ↪LDAP_SUCCESS ) {
                          report_ldap_error( "binding",
                          ↪GET_LDERROR( ld ));
28.                       ldap_unbind( ld );
29.                       exit( 1 );
30.              }

31.              if ( (msgid = ldap_search( ld, SEARCHBASE,
                 ↪LDAP_SCOPE_SUBTREE,
32.                   "(sn=Jensen)", NULL, 0 )) == -1 ) {
33.                       report_ldap_error( "initiating
                          ↪search", GET_LDERROR( ld ));
34.                       ldap_unbind( ld );
35.                       exit( 1 );
36.              }

37.              while ( (rc = ldap_result( ld, msgid, 0, NULL,
                 ↪&result ))
38.                   == LDAP_RES_SEARCH_ENTRY ) {

39.                       if ( (e = ldap_first_entry( ld, result
                          ↪)) == NULL ) {
40.                               report_ldap_error(
                                  ↪"getting entry",
```

```
41.                                             GET_LDERROR( ld
                                              ➥));
42.                         } else if (( dn = ldap_get_dn( ld, e
                          ➥)) == NULL ) {
43.                                     report_ldap_error(
                                      ➥"getting DN",
                                      ➥GET_LDERROR( ld ));
44.                         } else {
45.                                     printf( "Found: %s\n",
                                      ➥dn );
46.                                     ldap_memfree( dn );
47.                         }
48.                         ldap_msgfree( result );
49.             }

50.             if ( rc == LDAP_RES_SEARCH_RESULT ) {
51.                         lderr = ldap_result2error( ld,
                          ➥result, 1 );
52.                         if ( lderr != LDAP_SUCCESS ) {
53.                                     report_ldap_error(
                                      ➥"searching", lderr );
54.                         }
55.             } else {
56.                         report_ldap_error( "waiting for
                          ➥result", GET_LDERROR( ld ));
57.             }

58.             ldap_unbind( ld );
59.             return( 0 );
60.     }
```

There are several interesting things to notice about the code in this example. First, on lines 5–9 we define a macro called GET_LDERROR(), which retrieves the error code from the LDAP session handle. In the Netscape SDK, the ldap_get_lderrno() function is used for this purpose. If we are compiling with the University of Michigan SDK, the ld_errno field is accessed directly from the LDAP session structure.

Next we define a function on lines 10–16 called report_ldap_error() that uses the ldap_err2string() function to display LDAP errors in a slightly different format than ldap_perror() does. This is done mainly to show how the ldap_err2string() function can be used. If your application already includes error reporting facilities, you would make use of them instead of writing to standard error as report_ldap_error() does.

Most of the code in the main function is straightforward—we just use the asynchronous ldap_search() call to initiate a search and call ldap_result() in a loop to retrieve entries as they come. As each entry arrives, we print its DN. See Chapters 9 and 11 for more details on the functions used to do this. When we fall out of the loop, this code from lines 50–57 is used to report any errors that may have occurred:

```
if ( rc == LDAP_RES_SEARCH_RESULT ) {
        lderr = ldap_result2error( ld, result, 1 );
        if ( lderr != LDAP_SUCCESS ) {
                    report_ldap_error( "searching", lderr );
        }
} else {
        report_ldap_error( "waiting for result", GET_LDERROR( ld ));
}
```

rc contains the type of the last message returned by ldap_result(). If it is a search result, we call the ldap_result2error() function to extract the error code that was returned by the server (calling our error reporting function if the error code was not "success"). If rc is any other value, we did not actually receive the complete search result, and in this case the error code must be retrieved from the LDAP session handle instead of from the search result message. This sequence of code is a bit unintuitive, but it will become second nature after a while. Also note that by using the synchronous LDAP operation calls you can avoid a lot of the error handling complexity seen in this example.

The next section summarizes both the ldap_result2error() and the ldap_get_lderrno() functions.

Synopsis:

```
int ldap_result2error( LDAP *ld, LDAPMessage *res, int
freeit );
```

Retrieves the error code that was returned by an LDAP operation.

Return Value:

Type: `int`

One of the LDAP error codes listed in Table 8.1 later in this chapter.

Parameters:

`LDAP *ld`: A handle to an LDAP session, as returned by `ldap_init()` or `ldap_open()`.

`LDAPMessage *res`: An LDAP operation result, as returned by the `ldap_result()` function.

`int freeit`: A Boolean parameter that, if non-zero, causes `ldap_result2error()` to free the memory occupied by the res parameter for you by using `ldap_msgfree()`. If `freeit` is zero, res is not freed.

Synopsis:

```
int ldap_get_lderrno( LDAP *ld, char **matched, char **msg );
```

Retrieves information about the most recent error that occurred. This function is available in the Netscape SDK only. In the University of Michigan SDK, the `ld_errno`, `ld_matched`, and `ld_error` fields of the LDAP session handle can be accessed directly to obtain the information this function provides.

Return Value:

Type: `int`

The LDAP error code returned by the most recent operation or LDAP API call.

Parameters:

`LDAP *ld`: A handle to an LDAP session, as returned by `ldap_init()` or `ldap_open()`.

char **matched*: If a non-NULL pointer is passed, it will be set to point to a string that represents the portion of the DN that was matched by the last LDAP operation. This "matched DN" information is returned by an LDAP server when a DN was not found in the directory (that is, when an LDAP_NO_SUCH_OBJECT error is returned).

char **msg*: If a non-NULL pointer is passed, it will be set to point to the extra error message string that was returned by the server. The information returned depends entirely on the LDAP server implementation, but it may be helpful to display this along with other error information.

Tip

> Some implementations return extra information in the msg parameter. This information might be a more specific cause for some error condition or other information you may find useful in debugging problems with your application or even the LDAP server.

Example 8.3: A function that checks to see if an entry exists. If the entry does not exist, the portion of the entry's Distinguished Name that corresponds to its most immediate ancestor in the directory tree that does exist is displayed.

```
1.      int
2.      entry_exists( LDAP *ld, char *dn )
3.      {
4.              char    *attrs[ 2 ], *matched, *errmsg;
5.              int             lderr;
6.              LDAPMessage     *result;

7.              attrs[ 0 ] = "cn";
8.              attrs[ 1 ] = NULL;
9.              if ( (lderr = ldap_search_s( ld, dn,
                ➡LDAP_SCOPE_BASE,
10.                     "(objectclass=*)", NULL, 0, &result )) ==
                        ➡LDAP_SUCCESS ) {
11.                     printf( "Entry %s exists.\n", dn );
12.                     return( 1 );   /* entry exists */
13.             }
```

```
14.    #ifdef LDAP_OPT_SIZELIMIT                /* only defined in
       ➥Netscape SDK */
15.                    (void)ldap_get_lderrno( ld, &matched, &errmsg );
16.    #else
17.                    matched = ld->ld_matched;
18.                    errmsg = ld->ld_error;
19.    #endif

20.                    if ( lderr == LDAP_NO_SUCH_OBJECT ) {
21.                            printf( "Entry %s does not
                                ➥exist.\n", dn );
22.                            printf( "Matched DN:  %s\n",
                                ➥matched );
23.                            return( 0 );
24.                    }

25.                    printf( "Could not check existence of %s\n", dn
                       ➥);
26.                    printf( "because this error occurred: %s.\n",
27.                            ldap_err2string( lderr ));
28.                    if ( errmsg != NULL ) {
29.                            printf( "Server sent this
                                ➥additional info.: %s\n",
30.                                    errmsg );
31.                    }
32.                    return( -1 );   /* error */
33.    }
```

This function is fairly simple. It assumes that the LDAP session handle
that is passed in is valid and that a bind operation has already been
done. A base object search is done to read the entry we are interested
in. If the search succeeds, we know the entry exists.

If the search fails, we check the error code and treat "no such object"
as a special case. The code on lines 14–19 is conditional on whether we
are compiling using the Netscape SDK or University of Michigan SDK.
It sets the matched and errmsg variables that are used in the error reporting code on lines 20–32.

All of the LDAP Error Codes

A list of all the possible error codes and their symbolic names is shown in Table 8.1. Also given are the actual numbers associated with each error. As you can see, there are a lot of error codes!

Table 8.1

LDAP Error Codes and Messages

Symbolic Name (as defined in ldap.h)	Message
LDAP_SUCCESS	Success
LDAP_OPERATIONS_ERROR	Operations error
LDAP_PROTOCOL_ERROR	Protocol error
LDAP_TIMELIMIT_EXCEEDED	Time limit exceeded
LDAP_SIZELIMIT_EXCEEDED	Size limit exceeded
LDAP_COMPARE_FALSE	Compare false
LDAP_COMPARE_TRUE	Compare true
LDAP_STRONG_AUTH_NOT_SUPPORTED	Strong authentication not supported
LDAP_STRONG_AUTH_REQUIRED	Strong authentication required
LDAP_PARTIAL_RESULTS	Partial results and referral received
LDAP_NO_SUCH_ATTRIBUTE	No such attribute
LDAP_UNDEFINED_TYPE	Undefined attribute type
LDAP_INAPPROPRIATE_MATCHING	Inappropriate matching
LDAP_CONSTRAINT_VIOLATION	Constraint violation
LDAP_TYPE_OR_VALUE_EXISTS	Type or value exists
LDAP_INVALID_SYNTAX	Invalid syntax
LDAP_NO_SUCH_OBJECT	No such object
LDAP_ALIAS_PROBLEM	Alias problem
LDAP_INVALID_DN_SYNTAX	Invalid DN syntax

Symbolic Name (as defined in ldap.h)	Message
LDAP_IS_LEAF	Object is a leaf
LDAP_ALIAS_DEREF_PROBLEM	Alias dereferencing problem
LDAP_INAPPROPRIATE_AUTH	Inappropriate authentication
LDAP_INVALID_CREDENTIALS	Invalid credentials
LDAP_INSUFFICIENT_ACCESS	Insufficient access
LDAP_BUSY	Server is busy
LDAP_UNAVAILABLE	Server is unavailable
LDAP_UNWILLING_TO_PERFORM	Server is unwilling to perform
LDAP_LOOP_DETECT	Loop detected
LDAP_NAMING_VIOLATION	Naming violation
LDAP_OBJECT_CLASS_VIOLATION	Object class violation
LDAP_NOT_ALLOWED_ON_NONLEAF	Operation not allowed on nonleaf
LDAP_NOT_ALLOWED_ON_RDN	Operation not allowed on RDN
LDAP_ALREADY_EXISTS	Already exists
LDAP_NO_OBJECT_CLASS_MODS	Cannot modify object class
LDAP_RESULTS_TOO_LARGE	Results too large
LDAP_OTHER	Unknown error
LDAP_SERVER_DOWN	Cannot contact LDAP server
LDAP_LOCAL_ERROR	Local error
LDAP_ENCODING_ERROR	Encoding error
LDAP_DECODING_ERROR	Decoding error
LDAP_TIMEOUT	Timed out
LDAP_AUTH_UNKNOWN	Unknown authentication method
LDAP_FILTER_ERROR	Bad search filter
LDAP_USER_CANCELLED	User cancelled operation

continues

Table 8.1

LDAP Error Codes and Messages

Symbolic Name (as defined in ldap.h)	Message
LDAP_PARAM_ERROR	Bad parameter to an ldap routine
LDAP_NO_MEMORY	Out of memory
LDAP_CONNECT_ERROR	Cannot connect to the LDAP server

Summary

The following table summarizes the routines described in this chapter.

Name	Description
ldap_perror()	Prints a message that corresponds to the most recent LDAP error that occurred.
ldap_err2string()	Retrieves the error message that corresponds to an LDAP error code.
ldap_result2error()	Retrieves the error code that was returned by an LDAP operation.
ldap_get_lderrno()	Retrieves information about the most recent error that occurred (Netscape SDK only).

Looking Ahead

Now that we have discussed LDAP API error handling techniques, it is time to roll up our sleeves and learn how to find and retrieve entries from an LDAP directory server. The next chapter begins our detailed discussion of LDAP search, the most common and arguably the most useful LDAP operation.

Search

S earch is unquestionably the heart of LDAP. The LDAP search operation lets you select and retrieve entries from the directory using surprisingly complex criteria. Different starting points and scopes can be specified in order to search different portions of the LDAP directory. You can specify size and time limits on the search, restricting the number of entries that will be returned from the search and the amount of time to spend on the search.

The LDAP API allows you access to all these features of search and more. Once you get the results back from a search, the API allows you to parse the results and extract particular pieces of information from each entry returned, including the entry's name and associated attributes and values.

This chapter presents the LDAP API search calls in all their various forms. We'll describe both synchronous and asynchronous versions of the search calls. We also describe routines to retrieve and parse the results of the search. These routines are the same regardless of whether the results being parsed were retrieved synchronously or asynchronously.

There are routines to step through a list of entries returned from a search. Once you have an individual entry, there are routines to step through the entry's attributes. Once you have an attribute, there are routines to retrieve the attribute's values.

As in other chapters, we adopt an example-driven approach, introducing new features of the API as they appear in our examples. A summary of the routines covered appears at the end of this chapter. We start with the synchronous version of the search call, since it is somewhat simpler, and save the asynchronous calls for later. This chapter covers the basics of searching, parsing, and constructing search filters. The next chapter takes a more advanced look at search filters and how to construct them, and introduces some routines you can use to help you in this task.

Synchronous Searching

The following example illustrates a simple application of search.

Example 9.1: The goal of this program is to print out the number of people at Ace Industry who have a surname of "Jensen".

```
1.    #include <stdio.h>
2.    #include <ldap.h>

3.    #define SEARCHBASE      "o=Ace Industry, c=US"

4.    main()
5.    {
6.            LDAP         *ld;
7.            LDAPMessage  *result;
8.            int          nentries;

9.            if ( (ld = ldap_init( "ldap.netscape.com", LDAP_PORT ))
10.             == NULL) {
11.                   perror( "ldap_init" );
12.                   exit( 1 );
13.            }

14.            if ( ldap_simple_bind_s( ld, NULL, NULL ) != LDAP_SUCCESS
              ➥) {
15.                   ldap_perror( ld, "ldap_simple_bind_s" );
16.                   exit( 1 );
17.            }

18.            if ( ldap_search_s( ld, SEARCHBASE, LDAP_SCOPE_SUBTREE,
19.              "(sn=Jensen)", NULL, 0, &result ) != LDAP_SUCCESS ) {
```

```
20.                    ldap_perror( ld, "ldap_search_s" );
21.                    exit( 1 );
22.         }

23.         if ( (nentries = ldap_count_entries( ld, result )) == -1
➡) {
24.                    ldap_perror( ld, "ldap_count_entries" );
25.                    exit( 1 );
26.         }

27.         printf( "Found %d Jensens at Ace Industry\n", nentries );
28.         ldap_msgfree( result );
29.         ldap_unbind( ld );
30.         return( 0 );
31. }
```

The first things to notice about this example are the calls that we will not explain in this chapter, except very briefly. The ldap_init() call on line 9 initializes an LDAP session. It's described in more detail in Chapter 6. The ldap_simple_bind_s() call on line 14 authenticates to the directory, in this case as "nobody", the anonymous user. ldap_simple_bind_s() is also described briefly in Chapter 6 and in more detail in Chapter 13, "Authentication."

Tip

In version 2 of the LDAP protocol, the bind step is technically required, even if you are binding as the anonymous user and providing no authentication information. Some servers such as the Netscape Directory Server and the University of Michigan slapd server do not enforce this requirement (that is, you could call ldap_search_s() immediately following a successful call to ldap_init()). You should include the bind step to ensure interoperability of your program with stricter LDAP implementations.

Things get more interesting with the ldap_search_s() call at line 18. This is the routine that actually initiates an LDAP search protocol operation and waits for the server to send results back. When the server does return results, they are transmitted to your program via the result parameter of ldap_search_s().

ldap_search_s() returns a result code indicating the outcome of the search operation and any error that has occurred. In our simple example, we accept the predefined result LDAP_SUCCESS as the only indication of a successful search. As we will see later, there are other return codes that may indicate partial success of the operation if, for example, a size or time limit was exceeded.

At line 23 our program calls ldap_count_entries() to determine the number of entries that matched the search criteria. This is about the simplest thing we can do with a search result. The next section on basic results parsing shows more interesting and complete things you can do with a search result.

The next sections examine the parameters and calling convention of ldap_search_s() in more detail.

Synopsis:

    int ldap_search_s(LDAP *ld, char *base, int scope, char *fil-
    ter, char *attrs[], int attrsonly, LDAPMessage **result);

Performs a search of the LDAP directory using base as a starting point, covering entries described by scope, selecting entries matching filter, and returning attributes given by attrs. Matching entries are returned in result.

Return Value:

Type: int

The LDAP error code indicating the outcome of the operation. This code can be interpreted by calling ldap_err2string().

Parameters:

LDAP *ld: This parameter is a handle to an LDAP session, as returned by a successful call to ldap_init() or ldap_open(). In the Netscape LDAP SDK, this handle references an opaque data type. In the University of Michigan SDK, this handle is a pointer to a structure that is exposed to your program.

char *base*: This parameter specifies the base object for the search operation. The base object is the point in the LDAP tree at which you want to start searching. Its value is a distinguished name. In our example, we've set the base object to "o=Ace Industry, c=US". If you are running an LDAP server of your own, you could set the base object to the DN for your own organization.

int *scope*: This parameter specifies the portion of the LDAP tree, relative to the base object, to search. It can have one of three possible values. The value we've chosen for our example is LDAP_SCOPE_SUBTREE, indicating that we want to search the entire LDAP subtree rooted at and including the base object. Other possible values are LDAP_SCOPE_ONELEVEL to search only the immediate children of the base object, and LDAP_SCOPE_BASE to search only the base object entry itself.

char *filter*: This parameter specifies the criteria to use during the search to determine which entries to return. In our simple example, we've chosen to look for any entries with a surname of Jensen using the filter "(sn=Jensen)" (sn is LDAP shorthand for the surname attribute). We cover more complicated search filters in the next chapter.

char *attrs*[]: This parameter specifies the attributes to return along with each entry matching the search. It is a NULL-terminated array of character strings specifying the names of the attributes you want returned. Passing NULL for this argument, as we have done in our example, means that all available attributes should be returned.

int *attrsonly*: This parameter is a Boolean specifying whether both types and values should be returned with each attribute (zero) or types only should be returned (non-zero). In our example, we've requested both types and values.

LDAPMessage **result*: This parameter is a pointer to an LDAPMessage * used to hold the result of a successful search. The LDAPMessage is an opaque data type in the Netscape SDK. It is a structure available to your code in the University of Michigan SDK. If the ldap_search_s() call returns a value greater than or equal to zero, the `result` parameter will be filled in with the entries (if any) and final result of the search. A return of `LDAP_SUCCESS`, `LDAP_SIZELIMIT_EXCEEDED`, `LDAP_TIMELIMIT_EXCEEDED`, or `LDAP_PARTIAL_RESULTS` indicates that there may be entries present in the result, in addition to the success or error indication. The `result` parameter should be freed by calling `ldap_msgfree()` when it is no longer needed.

Tip

You can effectively read the attributes of a single entry by setting the scope of the search to `LDAP_SCOPE_BASEOBJECT` and the filter to `"(objectclass=*)"`, which is guaranteed to match any entry. This is useful when you know the name of the entry from which you'd like to retrieve some attributes.

Tip

You can effectively list the children of any entry in the directory by setting the scope of the search to `LDAP_SCOPE_ONELEVEL` and the filter to `"(objectclass=*)"`, which is guaranteed to match any entry. This is useful when you are writing a browsing application that displays the structure of the directory tree at a given level.

Additional Search Parameters

There are three additional parameters associated with the LDAP session that affect the search request. In the University of Michigan SDK, these parameters are fields you can set within the LDAP structure. In the Netscape SDK, these parameters are set by calling the `ldap_set_option()` routine, described in more detail in Chapter 6. The three additional parameters and their functions are described below, along with examples of how to set them in both the U of M and Netscape SDKs.

`sizelimit`: This parameter specifies the maximum number of entries the server should return from the search. A value of zero (the default) indicates that no limit should be imposed. The server itself may well impose an administrative limit on the number of entries it will return. Although you can ask for more entries than the server is willing to return, the server will not exceed its own administrative limit. In the University of Michigan SDK, this limit would be set to 10 like this:

```
LDAP      *ld;
...
/* after calling ldap_init() to get an LDAP * handle */
ld->ld_sizelimit = 10;
```

In the Netscape SDK, the LDAP handle is an opaque data type and the size limit would be set like this:

```
LDAP      *ld;
int       sizelimit;
...
/* after calling ldap_init() to get an LDAP * handle */
sizelimit = 10;
ldap_set_option( ld, LDAP_OPT_SIZELIMIT, &sizelimit );
```

timelimit: This parameter specifies the maximum number of seconds the client is willing to wait for an answer to its search request. A value of zero (the default) indicates that no limit should be imposed. The server itself may impose an administrative limit on the length of time it will spend answering any single request. Although you can ask for more time than the server is willing to spend, the server will not exceed its administrative limit. In the U-M SDK, this limit would be set to 30 seconds like this:

```
LDAP      *ld;
...
/* after calling ldap_init() to get an LDAP * handle */
ld->ld_timelimit = 30;
```

In the Netscape SDK, the LDAP handle is an opaque data type and the time limit would be set like this:

```
LDAP      *d;
int       timelimit;
...
/* after calling ldap_init() to get an LDAP * handle */
timelimit = 30;
ldap_set_option( ld, LDAP_OPT_TIMELIMIT, &timelimit );
```

Tip

It is important to realize that this time limit is simply transmitted to the server as part of the search parameters. The client does not enforce the limit itself. To enforce a client-side-imposed time limit on a search, use the `ldap_search_st()` call, described below, or use the asynchronous version of search.

deref: This parameter specifies how alias entries are to be handled by the server when evaluating the search request. The LDAP server answers a search request in two phases. The first phase involves locating the base object at which to start searching for entries. The second phase, once the base object has been located, involves actually searching for entries that match the filter. Aliases can be dereferenced or not during each of these two phases, leading to the four possible values of deref with the following meanings:

- LDAP_DEREF_NEVER   This value of deref prohibits aliases from being dereferenced by the server during either phase of the search. If the base object is an alias or the DN identifying it contains an alias component, the alias will not be dereferenced. Similarly, during the search itself, alias entries themselves are examined to determine whether they match the search filter, not the entries the aliases point to. This setting of deref is the default.

- LDAP_DEREF_FINDING   This value of deref specifies that aliases should be dereferenced when locating the base object of the search, but not when actually evaluating entries that match the search filter.

- LDAP_DEREF_SEARCHING   This value of deref specifies that aliases should be dereferenced when applying the filter to entries within the scope of the search after the base object has been located, but not when locating the base object itself. A consequence of this setting is that alias entries are never returned from the search, since it causes the entries pointed to by alias entries to be examined, rather than the alias entries themselves.

- LDAP_DEREF_ALWAYS   This value of deref specifies that aliases should be dereferenced both when locating the base object of the search and when evaluating entries that match the search filter. As with

LDAP_DEREF_SEARCHING, a consequence of this setting is that alias entries are never returned from the search, since it causes the entries pointed to by alias entries to be examined, rather than the alias entries themselves.

In the U-M SDK, the deref parameter is a field in the LDAP structure. It could be set to LDAP_DEREF_SEARCHING like this:

```
LDAP    *ld;
...
/* after calling ldap_init() to get an LDAP * handle */
ld->ld_deref = LDAP_DEREF_SEARCHING;
```

In the Netscape SDK, the LDAP handle is an opaque data type and the deref parameter would be set like this:

```
LDAP    *ld;
int     deref;
...
/* after calling ldap_init() to get an LDAP * handle */
deref = LDAP_DEREF_SEARCHING;
ldap_set_option( ld, LDAP_OPT_DEREF, &deref );
```

Tip

In some LDAP configurations and server implementations, dereferencing aliases during a search operation can be very expensive. Unless you really need this feature, it's recommended that you stick with the default value of deref, which is to never dereference aliases.

Retrieving No Attributes

You may have noticed that our first example has some room for improvement. For example, even though all we want to know is the number of entries returned, by passing NULL for the attrs parameter, we are requesting that all attributes be returned, a needless waste of bandwidth. If the entries returned contain many or large attributes, this waste could be substantial.

To be more efficient, we could ask only for a single specific attribute, even one we're sure the matching entries won't have. To be even more efficient, we can turn on the attrsonly flag, indicating that no values should be returned in the event one of the matching entries does contain the attribute. For example:

```
char    *attrs[2];
...
attrs[0] = "c";
attrs[1] = NULL;
if ( ldap_search_s( ld, SEARCHBASE, LDAP_SCOPE_SUBTREE,
    "(sn=Jensen)", attrs, 1, &result ) != LDAP_SUCCESS ) {
        ldap_perror( ld, "ldap_search_s" );
        exit( 1 );
}
```

 Tip

To retrieve entries without getting any attributes, ask for a type name the entry is unlikely to contain (such as "c", for country), and turn on the attrsonly flag.

Tip

To find out what attributes an entry has without actually retrieving the values (which might be very large) set the attrsonly ldap_search_s() parameter to one.

Searching with a Time Limit

One potential problem with the ldap_search_s() routine is that it will wait until the results of the search are returned, regardless of how long this might take. If the server is very slow, or certain kinds of undetectable network outages occur, this could be a long time.

The timelimit LDAP session parameter can be set to instruct the server not to spend more than a certain number of seconds on the search, but this does nothing in case of a network failure the client does not detect, and it also relies on the server to follow the time limit faithfully. The client itself may want to set a local timeout to ensure it spends only a certain amount of time on the search. The ldap_search_st() routine is provided to fill this need.

Synopsis:

```
int ldap_search_st( LDAP *ld, char *base, int scope, char *fil-
ter, char *attrs[], int attrsonly, LDAPMessage **result, struct
timeval *tv );
```

Performs a search of the LDAP directory using *base* as a starting point, covering entries described by *scope*, selecting entries matching *filter*, and returning attributes given by *attrs*. Do not spend more than the time limit specified in *tv* on the search. Matching entries are returned in *result*.

Return Value:

Type: int

The LDAP error code indicating the outcome of the search. This code can be interpreted by calling ldap_err2string().

Parameters:

Other parameters are the same as for ldap_search_s().

struct timeval *tv: A structure representing the maximum number of seconds and microseconds to wait for the search to complete. The structure is declared in the time.h system include file as follows:

```
struct timeval {
        unsigned long tv_sec;
        unsigned long tv_usec;
};
```

ldap_search_st() works just like ldap_search_s() with the following exception. It takes one additional parameter that allows you to specify a timeout on the search. The parameter is a pointer to a struct timeval, allowing pretty fine-grained timeout values to be specified.

We could change our simple example to specify a timeout on the search of 10 seconds by adding the following lines of code and replacing the call to ldap_search_s() with the following call to ldap_search_st().

```
struct timeval   *tv;
...
tv.tv_sec = 10;          /* seconds */
tv.tv_usec = 0;          /* microseconds */
if ( ldap_search_st( ld, BASE, LDAP_SCOPE_SUBTREE,
   "(sn=Jensen)", NULL, 0, &result, &tv ) != LDAP_SUCCESS ) {
        ldap_perror( ld, "ldap_search_s" );
        exit( 1 );
}
```

If ten seconds pass before the server responds, ldap_search_st() will return the LDAP_TIMEOUT error code.

Basic Result Parsing

So far, the example we've been following doesn't do much in the way of parsing the results it gets back from the search it performs. All it does is call ldap_count_entries() to determine the number of entries matching the search criteria. This section describes the ldap_count_entries() routine and then goes on to introduce the other basic result parsing routines.

It is important to understand that none of the parsing routines described in this section do any network I/O. They merely interpret data previously obtained from the LDAP server via routines that do network I/O, such as ldap_search_s() and ldap_search_st().

Synopsis:

```
int ldap_count_entries( LDAP *ld, LDAPMessage *result );
```

Counts the number of entries returned in an LDAP search result.

Return Value:

Type: int

The number of entries in the search result, or −1 if an error occurs.

Parameters:

> LDAP *`ld`: This parameter is the handle on the LDAP session, as returned by a successful call to `ldap_init()` or `ldap_open()`.
>
> LDAPMessage *`result`: This parameter is the search result, as returned by a successful call to `ldap_search_s()` or `ldap_search_st()` or `ldap_result()`, described later in this section. In the Netscape SDK, this parameter is a handle on an opaque data type. In the University of Michigan SDK, this parameter is a pointer to a structure defined in the `ldap.h` include file.

The `ldap_count_entries()` call returns the number of entries in the search result or −1 in case of error. If `ldap_count_entries()` returns zero, then no entries matching the search were returned. Note that this does not necessarily mean there are no entries in the LDAP directory that match your search criteria. The entries might be protected by access control, or the search may have returned `LDAP_SIZELIMIT_EXCEEDED` or `LDAP_TIMELIMIT_EXCEEDED`, indicating that some client- or server-imposed limit was exceeded before the search could be completed.

Retrieving Individual Entries

Usually you'll want to do more than simply count the entries returned from a search. More often, you'll want to step through the entries one at a time, perhaps retrieving a specific attribute or maybe even all attributes from each entry. Stepping through entries in a search result is accomplished by calling `ldap_first_entry()` and `ldap_next_entry()`.

The `ldap_first_entry()` routine is used to return the first entry in a chain of search results. The `ldap_first_entry()` routine is described as below.

Synopsis:

```
LDAPMessage *ldap_first_entry( LDAP *ld, LDAPMessage *result );
```

Returns the first entry in a chain of search results.

Return Value:

Type: `LDAPMessage *`

A pointer to an opaque data structure containing the first entry in the chain of search results. NULL is returned on error, or if no entries are in the chain. The only way to distinguish these two conditions is by examining the LDAP error code (see Chapter 8) when a NULL return occurs.

Parameters:

`LDAP *ld`: This parameter is the LDAP session handle, as returned from a successful call to `ldap_init()` or `ldap_open()`.

`LDAPMessage *result`: This parameter is the result of the search, obtained from a successful call to `ldap_search_s()`, `ldap_search_st()`, or `ldap_result()`. `ldap_result()` is described later in this chapter in the asynchronous searching section.

`ldap_first_entry()` returns a handle to the first entry in the result chain, or NULL if no entries are in the chain. A NULL return also can indicate an error condition. The only way to distinguish these two conditions is to examine the LDAP error after the call. Chapter 8 talks more about LDAP error evaluation.

The handle returned is passed to the various entry parsing routines, such as `ldap_get_dn()`, `ldap_first_attribute()`, `ldap_next_attribute()`, and so on. These routines are described later. The entry returned can also be passed on a subsequent call to the `ldap_next_entry()` routine to step through the chain of entries returned from a search.

Note that in the Netscape SDK, the `LDAPMessage` is an opaque data type. In the University of Michigan SDK, the `LDAPMessage` is a structure declared in the `ldap.h` header file.

The `ldap_next_entry()` routine is used to return the next entry in a chain of search results. The `ldap_next_entry()` routine is described as follows.

Synopsis:

```
LDAPMessage *ldap_next_entry( LDAP *ld, LDAPMessage *preventry
);
```

Returns the next entry in a chain of search results.

Return Value:

Type: `LDAPMessage *`

A pointer to an opaque data structure containing the next entry in the chain of search results. `NULL` is returned on error, or if no entries are in the chain. The only way to distinguish these two conditions is by examining the LDAP error code (see Chapter 8) when a `NULL` return occurs.

Parameters:

`LDAP *ld`: This parameter is the LDAP handle, as returned from a successful call to `ldap_init()` or `ldap_open()`.

`LDAPMessage *preventry`: This parameter is an entry returned from a previous successful call to `ldap_first_entry()` or `ldap_next_entry()`. The next entry in the chain will be returned.

`ldap_next_entry()` returns a handle to the next entry in the result chain, or `NULL` if no more entries are in the chain. A `NULL` return also can indicate an error condition. The only way to distinguish these two conditions is to examine the LDAP error after the call. Chapter 8 talks more about LDAP error evaluation.

The handle returned is passed to the various entry parsing routines, such as `ldap_get_dn()`, `ldap_first_attribute()`, `ldap_next_attribute()`, and so on, described later. The entry returned can also be passed to another `ldap_next_entry()` call to continue stepping through the chain of entries returned from a search.

Example 9.2: To illustrate the use of these two routines, the following example shows how the `ldap_count_entries()` function could be implemented using `ldap_first_entry()` and `ldap_next_entry()`.

```
int
ldap_count_entries( LDAP *ld, LDAPMessage *result )
{
        LDAPMessage     *e;
        int             nentries = 0;

        for ( e = ldap_first_entry( ld, result ); e != NULL;
          e = ldap_next_entry(ld, e ) ) {
            nentries++;
        }
        if ( ldap_get_lderrno( ld, NULL, NULL ) != LDAP_SUCCESS ) {
            return( -1 );
        } else {
            return( nentries );
        }
}
```

Note that in the Netscape SDK, the LDAPMessage is an opaque data type. In the University of Michigan SDK, the LDAPMessage is a structure declared in the ldap.h header file.

Getting the Name of an Entry

Once you have an entry, you can retrieve the entry's name using the ldap_get_dn() routine.

Synopsis:

```
char *ldap_get_dn( LDAP *ld, LDAPMessage *entry );
```

Returns a copy of the distinguished name of an entry.

Return Value:

Type: char *

A copy of the entry's distinguished name. NULL will be returned in case of error, and the LDAP error code set. The DN returned should be freed by calling ldap_memfree() when it is no longer needed.

Parameters:

> LDAP *ld*: This parameter is the LDAP session handle as returned from a successful call to ldap_init() or ldap_open().

> LDAPMessage *entry*: This parameter is the entry whose DN is to be returned. The entry must have been returned from a successful call to ldap_first_entry() or ldap_next_entry().

ldap_get_dn() returns a char *, which points to a copy of the entry's name in distinguished name format. This format is described in more detail in Chapter 3. The DN returned should be freed by the caller when it's no longer needed by calling ldap_memfree(). It is important to use ldap_memfree() instead of free(), because the LDAP library may not have used malloc() to allocate the DN.

Example 9.3: Combining this routine with the two entry stepping routines described previously, the following example function prints out the names of entries in a chain of search results.

```
void
print_entry_dns( LDAP *ld, LDAPMessage *result )
{
        LDAPMessage    *e;
        char           *dn;

        for ( e = ldap_first_entry( ld, result ); e != NULL;
            e = ldap_next_entry(ld, e ) ) {
                if ( (dn = ldap_get_dn( ld, e )) != NULL ) {
                        printf( "dn: %s\n", dn );
                        ldap_memfree( dn );
                } else {
                        ldap_perror( ld, "ldap_get_dn" );
                }
        }
}
```

Retrieving the Attributes of an Entry

Once you have an entry you may want to know what attributes it contains. Remember that just because you requested a particular set of attributes for the entry, not all of them may have been returned for access control or other reasons. The ldap_first_attribute() and ldap_next_attribute() routines are provided to step through the attribute names returned with a particular entry.

Synopsis:

```
char *ldap_first_attribute(LDAP *ld, LDAPMessage *entry,
➥BerElement **ber );
```

Returns a copy of the first attribute name contained in an entry.

Return Value:

Type: char *

The name of the first attribute in the entry. NULL will be returned in case of error, and the LDAP error code set. NULL is also returned if the entry contains no attributes. In the Netscape SDK, the attribute name returned should be freed by calling ldap_memfree() when it is no longer needed. In the University of Michigan SDK, the return value is a pointer to static data and does not need to be freed.

Parameters:

LDAP *ld: This parameter is the LDAP session handle as returned from a successful call to ldap_init() or ldap_open().

LDAPMessage *entry: This parameter is the entry whose first attribute is to be returned. The entry must have been returned from a successful call to ldap_first_entry() or ldap_next_entry().

BerElement **ber: This parameter is a pointer to a pointer to an opaque data type that the ldap_first_attribute() and ldap_next_attribute() routines fill in and use to keep track of their position in the current entry. If *ber is non-NULL upon return from ldap_first_attribute(), it should be freed by calling ber_free() with a second argument of zero.

ldap_first_attribute() returns a char * pointing to the string name of the first attribute in the entry. In the Netscape SDK, this memory must always be freed by the caller by calling ldap_memfree(). In the University of Michigan SDK, the pointer returned is to a static area that does not need to be freed.

If the returned entry contains no attributes or an error occurs, ldap_first_entry() will return NULL. To distinguish between these two conditions you must examine the value of the LDAP error from the last operation. LDAP error handling is described in more detail in Chapter 8.

The result parameter ber, used to keep track of the current position in the entry's list of attributes, may be passed to a subsequent call to ldap_next_attribute() to step through the entry's attributes. If *ber is non-NULL after the final call in a sequence of calls to ldap_first_attribute() and ldap_next_attribute(), it should be freed by calling ber_free() with a second argument of zero.

Synopsis:

```
char *ldap_next_attribute(LDAP *ld, LDAPMessage *entry, BerEle-
ment *ber );
```

Returns a copy of the next attribute name contained in an entry.

Return Value:

Type: char *

A copy of the name of the next attribute in the entry. NULL will be returned in case of error, and the LDAP error code set. NULL is also returned if there are no more attributes in the entry. In the Netscape SDK, the attribute name returned should be freed by calling ldap_memfree() when it is no longer needed. In the University of Michigan SDK, the return value is a pointer to static data and does not need to be freed.

Parameters:

> `LDAP *ld`: This parameter is the LDAP session handle as returned from a successful call to `ldap_init()` or `ldap_open()`.
>
> `LDAPMessage *entry`: This parameter is the entry whose next attribute is to be returned. The entry must have been returned from a successful call to `ldap_first_entry()` or `ldap_next_entry()`.
>
> `BerElement *ber`: This parameter is a pointer to an opaque data type that was allocated by a previous call to `ldap_first_attribute()`. When you are done with a sequence of calls to `ldap_first_attribute()` and `ldap_next_attribute()`, this argument, if non-`NULL`, should be freed by calling `ber_free()` with a second argument of zero.

`ldap_next_attribute()` returns a char * pointing to the string name of the next attribute in the entry. In the Netscape SDK, this memory must be freed by the caller by calling `ldap_memfree()`. In the University of Michigan SDK, the string is static storage that should not be freed.

If the returned entry contains no more attributes or an error occurs, `ldap_next_entry()` will return `NULL`. To distinguish between these two conditions you must examine the value of the LDAP error from the operation. LDAP error handling is described in more detail in Chapter 8.

The opaque data type pointed to by the `ber` parameter is updated to keep track of the current position in the entry's list of attributes. It may be passed to a subsequent call to `ldap_next_attribute()` to continue stepping through the entry's attributes. If `ber` is non-`NULL` after the final call in a sequence of calls to `ldap_first_attribute()` and `ldap_next_attribute()`, it should be freed by calling `ber_free()` with a second argument of zero.

Example 9.4: The following example combines the `ldap_first_attribute()` and `ldap_next_attribute()` routines with the other entry parsing routines we've described so far to implement a function that steps through the results of a search, and prints out each entry's name and the names of the attributes the entry contains.

```
void
print_entry_attr_names( LDAP *ld, LDAPMessage *result )
{
        LDAPMessage    *e;
        BerElement     *ber;
        char           *dn, *attr;

        for ( e = ldap_first_entry( ld, result ); e != NULL;
          e = ldap_next_entry(ld, e ) ) {
            if ( (dn = ldap_get_dn( ld, e )) != NULL ) {
                    printf( "dn: %s\n", dn );
                    ldap_memfree( dn );
            }
            for ( attr = ldap_first_attribute( ld, e, &ber );
              attr != NULL;
              attr = ldap_next_attribute( ld, e, ber ) {
                    printf( "attr: %s\n", attr );
                    ldap_memfree( attr );
            }
            if ( ber != NULL ) {
                    ber_free( ber, 0 );
            }
        }
}
```

Tip

It is important to distinguish the attributes you asked to be retrieved with an entry in an LDAP search operation from the entire set of attributes contained in the entry in the directory. The former list is stepped through by `ldap_first_attribute()` and `ldap_next_attribute()`. It is the same as the latter list only if you requested and have access to retrieve all attributes in the entry itself.

Retrieving the Values of an Attribute

The most common reason for searching the LDAP directory is to retrieve certain attributes and values from entries that match the search criteria. So far, we've described routines that let you do everything but this vital task, to which we now turn our attention. Two routines are provided for retrieving the values of an attribute: `ldap_get_values()` and ldap_get_values_len(). The ldap_get_values() routine is used to retrieve string values of an attribute from an entry.

Synopsis:

```
char **ldap_get_values( LDAP *ld, LDAPMessage *entry, char *attr );
```

Returns a copy of the attribute values for the given attribute from the given entry.

Return Value:

Type: char **

A NULL-terminated array of NULL-terminated strings, containing a copy of the given attribute's values. NULL will be returned if the entry does not contain the attribute, or in case of error, in which case the LDAP error code will be set. The values returned should be freed by calling ldap_value_free() when they are no longer needed.

Parameters:

LDAP *ld: This parameter is the LDAP session handle as returned from a successful call to ldap_init() or ldap_open().

LDAPMessage *entry: This parameter is the entry containing the attribute whose values are to be returned. The entry must have been returned from a successful call to ldap_first_entry() or ldap_next_entry().

char *attr: This parameter is the name of the attribute whose values are to be retrieved from the entry. It can be an attribute name as returned from ldap_first_attribute() or ldap_next_attribute(), or a literal string or variable referencing the name of the attribute.

The ldap_get_values() routine returns a NULL-terminated array of NULL-terminated strings containing the values of the given attribute from the given entry. This array of values should be freed by the caller calling the ldap_value_free() routine. ldap_get_values() will return NULL if the attribute does not exist in the entry, the attribute contains no values, or some error occurred. The error condition can be distinguished by examining the LDAP error in the event of a NULL return.

There is no way to tell the difference between "attribute does not exist" and "attribute has no values", aside from using ldap_first_attribute() and ldap_next_attribute() to step through the attribute types to see if the attribute you're interested in exists.

Tip

> ldap_get_values() is a convenient way to access data values that can be represented by NULL-terminated strings. In the case of binary data (for example, a jpegPhoto or audio attribute), the ldap_get_values() interface is insufficient, and the ldap_get_values_len() routine should be used instead.

Example 9.5: Using the ldap_get_values() routine, the following example implements a function that steps through a list of entries as returned by ldap_search_s() or ldap_search_st() and prints out the contents of each entry in an LDIF-like format. LDIF, the LDAP Data Interchange Format, is described in more detail in Chapter 17.

```
void
print_entries_with_values( LDAP *ld, LDAPMessage *result )
{
        LDAPMessage     *e;
        BerElement      *ber;
        char            *dn, *attr;
        char            **vals;
        int             i;

        for ( e = ldap_first_entry( ld, result ); e != NULL;
            e = ldap_next_entry(ld, e ) ) {
                if ( (dn = ldap_get_dn( ld, e )) != NULL ) {
                        printf( "dn: %s\n", dn );
                        ldap_memfree( dn );
                }
                for ( attr = ldap_first_attribute( ld, e, &ber );
                    attr != NULL;
                    attr = ldap_next_attribute( ld, e, ber ) {
```

```
                              if ( (vals = ldap_get_values( ld, e, attr ))
                                 != NULL ) {
                                      for ( i = 0; vals[i] != NULL; i++ ) {
                                              printf( "%s: %s\n", attr,
                                          ➥vals[i] );
                                      }
                                      ldap_value_free( vals );
                              }
                              ldap_memfree( attr );
                      }
                      printf( "\n" );
                      if ( ber != NULL ) {
                              ber_free( ber, 0 );
                      }
              }
      }
}
```

This example assumes you are using the Netscape SDK. Small changes would be needed to adapt it to the University of Michigan SDK.

Pay particular attention to the calls to ldap_memfree() that we make to free memory returned by ldap_get_dn(), ldap_first_attribute(), and ldap_next_attribute(). A similar call to ldap_value_free() is included to free the result of the call to ldap_get_values(). Note especially two things about the call to ber_free(). First, it is only made if ber itself is non-NULL, indicating that an opaque data type has been allocated. Second, the second argument to ber_free() is always zero when called in this context.

Not all data values can be represented as NULL-terminated C strings. JPEG photos, audio attributes, and other binary data may contain embedded NULL characters. The ldap_get_values_len() routine is provided to deal with such values.

Synopsis:

```
struct berval **ldap_get_values_len( LDAP *ld, LDAPMessage
➥*entry, char *attr );
```

Returns a copy of the attribute values for the given attribute from the given entry.

Return Value:

Type: struct berval **

A copy of the given attribute's values. NULL will be returned if the entry does not contain the attribute, or in case of error, in which case the LDAP error code will be set. The values returned should be freed by calling ldap_value_free() when it is no longer needed.

Parameters:

LDAP *ld: This parameter is the LDAP session handle as returned from a successful call to ldap_init() or ldap_open().

LDAPMessage *entry: This parameter is the entry attribute values are to be returned. The entry must have been returned from a successful call to ldap_first_entry() or ldap_next_entry().

char *attr: This parameter is the name of the attribute whose values are to be retrieved from the entry. It can be an attribute name as returned from ldap_first_attribute() or ldap_next_attribute(), or a literal string or variable referencing the name of the attribute.

The ldap_get_values_len() routine returns a NULL-terminated array of pointers to struct bervals containing the values of the given attribute from the given entry. This array of values should be freed when no longer in use by the calling the ldap_value_free_len() routine. ldap_get_values_len() will return NULL if the attribute does not exist in the entry, the attribute contains no values, or some error occurs. The error condition can be distinguished by examining the LDAP error in the event of a NULL return. There is no way to tell the difference between "attribute does not exist" and "attribute has no values", aside from using ldap_first_attribute() and ldap_next_attribute() to step through the attribute types to see if the attribute you're interested in exists.

Representing Binary Values

The berval structure is a simple data type used to represent data values of arbitrary size and composition. It is defined as follows.

```
struct berval {
        unsigned long  bv_len;
        char           *bv_val;
};
```

The bv_len field holds the length of the data pointed to by the bv_val field.

Asynchronous Searching

The search calls we've discussed so far may be appropriate for simple applications, or applications whose only purpose is to access the LDAP directory. But typically, a directory-enabled application, or a user-driven directory application would rather do other things while it is waiting for results from the directory server. Being blocked — even for a few seconds — inside an ldap_search_s() call is not acceptable.

Luckily, the LDAP API provides an asynchronous interface that allows searches to be initiated, and then the results to be polled for at the caller's convenience. It is this form of the API that you will undoubtedly find most useful when writing all but the simplest directory or directory-enabled applications. An example will be coming up soon. But first, we describe the basic approach to asynchronicity that the LDAP API follows.

The ldap_search() call is used to initiate an LDAP search operation. It takes the parameters you provide, packages them up, and actually sends them off in a search request to the LDAP server. Assuming that all goes well, ldap_search() then returns to the caller a message ID identifying the request. This message ID can be used in subsequent calls to ldap_result() to retrieve the results of the search.

ldap_result() is at the heart of all asynchronous use of the LDAP API. The LDAP server returns the results of operations, including entries and the final result of a search, as well as other operations, in separate packets, or protocol data units, delivered over the network. ldap_result() is essentially an interface to retrieving these packets as they come in.

ldap_result() lets you specify how long you're willing to wait for a packet to show up, whether you want an individual packet (result or search entry) or in the case of search, an entire chain of results (all entries plus the result of the search). ldap_result() also lets you indicate interest in the result of a particular LDAP operation or any result that happens to come in. The details of both ldap_search() and ldap_result() are next, followed by an example of their use.

Synopsis:

```
int ldap_search( LDAP *ld, char *base, int scope, char *filter,
char *attrs[], int attrsonly );
```

Initiates a search of the LDAP directory using *base* as a starting point, covering entries described by *scope*, selecting entries matching *filter*, and returning attributes given by *attrs*.

Return Value:

Type: int

The message ID of the search operation initiated. If the search cannot be successfully initiated, –1 is returned and the LDAP error code is set to indicate the error.

Parameters:

LDAP *ld: This parameter is a handle to an LDAP session, as returned by a successful call to ldap_init() or ldap_open(). In the Netscape LDAP SDK, this handle references an opaque data type. In the University of Michigan SDK, this handle is a pointer to a structure that is exposed to your program.

char *base: This parameter specifies the base object for the search operation. The base object is the point in the LDAP tree at which you want to start searching. Its value is a distinguished name. In our example, we've set the base object to "o=Ace Industry, c=US". If you are running an LDAP server of your own, you could set the base object to the DN for your own organization.

int *scope*: This parameter specifies the portion of the LDAP tree, relative to the base object, to search. It can have one of three possible values. The value we've chosen for our example is LDAP_SCOPE_SUBTREE, indicating that we want to search the entire LDAP subtree rooted at and including the base object. Other possible values are LDAP_SCOPE_ONELEVEL to search only the immediate children of the base object and LDAP_SCOPE_BASE to search only the base object entry itself.

char **filter*: This parameter specifies the criteria to use during the search to determine which entries to return. We cover more complicated search filters in the next chapter.

char **attrs*[]: This parameter specifies the attributes to return along with each entry matching the search. It is a NULL-terminated array of strings specifying the name of attributes you want returned to you. Passing NULL for this argument means that all attributes should be returned.

int *attrsonly*: This parameter is a Boolean parameter specifying whether both types and values should be returned with each attribute (zero) or types only should be returned (non-zero).

As you can see, the parameters of ldap_search() are the same as those for ldap_search_s(), except that the last parameter of ldap_search_s() is missing.

The value returned by ldap_search() is quite different from the value returned by ldap_search_s(). While the latter routine returns one of the error codes found in ldap.h indicating the ultimate success or failure of the search, ldap_search() returns the message ID of the request it has initiated.

Recall that ldap_search() only initiates the search. The message ID it returns is unique among other message IDs outstanding on the LDAP session and is used to reference the search on a later call to ldap_result(). It has no other significance. You must call ldap_result() to find out the status of the search (whether the server has responded

to your request yet and what that response is). ldap_search() will return
−1 if it was unable to initiate the request, which can happen if the network was down, memory could not be allocated, etc. The LDAP error
will be set to indicate the problem if −1 is returned.

Synopsis:

```
int ldap_result( LDAP *ld, int msgid, int all, struct timeval
*timeout, LDAPMessage **result );
```

Retrieves the results from previously initiated operations, or
checks the status of previously initiated operations.

Return Value:

Type: int

If greater than zero, the message type of the result retrieved. If
zero, the timeout was exceeded before the requested result(s) were
available. If −1 is returned, an internal error has occurred, and the
LDAP error code is set to indicate the error.

Parameters:

LDAP *ld: This parameter is a handle to an LDAP session, as returned by a successful call to ldap_init() or ldap_open().

int msgid: This parameter specifies the message ID for which results are desired, as returned from a successful call to
ldap_search() or any of the other asynchronous operation initiation routines. To request the result of any operation, the special
value LDAP_RES_ANY should be passed for msgid.

int all: This parameter only has meaning for search operations.
Recall that the result of a search operation as sent by the LDAP
server consists of zero or more entries followed by a final search
outcome packet indicating the ultimate success or failure of the
search. The all parameter is a Boolean that determines whether
ldap_result() should return single packets (either search entries or
the result of an operation) as they come in (zero), or if instead it
should wait and return the entire chain of search entries and final
outcome only after all the entries and the final outcome have been

received (non-zero). If `all` is non-zero, `ldap_result()` will always return at most one "packet" per call, either an entry from a search operation, or a final outcome result from any operation.

`struct timeval *timeout`: This parameter controls how long `ldap_result()` should wait for results to come in. A value of `NULL` for `timeout` indicates that `ldap_result()` should block indefinitely, until the requested results come in. A non-`NULL` value of `timeout` with the timeout value set to zero indicates that `ldap_result()` should effect a polling behavior. If results are available immediately, they will be returned. If not, `ldap_result()` will not wait for them.

`LDAPMessage **result`: This parameter is a pointer to an `LDAPMessage *` used to hold the result of a successful call to `ldap_result()`. If the `ldap_result()` call returns a value greater than zero, the `result` parameter will be filled in with the result, which, depending on what has been requested via the `msgid` and `all` parameters, may be a single search entry, an LDAP result from an operation, or an entire chain of search entries and a final search result. The `result` parameter should be freed by the caller by calling `ldap_msgfree()` when it is no longer in use.

The return value of `ldap_result()` follows a convention similar to that used by the `select()` system call. It returns values in one of three categories. A return of –1 indicates that some error has occurred. The LDAP error will be set to indicate the problem. A return of 0 (zero) indicates that a timeout has occurred. The timeout you specified in the timeout parameter expired before an appropriate result came in. A non-zero return indicates success, and that a result has been returned in the result parameter.

The value of the greater-than-zero return from `ldap_result()` indicates the type of result contained in the result parameter. It will be one of the result type constants declared in the `ldap.h` header file. Possible values and their meanings are described below. Only the first two values are relevant to search, but we list the other values for completeness.

`LDAP_RES_SEARCH_ENTRY`	A single entry matching a previously initiated search request.
`LDAP_RES_SEARCH_RESULT`	Either a result indicating the final outcome of a previously initiated search operation or an entire chain of entries matching a previously initiated search request, along with the final outcome.
`LDAP_RES_BIND_RESULT`	The result of a previously initiated bind operation.
`LDAP_RES_COMPARE_RESULT`	The result of a previously initiated compare operation.
`LDAP_RES_MODIFY_RESULT`	The result of a previously initiated modify operation.
`LDAP_RES_ADD_RESULT`	The result of a previously initiated add operation.
`LDAP_RES_DELETE_RESULT`	The result of a previously initiated delete operation.
`LDAP_RES_MODRDN_RESULT`	The result of a previously initiated modify RDN operation.

If you have specified `LDAP_RES_ANY` in the call to `ldap_result()`, it may be useful to know the message ID of the result finally returned; `ldap_result()` returns the type of the result, but not its message ID. In the University of Michigan SDK, the message ID of the result is available in the following field of the LDAPMessage structure.

```
int          msgid;
LDAPMessage  *result;
/* successful call to ldap_result() fills in result */
msgid = result->lm_msgid;
```

In the Netscape SDK, the LDAPMessage holding results is an opaque data type. The message ID associated with a result can be obtained by calling the following accessor function.

```
int          msgid;
LDAPMessage  *result;
/* successful call to ldap_result() fills in result */
msgid = ldap_msgid( ld, result );
```

Asynchronous Programming Example

Example 9.6: Having described the asynchronous searching routines in excruciating detail, we now present a complete example illustrating their use. This example is basically a rewrite of our previous example which dumped out an LDIF representation of the Jensen family.

We've made two changes to help illustrate the power of the asynchronous LDAP API. First, instead of just retrieving information about the Jensens, we've changed the example to retrieve information about everyone at Ace Industry. This will better illustrate the performance improvements that the asynchronous API can provide. Second, instead of waiting for the entire set of entries to come in before we begin printing them, we retrieve and print them out one at a time, as they are delivered to us by the server. You should experience a noticeably shorter time delay before the entries start printing with this asynchronous example.

```
1.   #include <stdio.h>
2.   #include <ldap.h>

3.   #define SEARCHBASE      "o=Ace Industry, c=US"

4.   /*
5.    * include definition of print_entries_with_values() routine
6.    * from the example above.
7.    */

8.   main()
9.   {
```

```
10.          LDAP        *ld;
11.          LDAPMessage *result;
12.          int         nentries, msgid, rc;

13.          if ( (ld = ldap_init( "ldap.netscape.com", LDAP_PORT ))
14.              == NULL) {
15.                  perror( "ldap_init" );
16.                  exit( 1 );
17.          }

18.          if ( ldap_simple_bind_s( ld, NULL, NULL ) !=
        ➥LDAP_SUCCESS ) {
19.                  ldap_perror( ld, "ldap_simple_bind_s" );
20.                  exit( 1 );
21.          }

22.          if ( (msgid = ldap_search( ld, SEARCHBASE,
        ➥LDAP_SCOPE_SUBTREE,
23.              "(objectclass=*)", NULL, 0 )) == -1 ) {
24.                  ldap_perror( ld, "ldap_search" );
25.                  exit( 1 );
26.          }

27.          nentries = 0;
28.          while ( (rc = ldap_result( ld, msgid, 0, NULL, &result ))
29.              == LDAP_RES_SEARCH_ENTRY ) {
30.                  nentries++;
31.                  print_entries_with_values( ld, result );
32.                  ldap_msgfree( result );
33.          }
34.          if ( rc == -1) {
35.                  ldap_perror( ld, "ldap_result" );
36.                  exit( 1 );
37.          }

38.          printf( "Found %d entries at Ace Industry\n", nentries );
39.          ldap_unbind( ld );
40.          return( 0 );
41.  }
```

This example makes use of the `print_entries_with_values()` routine we constructed above in the example for `ldap_get_values()`. This function works as well to print out single entries as it does to print out a whole chain of search entries.

Notice that we've changed the search filter used in this example from `(sn=Jensen)` to `(objectclass=*)`. The former filter selects entries with a surname attribute of Jensen. The latter filter matches any entry and will thus return to us everybody who works for Ace Industry. The next chapter talks in more detail about search filters and how to construct them.

Lines 29 through 34 call `ldap_result()` repeatedly, retrieving one entry from the search per call. `ldap_result()` is called with a blocking timeout (fourth parameter of `NULL`), which causes it to not return until an entry is received. The entry is returned in the result parameter. As long as the result returned is an entry from the search, identified by `ldap_result()` returning `LDAP_RES_SEARCH_ENTRY`, we continue to call `ldap_result()`.

If we had something else to do between calls to `ldap_result()`, for example, check for other network activity, spin a cursor, update a display, check for keyboard input, etc., we could have called `ldap_result()` in polling mode (fourth parameter pointing to a zero-valued timeval structure) instead.

We gain two key advantages from calling `ldap_result()` to retrieve one entry at a time, instead of calling `ldap_search_s()` to retrieve all entries at once. First, we can start processing and printing entries as soon as they come in, rather than waiting for the complete list of entries to accumulate before printing any. If the number of entries being returned is large, this can provide quite a perceived performance improvement. Second, since we process one entry at a time, we can free up each entry after we print it out, resulting in much smaller memory use. Such savings are important in memory-constrained environments.

Summary

The following table summarizes the routines and data types described in this chapter.

Name	Description
ber_free()	Frees memory allocated to keep track of position between calls to ldap_first_attribute() and ldap_next_attribute().
ldap_count_entries()	Counts the number of entries in a search result.
ldap_first_attribute()	Retrieves the name of the first attribute in an entry.
ldap_first_entry()	Retrieves the first entry in a chain of search results.
ldap_get_dn()	Retrieves the DN of an entry.
ldap_get_values()	Retrieves a NULL-terminated array of NULL-terminated string values of an attribute.
ldap_get_values_len()	Retrieves a NULL-terminated array of arbitrary data values of an attribute.
ldap_memfree()	Frees memory allocated by the LDAP library and returned via ldap_get_dn(), ldap_first_attribute(), or ldap_next_attribute().
ldap_msgid()	Retrieves the message ID of a result returned from ldap_result().
ldap_msgfree()	Frees a chain of search results returned from ldap_search_s() and friends.
ldap_next_attribute()	Retrieves the name of the next attribute in an entry.
ldap_next_entry()	Retrieves the next entry in a chain of search results.
ldap_result()	Asynchronously retrieves results of previously initiated operations.
ldap_search()	Initiates an asynchronous search of the LDAP directory.
ldap_search_s()	Synchronously searches the LDAP directory.

continues

Name	Description
`ldap_search_st()`	Synchronously searches the LDAP directory with time-out.
`ldap_value_free()`	Frees memory allocated by a call to `ldap_get_values()`.
`ldap_value_free_len()`	Frees memory allocated by a call to `ldap_get_values_len()`.
`struct timeval`	Used to specify a local time limit on search operations.
`struct berval`	Used to represent binary data values.

Looking Ahead

This chapter has introduced you to the core LDAP API calls needed to search an LDAP directory. Some topics have been glossed over a bit, such as how to construct search filters and some interesting things you can do with distinguished names. These topics are tackled in the next chapters.

CHAPTER 10

Search Filters

I n the last chapter, you learned the basics of LDAP searching, how to parse the entries returned, and how to construct simple search filters. In this chapter we take a detailed look at search filters, their syntax, and how to construct them. We also introduce the `getfilter` routines. This set of routines is included with the LDAP SDK and can greatly simplify and automate the process of constructing search filters.

The following section presents a formal definition of LDAP search filters, showing you the full range of capabilities they possess, and how you can construct arbitrarily complex filters. The next section describes the LDAP `getfilter` routines, which can be used in some circumstances to automate the process of filter construction.

Search Filters

As you saw in the previous chapter, the LDAP API search calls accept a search filter in the form of a simple string. The format of this string is defined in RFC 1960. We did not go into detail about the format of this string, choosing instead to focus on other aspects of the search routines and show only simple examples of search filters. This section describes search filters in detail.

The string representation of LDAP search filters allows you to access the full range of search filters possible in the LDAP protocol. You can construct filters to find entries satisfying quite complex criteria. In the last chapter we saw how to use the following simple filters.

Filter Example	Matches
(sn=Jensen)	Entries that have a surname of Jensen
(objectclass=*)	All entries

Search Filters Explained

Search filters can go way beyond these simple examples. Before we get to the formal definition, consider the following examples of more complicated LDAP search filters.

Filter Example	Matches
(cn=*bert*)	All entries with the string "bert" somewhere in the name.
(cn>=Fred)	All entries with a common name lexicographically greater than "Fred".
(&(objectclass=person)(mail=*))	All people with an e-mail address.

`(&(title=*director*)(ou=marketing)` `(mail=*))`	All entries with the string "director" in their title and who are in marketing and who have an e-mail address.

`(&(objectclass=person)`
`(|(title=*director*)`
`(title=*executive*)))`
	All people entries with the string "director" or the string "executive" in their title.

As you can see, filters can be pretty powerful. The format is relatively simple, though a little bit obscure unless you are familiar with prefix notation. The formal grammar defining a search filter follows at the end of this section, but first we present the search filter in what we hope is an easier-to-understand format.

There are six kinds of basic search filters that take an `<attribute>` `<operator><value>` format. More complicated search filters are constructed by combining these basic search filters (and other complex filters) using the Boolean operations AND, OR, and NOT. The six basic filter components and their meanings are as follows.

Filter Type	Format	Example	Matches
Equality	`(<attr>=<value>)`	`(sn=Jensen)`	Surnames exactly equal to Jensen.
Approximate	`(<attr>~=<value>)`	`(sn~=Jensin)`	Surnames approximately equal to Jensin (for example, that sounds like Jensin—note the misspelling).
Substring	`(<attr>=[<leading>]*` `[<any>]*[<trailing>])`	`(sn=*jensen*)`	Surnames containing the string "jensen".

continues

Filter Type	Format	Example	Matches
		`(sn=jensen*)`	Surnames starting with "jensen".
		`(sn=*jensen)`	Surnames ending in "jensen".
		`(sn=jen*s*en)`	Surnames starting with "jen", containing an "s", and ending with "en".
Greater than or equal	`(<attr>>=<value>)`	`(sn>=Jensen)`	Surnames lexicographically greater than or equal to Jensen.
Less than or equal	`(<attr><=<value>)`	`(sn<=Jensen)`	Surnames lexicographically less than or equal to Jensen.
Presence	`(<attr>=*)`	`(sn=*)`	All surnames.

These basic filters can be combined to form more complex filters using the Boolean operators and a prefix notation. The '&' character represents AND, the '|' character represents OR, and the '!' character represents NOT. The following table explains how to combine simple filters to produce more complicated ones.

Filter Type	Format	Example	Matches
AND	`(&(<filter1>)` `(<filter2>)…))`	`(&(sn=Jensen)` `(objectclass=person))`	Entries with an object class of person and a surname exactly equal to Jensen.

		`(&(sn=Jensen)` `(mail=*)` `(title=*director*)` `(objectclass=person))`	Entries with an object class of person and a title containing "director" and an object class of person and a mail attribute.
OR	`(|(<filter1>)` `(<filter2>)…)`	`(|(sn~=Jensin)` `(cn=*jensin))`	Entries with a surname approximately equal to Jensin or a common name ending in "jensin".
		`(|(cn=bob)` `(cn=robert)` `(cn=*bert*)` `(objectclass=person))`	Entries with an object class of person and with a common name of "bob" or "robert" or containing "bert".
NOT	`(!(<filter>))`	`(!(mail=*))`	Entries without a mail attribute.

Tip

> Often it is wise to create a filter that weeds out unwanted entries based on their object class. For example, in an address book application, you might only want to retrieve people entries with a common name of John, leaving out the entry for your neighbor John's self-titled machine. A filter like this would do the trick:
>
> `(&(objectclass=person)(cn=john))`

Complex filters themselves can be combined to create arbitrarily complex nested filters. For example, in the previous example if you wanted to search for people or groups named John, while still leaving out printers, machines, or other things named John, you could do so with the following filter:

`(&(|(objectclass=person)(objectclass=group))(cn=john))`

Any number of components can be combined under the AND and OR filters. For example, you could construct this filter to search for people by several names at once:

`(|(cn=Bob)(cn=Robert)(cn=Rob)(cn=Rob-Bob)(cn=Bobby))`

A NOT filter can only have a single filter associated with it, though that single filter may be as complex as desired. For example, to search for people not named in the preceding search, you could construct this filter:

`(!(|(cn=Bob)(cn=Robert)(cn=Rob)(cn=Rob-Bob)(cn=Bobby)))`

Tip

Keep in mind that the kind of filter you construct is likely to have a large impact on how quickly the search you're doing takes place. If you construct filters that involve attributes that the directory server does not index, or constructs that it can't evaluate efficiently, performance is likely to suffer. Unfortunately, aside from being familiar with the administration and/or inner workings of the server itself, there is only trial and error to tell you whether your search filter will be handled efficiently.

Search Filters Defined

Now that you've seen a number of examples of search filters and have a good idea of their full power, it's time for a formal definition. The following grammar is in a BNF-like format, as is used in many Internet RFCs.

```
<filter> ::= '(' <filtercomp> ')'
<filtercomp> ::= <and> | <or> | <not> | <item>
<and> ::= '&' <filterlist>
```

```
<or> ::= '|' <filterlist>
<not> ::= '!' <filter>
<filterlist> ::= <filter> | <filter> <filterlist>
<item> ::= <simple> | <present> | <substring>
<simple> ::= <attr> <filtertype> <value>
<filtertype> ::= <equal> | <approx> | <greater> | <less>
<equal> ::= '='
<approx> ::= '~='
<greater> ::= '>='
<less> ::= '<='
<present> ::= <attr> '=*'
<substring> ::= <attr> '=' <initial> <any> <final>
<initial> ::= NULL | <value>
<any> ::= '*' <starval>
<starval> ::= NULL | <value> '*' <starval>
<final> ::= NULL | <value>
```

BNF aficionados may notice that there are two ways to produce the
<attr>=* construct, both through the <present> production and
through the <substring> production. This is an artifact of the grammar
only. Any filter of the form <attr>=* denotes a presence filter.

Automatic Filter Generation

Sometimes it's possible to know in advance the kind of filter you want
to use in a search. Other times, you can ask the user to construct the
appropriate filter through some GUI query builder or the equivalent.
Occasionally, if your application is targeted at a knowledgeable user, it's
acceptable to have the user type in the search filter directly.

More often, though, your application is targeted at much less sophisti-
cated users and is far too limited to include a general query builder
GUI component. This is typical of a directory component embedded
within a larger application. In these situations, you may have only a
single box of input for the user to type into, and it's up to your application to figure out based on what the user typed the best kind of LDAP
search to perform.

Enter the getfilter routines. These routines are designed to work in
this limited user-interaction, unsophisticated user environment. They

take some input, typically a search string of some kind typed in by a user, and return a series of search filters to try. Each filter may be based on the input itself, or may be some constant filter that is always tried.

The `getfilter` routines work from a configuration file. They compare the input they are given to regular expressions in the configuration file. If they find a match, the routines construct the associated filter(s) specified in the file. The input string being matched can be broken into tokens, which can then be substituted into the filters produced. The whole scheme provides a pretty flexible way to generate filters.

Example 10.1: An example should help explain things. Suppose we have a simple search application that collects user input and searches the directory for matching entries. If the user types in what looks like a phone number, we want to search by phone number. If the user types in what looks like an e-mail address, we want to search by e-mail address. A text string should cause a search by common name and surname to be done. A text string with no spaces should cause a search by common name and surname and uid. And finally, for those users who are really cool, if they type in something that looks like a raw search filter, we want to search using the filter itself, unchanged. The following program implements this algorithm, all with the `getfilter` routines.

```
1.    #include <stdio.h>
2.    #include <ldap.h>

3.    #define FILTERFILE  "/tmp/getfilter.conf"
4.    #define SEARCHBASE       "o=Ace Industry, c=US"

5.    main( int argc, char **argv )
6.    {
7.            LDAP                          *ld;
8.            LDAPMessage        *result;
9.            LDAPFiltInfo                   *fi;
10.           LDAPFiltDesc       *fd;

11.           if ( argc != 2 ) {
12.                   fprintf( stderr, "usage: %s searchstring\n",
                      ➥argv[0] );
13.                   exit( 1 );
```

```
14.             }
15.         if ( (ld = ldap_init( "ldap.netscape.com", LDAP_PORT ))
16.             == NULL ) {
17.                 perror( "ldap_init" );
18.                 exit( 1 );
19.         }
20.         if ( ldap_simple_bind_s( ld, NULL, NULL ) != LDAP_SUCCESS ) {
21.                 ldap_perror( ld, "ldap_simple_bind_s" );
22.                 exit( 1 );
23.         }
24.         if ( (fd = ldap_init_getfilter( FILTERFILE )) == NULL ) {
25.                 perror( FILTERFILE );
26.                 exit( 1 );
27.         }
28.         for ( fi = ldap_getfirstfilter( fd, "myapp", argv[1] );
29.             fi != NULL; fi = ldap_getnextfilter( fd ) ) {
30.                 if ( ldap_search_s( ld, SEARCHBASE,
                    ➥LDAP_SCOPE_SUBTREE,
31.                     fi->lfi_filter, NULL, 0, &result )
32.                     != LDAP_SUCCESS ) {
33.                         ldap_perror( ld, "ldap_search_s" );
34.                         exit( 1 );
35.                 }
36.                 if ( (matches = ldap_count_entries( ld, result ))
37.                     != 0 ) {
38.                         printf( "Found %d matches with filter
                            ➥\"%s\"\n",
39.                             matches, fi->lfi_filter );
40.                         return( 0 );
41.                 }
42.                 ldap_msgfree( result );
43.         }
44.         printf( "Could not find any matches for \"%s\"\n",
            ➥argv[1] );
45.         ldap_getfilter_free( fd );
46.         return( 1 );
47.  }
```

This application doesn't do much with what it finds. That's not the point of the application, so we didn't want to clutter it up. But it does illustrate the use of the getfilter routines.

Of course, all the magic that makes this happen is contained in the getfilter routines, which are called in the loop on lines 28–43, after having been initialized by lines 24–27. The initialization routine, ldap_init_getfilter(), reads the configuration file given in its argument. The configuration file consists of a series of stanzas, each identified by a unique tag. This tag is used later in the call to ldap_getfirstfilter(), and allows the sets of filters for multiple applications to live in the same getfilter file.

Each stanza in the getfilter file consists of a series of lines beginning with regular expressions that are matched by the input to ldap_getfirstfilter() and ldap_getnextfilter(). If one of the regular expressions matches, the filter patterns on the remainder of the line are filled in using the given input and returned in the lfi_filter field of the LDAPFiltInfo structure.

For example, the following getfilter file implements the policy for the preceding example.

```
"myapp"
     "="                 " "    "%v"                              "arbitrary
                                                                   filter"
     "^[0-9][0-9-]*$" " "      "(telephoneNumber=*%v)"            "phone
                                                                   number"
     "@"                 " "    "(mail=%v)"                        "email
                                                                   address"
                                "(mail=%v*)"                       "start of
                                                                   email
                                                                   address"
     "^.[. _].*"      ". _"    "(cn=%v1* %v2-)"                   "first
                                                                   initial"
     ".*[. _].$"      ". _"    "(cn=%v1-*)"                       "last
                                                                   initial"
     "[. _]"          ". _"    "(|(sn=%v1-)(cn=%v1-))"            "exact"
                                "(|(sn~=%v1-)(cn~=%v1-))"          "approximate"
     ".*"             ". "     "(|(cn=%v1)(sn=%v1)(uid=%v1))" "exact"
                                "(|(cn~=%v1)(sn~=%v1))"            "approximate"
```

If the user inputs something with an equals sign in it, the first line is matched, and the user input is used unchanged as the search filter (%v stands for the entire user-supplied value). If the user types something with all numbers in it, the second expression is matched, and a search for a telephone number ending in what the user typed is done. An @ sign causes a search by e-mail address, and other inputs cause various searches by common name (cn), surname (sn), and uid.

Notice the use of %v in the filter pattern (column three) to indicate the input value. Also allowed are constructs such as %v1, %v2, and so on to indicate individual "words" in the input string. A word is defined by the word-break characters, given in column two. %vN- can be used to indicate word N and all following words.

The final column is used to contain a descriptive string for the match. This string is available as the lfi_description field in the LDAPFiltInfo structure. The idea is that the string should be suitable for display to a user in a sentence like "Found three %s matches for your search query," where the string is substituted for %s, but you could put whatever you want there because it is only to be interpreted by your program.

The list of possible variable substitutions referring to portions of the user input you can use in a filter pattern is given in the following table. Where a number is provided, as in the %vN construct, the number must be a single digit from 0–9.

Format	Meaning
%v	The entire value.
%vN	Word N in the value.
%vN-	Word N in the value and all following words.
%vN-M	Words N through M in the value.
%v$	The last word in the value.

The getfilter routines are described in detail next. The ldap_init_getfilter() routine must be called first.

Synopsis:

```
LDAPFilterDesc *ldap_init_getfilter( char *filterfile );
```

Initializes the LDAP getfilter routines. The given configuration file containing getfilter configuration information is parsed and read.

Return Value:

Type: LDAPFilterDesc *

On success, the ldap_init_getfilter() routine will return a handle to the initialized filter file. This handle should be supplied to subsequent calls to ldap_getfirstfilter() or ldap_getnextfilter(). If the filter file cannot be opened, read, or contains faulty configuration information, NULL will be returned and the LDAP error code will be set to indicate the problem.

Parameters:

char *filterfile: This parameter is the name of the getfilter configuration file. It must be accessible for read by your program.

The LDAP API contains a related call, ldap_init_getfilter_buf(), that performs the same function as ldap_init_getfilter(), but it reads from an in-memory buffer instead of from a file. This routine is useful to applications that don't want to rely on configuration files, perhaps choosing instead to store their filter configuration information in an application resource.

Once the getfilter routines have been successfully initialized, the ldap_getfirstfilter() and ldap_getnextfilter() routines can be called to retrieve LDAP search filters appropriate to user input.

Synopsis:

```
LDAPFiltInfo *ldap_getfirstfilter( LDAPFilterDesc *fd,
char *tag, char *input );
```

Retrieves the first matching filter string from the given initialized `getfilter` file. This routine is used along with `ldap_getnextfilter()` to step through a list of matching filters.

Return Value:

Type: `LDAPFiltInfo *`

On success, `ldap_getfirstfilter()` returns a pointer to an `LDAPFiltInfo` structure containing information about the filter that was matched. The `LDAPFiltInfo` structure is defined below. The `ldap_getfirstfilter()` routine returns `NULL` if no filters match the given input, or in case of trouble (memory allocation failure and so on).

Parameters:

`LDAPFilterDesc *fd`: This parameter is a handle to an initialized `getfilter` configuration file, as returned from a successful call to `ldap_init_getfilter()`. In the Netscape SDK, this is a handle to an opaque data type. In the University of Michigan SDK, this is a pointer to a structure available to your program.

`char *tag`: This parameter is the tag at the head of the desired stanza within the filter configuration file. Tags are examined in the order in which they appear in the file to find a match.

`char *input`: This is the input to match against the regular expressions in column one of the matching stanza of the `getfilter` file. Usually, this input comes from the user.

The `LDAPFiltInfo` structure is used to return information about a matching search filter. It is defined as follows.

```
typedef struct ldap_filt_info {
  char                    *lfi_filter;
  char                    *lfi_desc;
  int                     lfi_scope;
  int                     lif_isexact;
  struct ldap_filt_info   *lfi_next;
} LDAPFiltInfo;
```

The fields have the following meaning.

char *lfi_filter: This field contains an LDAP search filter that has been constructed from the filter pattern contained in the getfilter configuration file and the input parameter to ldap_getfirstfilter(). It is suitable for passing to ldap_search().

char *lfi_desc: This field contains the match description associated with the matching filter. It is the string in the last column of the getfilter configuration file.

int lfi_scope: This field will be set to one of the valid LDAP search scopes, corresponding to the contents of the optional fifth and last column in the filter description file, which should contain one of the strings "base", "onelevel", or "subtree".

int lfi_isexact: This field is a Boolean flag that is zero if the filter pattern given in column one of the filter description file contains a '*' or '~' character, indicating a substring or approximate matching filter, respectively.

The filter configuration file can contain multiple filters matching each regular expression. Subsequent matching filters may be retrieved by calling the ldap_getnextfilter() routine.

Synopsis:

LDAPFiltInfo *ldap_getnextfilter(LDAPFilterDesc *fd);

Retrieves the next matching filter string in a sequence of matching filters from the given initialized getfilter file. This routine is used along with ldap_getfirstfilter() to step through a list of matching filters.

Return Value:

Type: LDAPFiltInfo *

On success, ldap_getnextfilter() returns a pointer to an LDAPFiltInfo structure containing information about the filter that was matched. The LDAPFiltInfo structure was defined previously and is the same as that returned by ldap getfirstfilter(). The ldap_getnextfilter() routine returns NULL if no filters match the given input, or in case of trouble (memory allocation failure and so on).

Parameters:

> LDAPFilterDesc *fd: This parameter is a handle to an initialized getfilter configuration file, as returned from a successful call to ldap_init_getfilter(). In the Netscape SDK, this is a handle to an opaque data type. In the University of Michigan SDK, this is a pointer to a structure available to your program. This parameter should have also been passed to a successful call to ldap_getfirstfilter().

Once you are done with an LDAP getfilter session, you should call the ldap_getfilter_free() routine to dispose of the LDAPFilterDesc handle allocated by ldap_init_getfilter().

Synopsis:

> void ldap_getfilter_free(LDAPFilterDesc *fd);

> Initializes the LDAP getfilter routines. The given configuration file containing getfilter configuration information is parsed and read.

Return Value:

> Type: void

Parameters:

> LDAPFilterDesc *fd: This parameter is the LDAPFilterDesc handle returned by a matching call to ldap_init_getfilter().

After calling ldap_getfilter_free() it is an error to refer to the LDAPFilterDesc handle that has been freed.

Summary

The following table summarizes the routines described in this chapter.

Name	Description
ldap_init_getfilter()	Opens a getfilter configuration file and initialize the getfilter routines.
ldap_init_getfilter_buf()	Initializes the getfilter routines from a buffer.
ldap_getfilter_free()	Deallocates the resources allocated by ldap_init_getfilter().
ldap_getfirstfilter()	Retrieves the first filter matching a given input.
ldap_getnextfilter()	Retrieves the next filter matching a given input.
LDAPFiltDesc	Opaque data type representing an LDAP getfilter configuration file.
LDAPFiltInfo	Data structure representing a filter matching user input constructed from the getfilter configuration file.

Looking Ahead

If you've made it through this chapter, you are an expert on LDAP searching and filter construction. In the next chapter we round out our coverage of search by describing a few more routines to deal with distinguished names and sort the entries returned from a search. The chapter after that finishes our coverage of operations to interrogate the LDAP directory by talking about compare. After that, we turn our attention to the task of updating the LDAP directory.

Distinguished Names and Sorting

I n the last two chapters you have learned how to search for and
retrieve information from LDAP directory entries. A number of
routines for pulling information out of the entries returned were also
covered. There are a few routines that were left out of that discussion.
In this chapter, we serve up these leftover functions. Note that this
chapter assumes you have already read about searching in Chapter 9.

The first category of functions we look at let you do interesting things
with an entry's Distinguished Name, including converting the DN into
a friendlier format and breaking it up into pieces. The second category
of functions we look at can be used to sort a list of entries or a set of
values. Because end-users expect to view sorted information but most
LDAP servers do not return entries and values in any particular order,
these sorting functions can be very important.

A Friendly Way to Display Distinguished Names

Example 11.1: Search an LDAP directory for all people with a surname of "Jensen" and display the entry names as a traditional DN and in a "user friendly" form.

```
1.     #include <stdio.h>
2.     #include <ldap.h>

3.     #define SEARCHBASE    "o=Ace Industry, c=US"

4.     main()
5.     {
6.             LDAP          *ld;
7.             LDAPMessage   *result, *e;
8.             char          *dn, *ufn;

9.             if ( (ld = ldap_init( "ldap.netscape.com", LDAP_PORT ))
10.                == NULL ) {
11.                    perror( "init" );
12.                    exit( 1 );
13.            }

14.            if ( ldap_simple_bind_s( ld, NULL, NULL ) !=
       ➡LDAP_SUCCESS ) {
15.                    ldap_perror( ld, "bind" );
16.                    ldap_unbind( ld );
17.                    exit( 1 );
18.            }

19.            if ( ldap_search_s( ld, SEARCHBASE,
       ➡LDAP_SCOPE_SUBTREE,
20.                "(sn=Jensen)", NULL, 0, &result ) != LDAP_SUCCESS
       ➡) {
21.                    ldap_perror( ld, "search" );
22.                    ldap_unbind( ld );
23.                    exit( 1 );
24.            }

25.            for ( e = ldap_first_entry( ld, result ); e != NULL;
26.                e = ldap_next_entry( ld, e )) {
27.                    if (( dn = ldap_get_dn( ld, e )) != NULL &&
```

```
28.                      ( ufn = ldap_dn2ufn( dn )) != NULL ) {
29.                           puts( dn );
30.                           puts( ufn );
31.                           putchar( '\n' );
32.                           ldap_memfree( dn );
33.                           ldap_memfree( ufn );
34.                      }
35.                 }

36.            ldap_unbind( ld );
37.            exit( 0 );
38.      }
```

This example is very similar to several that we saw in Chapter 9. It performs an LDAP search and steps through all of the entries returned. The only new call is the one to ldap_dn2ufn() that appears on line 28. This function takes a DN and returns a new, allocated string that is derived from the DN. This new form of the DN is called a "User Friendly Name" (UFN), and it differs from a DN in that the attribute type tags are removed. To illustrate, let's look at some sample output from a run of this example program:

```
cn=Kurt Jensen, ou=Product Development, o=Ace Industry, c=US
Kurt Jensen, Product Development, Ace Industry, US

cn=Barbara Jensen, ou=Product Development, o=Ace Industry, c=US
Barbara Jensen, Product Development, Ace Industry, US

cn=Gern Jensen, ou=Human Resources, o=Ace Industry, c=US
Gern Jensen, Human Resources, Ace Industry, US

cn=Jody Jensen, ou=Accounting, o=Ace Industry, c=US
Jody Jensen, Accounting, Ace Industry, US

cn=Allison Jensen, ou=Product Development, o=Ace Industry, c=US
Allison Jensen, Product Development, Ace Industry, US

cn=Bjorn Jensen, ou=Accounting, o=Ace Industry, c=US
Bjorn Jensen, Accounting, Ace Industry, US

cn=Ted Jensen, ou=Accounting, o=Ace Industry, c=US
Ted Jensen, Accounting, Ace Industry, US
```

```
cn=Richard Jensen, ou=Accounting, o=Ace Industry, c=US
Richard Jensen, Accounting, Ace Industry, US

cn=Randy Jensen, ou=Product Testing, o=Ace Industry, c=US
Randy Jensen, Product Testing, Ace Industry, US
```

The first of each pair of lines shows the Distinguished Name of the entry and the second shows the User Friendly Name. Most people would agree that the UFN form is easier to read and that not much information is lost by removing the tags.

Tip

Most polished LDAP applications hide DNs from their users whenever possible. The attribute types and tags are ugly and confusing to the uninitiated, and the `ldap_dn2ufn()` function is a very low-cost way to improve the readability of entry names.

The next section provides a summary of the `ldap_dn2ufn()` LDAP API function.

Synopsis:

```
char *ldap_dn2ufn( char *dn);
```

Converts a Distinguished Name (DN) into an easier to read form called a User Friendly Name (UFN). UFNs differ from DNs in that they do not contain any attribute type tags.

Return Value:

Type: char *

If successful, a pointer to a string that contains the UFN-form of a DN is returned. This string should be freed by calling `ldap_memfree()`. If the DN cannot be converted for some reason, NULL is returned (this usually only occurs if memory allocation fails or the DN passed into `ldap_dn2ufn()` was invalid).

Parameters:

> char *dn: An LDAP Distinguished Name (the name of an entry),
> as returned by a call such as ldap_get_dn(). The DN should con-
> form to the format described in RFC-1779, A String Representa-
> tion of Distinguished Names.

Breaking Up a Distinguished Name into Its Component Parts

You may recall from Chapter 3 that all DNs are made up of a series of components called Relative Distinguished Names (RDNs). Each RDN is unique among its siblings, that is, no two entries that exist below a common parent entry in the directory have the same RDN. This re-striction ensures that every entry within the same LDAP directory has a unique name.

Sometimes it is useful to pull a DN apart into its RDN components and use the pieces. The ldap_explode_dn() function can be used to break up a DN into its component parts.

Example 11.2: A function that returns the DN of the parent of an entry. If the DN has no parent (that is, it is NULL or a zero-length string already), we return a zero-length string.

```
1.    char *
2.    parentDN( char *dn )
3.    {
4.        char    *parent, **rdns;
5.        int     i, len;

6.        if ( dn == NULL || *dn == '\0' ) {
7.                return( strdup( "" ));
8.        }

9.        if ( (rdns = ldap_explode_dn( dn, 0 )) == NULL ) {
10.               return( NULL );
11.       }
```

```
12.        /* calculate total length of parent DN */
13.        len = 1;    /* room for zero byte used to terminate
           ➥strings */
14.        for ( i = 1; rdns[ i ] != NULL; ++i ) {
15.                len += ( 2 + strlen( rdns[ i ] )); /* room for ",
                   ➥" and RDN */
16.        }
17.        /* allocate space to hold the parent DN */
18.        if ( (parent = malloc( len )) == NULL ) {
19.                ldap_value_free( rdns );
20.                return( NULL );
21.        }

22.        /* construct parent DN from RDNs */
23.        *parent = '\0';
24.        for ( i = 1; rdns[ i ] != NULL; ++i ) {
25.                if ( i > 1 ) {
26.                        strcat( parent, ", " );
27.                }
28.                strcat( parent, rdns[ i ] );
29.        }

30.        ldap_value_free( rdns );
31.        return( parent );
32.}
```

This function looks pretty complicated but it is simpler than it appears. The hard work is done by ldap_explode_dn(), which is called on line 9. The ldap_explode_dn() function returns a NULL-terminated array of strings that contains the components of the DN passed into the function. The second parameter to ldap_explode_dn() is a flag that, if non-zero, tells it to remove attribute type tags. Because we need these to consruct the parent DN, we pass zero so that we are returned an array of RDNs. Our basic strategy is to use this array of RDNs to construct a new DN, which is the parent of our original one. This is easily done by skipping over the first RDN and concatenating the rest together with a comma placed between them as a separator.

The code on lines 12–16 steps through the RDNs and calculates the length of the parent DN. Once we have allocated space, lines 22–29 construct the parent DN by using the standard `strcat()` function. Finally, on lines 30 and 31, we free the RDN array and return the parent DN.

You may be wondering why we bother using `ldap_explode_dn()` at all. It seems like we could replace our entire function body with something much simpler, like this:

```
/* skip past first DN component */
if ( (s = strchr( parent, ',' )) == NULL ) {
        return( NULL );
}
/* skip past intervening whitespace */
while ( *s == ' ' ) {
        ++s;
}

return( strdup( s ));
```

This will return the correct result most of the time, but it doesn't take into account the fact that the first component of the DN may itself contain a comma that is quoted, or the fact that DN components may be separated with semicolons instead of commas. The `ldap_explode_dn()` function takes all of this and more into account for you. It also includes an option to remove the tags from the RDN components, which we use in our next example.

Example 11.3: A function that prints the first few components of a DN minus the attribute type tags. You can think of this as a shortened UFN-form of the DN.

```
1.    void
2.    print_leading_components( char *dn, int limit )
3.    {
4.        char    **comps;
5.        int     i;

6.        if ( (comps = ldap_explode_dn( dn, 1 )) == NULL ) {
7.                return;
8.        }
```

```
9.          for ( i = 0; i < limit && comps[ i ] != NULL; ++i ) {
10.              printf( "%s%s", ( i > 0 ? ", " : "" ), comps[ i ]
             ➥ );
11.          }
12.          putchar( '\n' );

13.          ldap_value_free( comps );
14.}
```

The call to `ldap_explode_dn()` appears on line 6. This time, the second parameter is 1, which causes `ldap_explode_dn()` to remove the attribute type tags from the DN components. The `for` loop on lines 9–11 steps through the component array returned and prints each component in turn. The DN components are separated by the customary comma-space pair, and printing stops when we run out of components or we exceed the `limit` parameter.

If we call `print_leading_components()` like this:

```
print_leading_components( "ou=Product Development, ou=Ace Industry,
c=US", 2 );
```

the output will look like this:

```
Product Development, Ace Industry
```

The next section provides a summary of the `ldap_explode_dn()` LDAP API function.

Synopsis:

```
char **ldap_explode_dn( char *dn, int notypes );
```

Breaks a Distinguished Name (DN) into its component parts. Each part is known as a Relative Distinguished Name (RDN).

Return Value:

Type: `char **`

If successful, a pointer to a NULL-terminated array of character strings is returned. This array should be freed by calling ldap_free_values(). If the DN cannot be broken up, NULL is returned (this usually only occurs if memory allocation fails or the DN passed into ldap_explode_dn() was invalid or of zero length).

Parameters:

char *dn: An LDAP Distinguished Name (the name of an entry), as returned by a call such as ldap_get_dn(). The DN should conform to the format defined in RFC-1779, A String Representation of Distinguished Names, and described in Chapter 3.

int notypes: A Boolean parameter that, if non-zero, causes the attribute type tags to be removed from the components returned.

Sorting Entries

Now we are going to switch gears a bit and turn our attention to sorting entries. Most LDAP directory servers do not make any effort to sort the entries that are returned from a search operation. This is in conflict with our human desire to be presented with ordered lists, which make finding the information we are looking for much easier. Fortunately, the LDAP client library provides a handy function called, not surprisingly, ldap_sort_entries() that can be used to sort entries by Distinguished Name or by an attribute value.

LDAPv3 Feature: A feature proposed for inclusion in version 3 of the LDAP protocol is server-side sorting. This feature would allow a client to request that search results be sorted by one or more attribute values. This feature is especially useful in environments where many entries will be returned, perhaps more than can easily be sorted by the client.

Example 11.4: Search an LDAP directory for all people with a surname of "Jensen" and display the names of the entries found in alphabetical order.

```
1.    #include <stdio.h>
2.    #include <string.h>
3.    #include <ldap.h>
```

```
4.      #define SEARCHBASE      "o=Ace Industry, c=US"

5.      main()
6.      {
7.              LDAP            *ld;
8.              LDAPMessage     *result, *e;
9.              char            *dn, *ufn;

10.             if ( (ld = ldap_init( "ldap.netscape.com", LDAP_PORT
                ➡)) == NULL ) {
11.                     perror( "init" );
12.                     exit( 1 );
13.             }

14.             if ( ldap_simple_bind_s( ld, NULL, NULL ) !=
                ➡LDAP_SUCCESS ) {
15.                     ldap_perror( ld, "bind" );
16.                     ldap_unbind( ld );
17.                     exit( 1 );
18.             }

19.             if ( ldap_search_s( ld, SEARCHBASE,
                ➡LDAP_SCOPE_SUBTREE,
20.                 "(sn=Jensen)", NULL, 0, &result ) != LDAP_SUCCESS
                    ➡) {
21.                     ldap_perror( ld, "search" );
22.                     ldap_unbind( ld );
23.                     exit( 1 );
24.             }

25.             if ( ldap_sort_entries( ld, &result, NULL, strcmp ) !=
                ➡0 ) {
26.                     ldap_perror( ld, "sort" );
27.                     /* keep going anyways */
28.             }

29.             for ( e = ldap_first_entry( ld, result ); e != NULL;
30.                 e = ldap_next_entry( ld, e )) {
31.                     if (( dn = ldap_get_dn( ld, e )) != NULL &&
32.                         ( ufn = ldap_dn2ufn( dn )) != NULL ) {
33.                             puts( dn );
34.                             puts( ufn );
35.                             putchar( '\n' );
```

```
36.                              ldap_memfree( dn );
37.                              ldap_memfree( ufn );
38.                      }
39.              }

40.             ldap_unbind( ld );
41.             exit( 0 );
42.     }
```

This code is identical to that in Example 1, except for the addition on lines 25–28 of a call to the ldap_sort_entries() function. By adding just a few lines of code, we improve our output considerably by sorting the list of entries before printing them! By passing NULL for the third parameter to ldap_sort_entries(), we tell it to reorder the entries based on the components of the entry DNs. The strcmp function, passed as the fourth parameter, is used by ldap_sort_entries() to compare the DNs.

The output from a run of this example program might look like this:

```
cn=Allison Jensen, ou=Product Development, o=Ace Industry, c=US
Allison Jensen, Product Development, Ace Industry, US

cn=Barbara Jensen, ou=Product Development, o=Ace Industry, c=US
Barbara Jensen, Product Development, Ace Industry, US

cn=Bjorn Jensen, ou=Accounting, o=Ace Industry, c=US
Bjorn Jensen, Accounting, Ace Industry, US

cn=Gern Jensen, ou=Human Resources, o=Ace Industry, c=US
Gern Jensen, Human Resources, Ace Industry, US

cn=Jody Jensen, ou=Accounting, o=Ace Industry, c=US
Jody Jensen, Accounting, Ace Industry, US

cn=Kurt Jensen, ou=Product Development, o=Ace Industry, c=US
Kurt Jensen, Product Development, Ace Industry, US

cn=Randy Jensen, ou=Product Testing, o=Ace Industry, c=US
Randy Jensen, Product Testing, Ace Industry, US
```

```
cn=Richard Jensen, ou=Accounting, o=Ace Industry, c=US
Richard Jensen, Accounting, Ace Industry, US

cn=Ted Jensen, ou=Accounting, o=Ace Industry, c=US
Ted Jensen, Accounting, Ace Industry, US
```

If you are, for example, looking for Barbara Jensen's entry, it is easy to pick it out among the sorted entries.

The next section provides a summary of the `ldap_sort_entries()` LDAP API function.

Synopsis:

> `int ldap_sort_entries( LDAP *ld, LDAPMessage **chain,char *attr, int (*cmp)( char *a, char *b ) );`

Sorts a list of LDAP entries either by Distinguished Name or by an attribute value.

Return Value:

> Type: `int`
>
> An error indication that will be zero if all goes well and −1 if an error occurs. A specific LDAP error code can be obtained from the LDAP session handle `ld`. Error handling is discussed in more detail in Chapter 8.

Parameters:

> `LDAP *ld`: A handle to an LDAP session as returned by `ldap_init()` or `ldap_open()`.
>
> `LDAPMessage **chain`: A pointer to the list of entries to be sorted. The `result` parameter in calls to LDAP API functions such as `ldap_search_s()` and `ldap_result()` is set to a suitable chain of entries that can be passed for this parameter. The head of the list may be changed by the sorting process.

char *`attr`: The name of the attribute whose values are used when sorting the entries. If NULL is passed, the components of Distinguished Names of the entries are used to reorder them.

int *(*cmp)(char *a, char *b)*: Pointer to a function that is used to compare two strings. This function is called just like the standard `strcmp` function, and should return zero if a and b are identical, a negative number if a is less than b, and a positive number if b is greater than a.

Note

The `ldap_sort_entries()` function applies the comparison function to each value of the attribute in the array of values returned by a call to `ldap_get_values()` until a mismatch is found. This works fine for attributes that only have a single value, but may produce unexpected results for multi-valued attributes. When sorting by DN, the comparison function is applied to an exploded version of the DN without types.

Example 11.5: Search an LDAP directory for all people whose name begins with "Jo" and display the entries in order by their surname.

```
1.    #include <stdio.h>
2.    #include <ldap.h>
3.    #include <string.h>

4.    #define SEARCHBASE     "o=Ace Industry, c=US"

5.    main()
6.    {
7.           LDAP            *ld;
8.           LDAPMessage     *result, *e;
9.           char            *dn, *ufn, *attrs[ 2 ];

10.          if ( (ld = ldap_init( "ldap.netscape.com", LDAP_PORT
             )) == NULL ) {
11.                  perror( "init" );
12.                  exit( 1 );
13.          }

14.          if ( ldap_simple_bind_s( ld, NULL, NULL ) !=
             LDAP_SUCCESS ) {
```

```
15.                      ldap_perror( ld, "bind" );
16.                      ldap_unbind( ld );
17.                      exit( 1 );
18.             }

19.            attrs[ 0 ] = "sn";
20.            attrs[ 1 ] = NULL;
21.            if ( ldap_search_s( ld, SEARCHBASE,
               ➥LDAP_SCOPE_SUBTREE,
22.                "(cn=Jo*)", attrs, 0, &result ) != LDAP_SUCCESS )
                   ➥{
23.                      ldap_perror( ld, "search" );
24.                      ldap_unbind( ld );
25.                      exit( 1 );
26.             }

27.            if ( ldap_sort_entries( ld, &result, "sn", strcmp ) !=
               ➥0 ) {
28.                      ldap_perror( ld, "sort" );
29.                      /* keep going anyways */
30.             }

31.            for ( e = ldap_first_entry( ld, result ); e != NULL;
32.                e = ldap_next_entry( ld, e )) {
33.                    if (( dn = ldap_get_dn( ld, e )) != NULL &&
34.                       ( ufn = ldap_dn2ufn( dn )) != NULL ) {
35.                            puts( dn );
36.                            puts( ufn );
37.                            putchar( '\n' );
38.                            ldap_memfree( dn );
39.                            ldap_memfree( ufn );
40.                    }
41.            }

42.            ldap_unbind( ld );
43.            exit( 0 );
44.     }
```

This code is similar to that in Example 4. The filter we pass to
ldap_search_s() on lines 21–22 is different because we want to find
entries whose name begins with "Jo". Also, we explicitly ask that only
values of the surname (sn) attribute be returned. Finally, by passing

"sn" as the third parameter to `ldap_sort_entries()`, we are able to print a list that is sorted by surname.

The output from a run of this example program might look like this:

```
cn=Jon Bourke, ou=Product Development, o=Ace Industry, c=US
Jon Bourke, Product Development, Ace Industry, US

cn=Jody Campaigne, ou=Product Development, o=Ace Industry, c=US
Jody Campaigne, Product Development, Ace Industry, US

cn=John Falena, ou=Human Resources, o=Ace Industry, c=US
John Falena, Human Resources, Ace Industry, US

cn=Jon Goldstein, ou=Human Resources, o=Ace Industry, c=US
Jon Goldstein, Human Resources, Ace Industry, US

cn=Jody Jensen, ou=Accounting, o=Ace Industry, c=US
Jody Jensen, Accounting, Ace Industry, US

cn=Jody Rentz, ou=Human Resources, o=Ace Industry, c=US
Jody Rentz, Human Resources, Ace Industry, US

cn=John Walker, ou=Product Testing, o=Ace Industry, c=US
John Walker, Product Testing, Ace Industry, US
```

Sorting Attribute Values

When attributes have multiple values, it can be useful to sort these values. Since the attributes are returned as a NULL-terminated array by `ldap_get_values()`, you can easily write your own function to sort the values. For completeness and your convenience, the LDAP client library provides a ready-made routine that can be used to sort attribute values.

Example 11.6: A pair of functions that can be used to display an entry's surname, common name, and favorite drink attribute values. The common name and favorite drink values are sorted before they are displayed.

```
1.    void
2.    print_entry( LDAP *ld, LDAPMessage *entry )
3.    {
4.            char    **vals;

5.            if (( vals = ldap_get_values( ld, entry, "sn" )) !=
              ➡NULL ) {
6.                print_values( "Surname", vals );
7.                ldap_value_free( vals );
          }

8.            if (( vals = ldap_get_values( ld, entry, "cn" )) !=
              ➡NULL ) {
9.                (void)ldap_sort_values( ld, vals,
                  ➡ldap_sort_strcasecmp );
10.               print_values( "Common Name", vals );
11.               ldap_value_free( vals );
12.           }

13.           if (( vals = ldap_get_values( ld, entry, "drink" )) !=
              ➡NULL ) {
14.               (void)ldap_sort_values( ld, vals,
                  ➡ldap_sort_strcasecmp );
15.               print_values( "Favorite Drink", vals );
16.               ldap_value_free( vals );
17.           }
18.   }


19.   void
20.   print_values( char *label, char **vals )
21.   {
22.           int     i;

23.           puts( label );
24.           for ( i = 0; vals[ i ] != NULL; ++i ) {
25.                   printf( "\t%s\n", vals[ i ] );
26.           }
27.   }
```

We have seen a lot of examples similar to this one before. The print_values() utility function defined on lines 19–27 just prints a label and all of the values for an attribute. It is called three times by the main print_entry() function (from lines 6, 10, and 15).

The print_entry() function makes three calls to ldap_get_values() to retrieve the values for the attributes we are interested in printing. The interesting code appears on lines 9 and 14 where we call the ldap_sort_values() function to reorder the "cn" and "drink" values before we print them. Because we want a case-insensitive ordering, we can use the comparison function ldap_sort_strcasecmp() that is provided by the LDAP library. Note that you can not pass the standard strcmp() or strcasecmp() functions to ldap_sort_values(); the calling convention of those functions is not correct.

The next section provides a summary of the ldap_sort_values() LDAP API function and also provides a summary of the ldap_sort_strcasecmp() comparison function.

Synopsis:

```
int ldap_sort_values( LDAP *ld, char **vals int (*cmp)
( char **ap, char **bp ) );
```

Sorts an array of attribute values.

Return Value:

Type: int

An error indication that will be zero if all goes well and −1 if an error occurs. A specific LDAP error code can be obtained from the LDAP session handle. Error handling is discussed in more detail in Chapter 8.

Parameters:

LDAP *ld: A handle to an LDAP session as returned by ldap_init() or ldap_open().

char **vals: A NULL-terminated array of string values as returned by a call to ldap_get_values().

int *(*cmp)(char *ap, char *bp)*: Pointer to a function that is used to compare two strings. This function is called with two parameters that are pointers to pointers to two strings to be compared, not pointers to the strings themselves. The comparison function should return zero if *ap and *bp are identical, a negative number if *ap is less then *bp, and a positive number if *ap is greater than *bp.

Tip

> The `ldap_sort_strcasecmp()` function, described next, is designed to be passed as the third parameter of `ldap_sort_values()`. You can also write your own comparison functions if a case-insensitive ascending sort does not meet your needs. For example, if you want to do a descending sort or handle non-ASCII characters, you will need to write your own comparison function.

Synopsis:

```
int ldap_sort_strcasecmp( char **ap, char **bp );
```

Performs an ASCII case-insensitive comparision of two strings.

Return Value:

Type: int

An indication of the relative ordering of the two strings. If the strings *ap and *bp are identical, zero is returned. If *ap should come before *bp, a negative number is returned. If *ap should come after *bp, a positive number is returned.

Parameters:

char *ap: A pointer to a pointer to the first string to be compared.

char *bp: A pointer to a pointer to the second string to be compared.

Summary

The following table summarizes the routines described in this chapter.

Name	Description
`ldap_dn2ufn()`	Converts a Distinguished Name (DN) into an easier-to-read form called a User Friendly Name (UFN).
`ldap_explode_dn()`	Breaks up a DN into its component parts.
`ldap_explode_rdn()`	Breaks up a Relative Distinguished Name (RDN) into its component parts.
`ldap_sort_entries()`	Sorts a list of entries.
`ldap_sort_values()`	Sorts an array of attribute values.
`ldap_sort_strcasecmp()`	Case-insensitive comparison function that can be used with the `ldap_sort_values()` function.

Looking Ahead

We have now covered all of the LDAP API functions related to searching and parsing directory entries. Before turning our attention to the task of updating the directory, the next chapter finishes our coverage of directory interrogation by introducing the LDAP compare operation.

CHAPTER 12

Compare

In the last three chapters, you learned how to use the family of LDAP search routines to retrieve information from an LDAP directory and to parse and interpret the results. In this chapter, you'll learn how to use the LDAP compare operation to see whether an entry contains a given attribute value.

The compare operation is simple, especially when compared to search. It takes a DN, identifying the entry to compare, and an attribute value assertion, consisting of a type and a value. The operation is designed to return TRUE if the entry contains the given attribute value, and FALSE otherwise. As for other protocol operations, the LDAP SDK provides both synchronous and asynchronous API interfaces to compare.

The next sections contrast the compare operation and the search operation. Then, we present quick examples showing how to use compare in both synchronous and asynchronous mode, followed by the formal function definitions.

Compare versus Search

You may be wondering why you can't just use one of the search calls to achieve the same effect as a compare. After all, the LDAP search operation takes a DN, and with a simple filter of the form (`<attr>=<value>`), it takes the equivalent of an attribute value assertion. With a scope of base object, restricting the search to a single entry, the effect is to return the entry if it contains the attribute value, and to return no entries otherwise. This is remarkably similar to what the compare operation does. The main reason both compare and search operations exist is historical, but there are some differences between the two operations.

There is only one condition that the compare operation handles differently from search. In a search operation, if an entry being searched does not contain the attribute requested (that is, the attribute does not exist in the entry), the entry is simply not returned. In a compare operation, the error `LDAP_NO_SUCH_ATTRIBUTE` is returned (as opposed to a FALSE compare result, which you might expect).

The ability to distinguish between "entry has the attribute but contains no matching value" and "entry does not have the attribute at all" can be convenient in some situations. Aside from this semantic difference, compare can be emulated by search.

There is one other advantage of compare over search. The compare protocol operation is somewhat smaller, and therefore more efficient. The result of the compare operation is a single packet containing the TRUE/FALSE or error indication. The result of the search is two packets, one containing the entry (in the case of the equivalent TRUE return), and another containing the result of the search.

Comparing Entries (Synchronous)

To illustrate the use of compare, we've chosen a simple example.

Example 12.1: Our goal is to write a small program that takes a DN, a type, and a value on the command line and outputs either TRUE of FALSE, depending on what the compare returns. Our program also exits with a different value depending on the result of the compare, allowing it to be easily used as a building block in some scripting language like Perl.

```
1.    #include <stdio.h>
2.    #include <ldap.h>

3.    main( int argc, char **argv )
4.    {
5.            LDAP        *ld;
6.            int rc;

7.            if ( argc != 4 ) {
8.                    fprintf(stderr, "usage: %s dn type value\n",
                    ➥argv[0]);
9.                    exit( 1 );
10.           }

11.           /* initialize the LDAP session */
12.           if ( (ld = ldap_init( "ldap.netscape.com", LDAP_PORT ))
13.              == NULL) {
14.                   perror( "ldap_init" );
15.                   exit( 1 );
16.           }

17.           /* authenticate to the LDAP server */
18.           if ( ldap_simple_bind_s( ld, NULL, NULL ) !=
              ➥LDAP_SUCCESS ) {
19.                   ldap_perror( ld, "ldap_simple_bind_s" );
20.                   exit( 1 );
21.           }

22.           /* do the compare */
23.           rc = ldap_compare_s( ld, argv[1], argv[2], argv[3] );

24.           /* clean up */
25.           ldap_unbind( ld );

26.           if ( rc == LDAP_COMPARE_TRUE ) {
27.                   printf( "TRUE\n" );
28.                   return( 0 );
29.           } else if ( rc == LDAP_COMPARE_FALSE ) {
30.                   printf( "FALSE\n" );
31.                   return( 1 );
```

```
32.          } else {
33.                  ldap_perror( ld, "Error:" );
34.                  return( -1 );
35.          }
36.  }
```

Much of this example we've seen before. After checking to make sure the program is invoked with the correct number of arguments on lines 7–10, the LDAP initialization and authentication code on lines 11–21 are similar to our previous examples. As usual, we have provided a NULL DN and password, resulting in an unauthenticated connection.

The interesting part of this example happens on lines 22 and 23, where we call the synchronous version of the compare routine, ldap_compare_s(). Arguments two through four are the DN of the entry to compare against, a type, and the value of that type to test the entry for. The LDAP session is closed and its resources freed on line 25.

If ldap_compare_s() returned LDAP_COMPARE_TRUE, indicating that the entry in question does contain the given attribute value, TRUE is printed. If ldap_compare_s() returns LDAP_COMPARE_FALSE, FALSE is printed. Any other return causes an error message to be printed and –1 to be returned.

A sample run of this program, if it were called "compare", might look like this:

```
% compare "o=Ace Industry, c=US" o "Ace Industry"
TRUE
% compare "o=Ace Industry, c=US" o "LoTech Institute"
FALSE
% compare "o=Ace Industry, c=US" c "XX"
Error: No such attribute
```

The next section examines the parameters of the ldap_compare_s() routine in more detail.

Synopsis:

```
int ldap_compare_s( LDAP *ld, char *entrydn, char *type,
char *value );
```

Compares the given attribute type and value against the given entry. The caller is blocked until the compare completes.

Return Value:

Type: int

The `ldap_compare_s()` routine returns the LDAP error code indicating the success or failure of the compare operation. A return value of `LDAP_COMPARE_TRUE` indicates that the entry contained the given attribute value assertion. A return value of `LDAP_COMPARE_FALSE` means that the compare operation was completed successfully, but the entry contained no matching attribute value assertion. Any other return indicates some kind of error with the operation.

Parameters:

`LDAP *ld`: This parameter is a handle to an LDAP session, as returned by a successful call to `ldap_init()` or `ldap_open()`. In the Netscape LDAP SDK, this handle references an opaque data type. In the University of Michigan SDK, this handle is a pointer to a structure that is exposed to your program.

`char *entrydn`: This parameter specifies the name of the directory entry to perform the compare against.

`char *type`: This parameter specifies the type portion of the attribute value assertion to test the entry for.

`char *value`: This parameter specifies the value portion of the attribute value assertion for which to test the entry.

Tip

You may have noticed that the value parameter is a `char *`, a pointer to a NULL-terminated string. This means that binary values cannot be compared. The Netscape SDK will soon contain `ldap_compare_bin()` and `ldap_compare_bin_s()` routines that allow comparisons against binary attributes. The University of Michigan SDK does not support these new routines.

The ldap_compare_s() routine is synchronous. It sends the compare request to the LDAP server and blocks the caller until the LDAP server responds. The next section describes the asynchronous interface to compare, ldap_compare().

Comparing Entries (Asynchronous)

To illustrate the asynchronous use of compare, we've expanded our simple synchronous example.

Example 12.2: Our goal is the same, to take a DN, a type, and a value on the command line and output either TRUE of FALSE, depending on what the compare returns. The difference is that we use the ldap_compare() and ldap_result() routines to implement a 10-second timeout on the operation.

```
1.    #include <stdio.h>
2.    #include <ldap.h>

3.    main( int argc, char **argv )
4.    {
5.          LDAP                    *ld;
6.          LDAPMessage        *res;
7.          struct timeval     tv;
8.          int                msgid, rc;

9.          if ( argc != 4 ) {
10.                fprintf(stderr, "usage: %s dn type value\n",
                   ➥argv[0]);
11.                exit( 1 );
12.         }

13.         /* initialize the LDAP session */
14.         if ( (ld = ldap_init( "ldap.netscape.com", LDAP_PORT ))
15.            == NULL) {
16.                perror( "ldap_init" );
17.                exit( 1 );
18.         }

19.         /* authenticate to the LDAP server */
20.         if ( ldap_simple_bind_s( ld, NULL, NULL ) != LDAP_SUCCESS ) {
```

```
21.              ldap_perror( ld, "ldap_simple_bind_s" );
22.              exit( 1 );
23.          }

24.          /* initiate the compare */
25.          msgid = ldap_compare( ld, argv[1], argv[2], argv[3] );

26.          /* wait 10 seconds for the result */
27.          tv.tv_sec = 10;
28.          tv.tv_usec = 0;
29.          if ( ldap_result( ld, msgid, 1, &tv, &res )
30.              != LDAP_RES_COMPARE ) {
31.                  ldap_unbind( ld );
32.                  printf( "TIMEOUT\n" );
33.                  return( -1 );
34.          }
35.          rc = ldap_result2error( ld, res, 1 );

36.          /* clean up */
37.          ldap_unbind( ld );

38.          if ( rc == LDAP_COMPARE_TRUE ) {
39.                  printf( "TRUE\n" );
40.                  return( 0 );
41.          } else if ( rc == LDAP_COMPARE_FALSE ) {
42.                  printf( "FALSE\n" );
43.                  return( 1 );
44.          } else {
45.                  ldap_perror( ld, "Error:" );
46.                  return( -1 );
47.          }
48.  }
```

The difference between this example and the previous synchronous example is apparent in lines 24–35. Instead of the call to ldap_compare_s(), we call ldap_compare() to initiate the compare operation. Then, we call ldap_result() with a timeout of 10 seconds. If it returns with a result in that time, we proceed as before. If the call to ldap_result() times out, we print a message and exit.

The next sections examine the parameters of the ldap_compare() and ldap_result() routines in more detail.

Synopsis:

```
int ldap_compare( LDAP *ld, char *entrydn, char *type,
char *value );
```

Initiates an operation comparing the given attribute type and value against the given entry. The compare is done asynchronously. The result of the operation is retrieved by a subsequent call to `ldap_result()`.

Return Value:

Type: `int`

The `ldap_compare()` routine sends a compare request to the LDAP server and returns the message ID of the operation it initiates. The result of the operation can be retrieved by a subsequent call to `ldap_result()`. If the operation could not be successfully initiated, –1 is returned and the LDAP error code is set to indicate the nature of the error.

Parameters:

`LDAP *ld`: This parameter is a handle to an LDAP session, as returned by a successful call to `ldap_init()` or `ldap_open()`. In the Netscape LDAP SDK, this handle references an opaque data type. In the University of Michigan SDK, this handle is a pointer to a structure that is exposed to your program.

`char *entrydn`: This parameter specifies the name of the directory entry to perform the compare against.

`char *type`: This parameter specifies the type portion of the attribute value assertion to test the entry for.

`char *value`: This parameter specifies the value portion of the attribute value assertion to test the entry for.

The `ldap_compare()` routine is asynchronous. It only sends the compare request to the LDAP server and then returns to the caller. The success or failure of the compare operation must be determined by calling `ldap_result()`, described below.

The parameters of the `ldap_result()` routine are described next. They are exactly the same as those described for `ldap_result()` in the search and update chapters, and are reproduced here only to save you the trouble of having to flip back through this book to find them.

Synopsis:

```
int ldap_result( LDAP *ld, int msgid, int all, struct
➥timeval *timeout, LDAPMessage **result );
```

Checks the status or retrieve the result of an operation previously initiated (e.g., by a call to `ldap_compare()`).

Return Value:

Type: `int`

`Return value`: The return value of `ldap_result()` follows a convention similar to that used by the `select()` system call. It returns values in one of three categories.

A return of –1 indicates that some error has occurred. The LDAP error will be set to indicate the problem.

A return of 0 (zero) indicates that a timeout has occurred. The timeout you specified in the timeout parameter expired before an appropriate result came in.

A greater-than-zero return indicates success, and that a result has been returned in the result parameter. The value of the greater-than-zero return from `ldap_result()` indicates the type of result contained in the result parameter. It will be one of the result type constants declared in the `ldap.h` header file. Possible values and their meanings are described in the following section. Only the first value is relevant to compare, and the next three values are relevant to other update operations, but we list the other values for completeness.

Parameters:

LDAP *ld: This parameter is a handle to an LDAP session, as returned by a successful call to ldap_init() or ldap_open().

int msgid: This parameter specifies the message ID for which results are desired, as returned from a successful call to ldap_compare() or any of the other asynchronous operation initiation routines. If the result of any operation is desired, the special value LDAP_RES_ANY may be passed for *msgid*.

int *all*: This parameter only has meaning for search operations. For a compare operation, this parameter should be set to zero.

struct timeval *timeout*: This parameter controls how long ldap_result() should wait for results if none have already come in and are waiting to be returned. A value of NULL for *timeout* indicates that ldap_result() should block indefinitely, until the requested results come in. A non-NULL value of *timeout* with the timeout set to zero indicates that ldap_result() should effect a polling behavior. If results are available immediately, they will be returned. If not, ldap_result() will not wait for them.

LDAPMessage **result*: This parameter is a pointer to an LDAPMessage * used to hold the result of a successful call to ldap_result(). If the ldap_result() call returns a value greater than zero, the *result* parameter will be filled in with the result retrieved, which in the case of a compare result, is a simple packet indicating success or failure of the operation. The *result* parameter should be freed by the caller by calling ldap_msgfree() when it is no longer in use.

Tip

A greater-than-zero return from ldap_result() means that ldap_result() was successfully able to retrieve the result of the operation you requested from the LDAP server. It does not tell you anything about the success or failure of the operation itself. This status can be obtained by calling ldap_result2error() on the result parameter returned from ldap_result().

Possible greater-than-zero return values for `ldap_result()` are given below. Each return value indicates the result of a different type of LDAP operation.

`LDAP_RES_COMPARE_RESULT`	The result of a previously initiated compare operation.
`LDAP_RES_MODIFY_RESULT`	The result of a previously initiated modify operation.
`LDAP_RES_ADD_RESULT`	The result of a previously initiated add operation.
`LDAP_RES_DELETE_RESULT`	The result of a previously initiated delete operation.
`LDAP_RES_MODRDN_RESULT`	The result of a previously initiated modify RDN operation.
`LDAP_RES_SEARCH_ENTRY`	A single entry matching a previously initiated search request.
`LDAP_RES_SEARCH_RESULT`	Either a result indicating the final outcome of a previously initiated search operation or an entire chain of entries matching a previously initiated search request, along with the final outcome.
`LDAP_RES_BIND_RESULT`	The result of a previously initiated bind operation.

If you have specified `LDAP_RES_ANY` in the call to `ldap_result()`, it may be useful to know the message ID of the result finally returned. `ldap_result()` returns the type of the result, but not its message ID. In the University of Michigan SDK, the message ID of the result is available in the following field of the LDAPMessage structure.

```
int         msgid;
LDAPMessage *result;
/* successful call to ldap_result() fills in result */
msgid = result->lm_msgid;
```

In the Netscape SDK, the LDAPMessage holding results is an opaque data type. The message ID associated with a result can be obtained by calling the following accessor function.

```
int         msgid;
LDAPMessage *result;
/* successful call to ldap_result() fills in result */
msgid = ldap_msgid( ld, result );
```

Summary

The following table summarizes the routines described in this chapter.

Name	Description
ldap_compare_s()	Synchronously performs a compare operation.
ldap_compare()	Asynchronously initiates a compare operation.
ldap_result()	Asynchronously retrieves the result of a previously initiated compare operation.
ldap_msgid()	Retrieves the message ID of an LDAP result in the Netscape SDK.

Looking Ahead

Having pretty thoroughly covered functions that allow you to interrogate the LDAP directory, we now turn our attention to updating the information in the directory. The next chapter explains how to authenticate to an LDAP server, setting the stage for Chapter 14, which describes the update functions themselves.

13

Authentication

Authentication can be loosely defined as the process of identifying yourself or your application to the directory server. In LDAP, a variety of authentication methods are supported by the LDAP bind operation. The bind operation allows you to identify yourself to the directory server by using a Distinguished Name and some authentication credentials (a password or other information).

When a bind operation is successfully completed, the directory server remembers the new identity until another bind is done or the LDAP session is terminated (usually this is done by calling `ldap_unbind()`). The identity is used by the server to make decisions about what information your application has access to and what kind of changes (if any) can be made to the directory.

Depending on the needs of the site running a particular directory server, use of certain authentication methods may be encouraged, discouraged, or forbidden. Most directory servers are configured to allow anonymous access to at least some of the information they contain. Authentication is usually required before a server will allow access to sensitive information and it is almost always required before changes to the directory are permitted.

In this chapter, we cover simple password-based authentication. Note that in the absence of a secure or encrypted network connection, passwords are passed over the network in the clear and may be intercepted by unscrupulous individuals. The Secure Sockets Layer (SSL) protocol is supported by the Netscape LDAP SDK and can be used to protect passwords and other information passed over LDAP. The University of Michigan SDK does not support SSL, but it does support Kerberos authentication.

Kerberos Authentication

Kerberos is an authentication system that was originally developed in the mid-eighties at the Massachusetts Institute of Technology as part of an ambitious network computing initiative called Project Athena. It uses the Data Encryption Standard (DES) for encryption. The security and authentication services Kerberos provides are based on a system of shared secrets. Passwords are never passed over the network in the clear, and client/server authentication is based on a clever system of temporary tickets that are issued by a secure server called the Key Distribution Center (KDC).

Due to its origin and the ability to scale to support tens of thousands of users, Kerberos is popular in university environments. The LDAP SDK produced by the University of Michigan includes a family of LDAP bind calls that use Kerberos, and the U-M LDAP servers also support Kerberos. Note that most other LDAP directory servers do not support Kerberos at the time of this writing.

Once again, we use an example-driven approach to present the LDAP bind API calls. A detailed description of each call is presented when it is introduced, and a summary of all routines covered appears at the end of this chapter. The material in this chapter is a prerequisite for the material in the next chapter on modification of LDAP directory information. If your application will not be making changes to LDAP directories and you know that anonymous access is sufficient for retrieving information at your site, you can safely skip this entire chapter.

LDAP and Secure Sockets Layer (SSL)

Before we take a detailed look at the LDAP API calls used for simple password-based authentication, it is useful to spend a little time discussing a relatively new communications technology called Secure Sockets Layer or SSL. SSL is already commonly used by users of World Wide

Web browsers to conduct secure transactions over HTTP. Netscape and other vendors of TCP/IP server and client software are implementing SSL across their entire product lines, and the SSL protocol itself is being advanced within the Internet standards process.

Figure 1 shows how the Secure Sockets Layer fits into the protocol puzzle. SSL is designed to be used in conjunction with standard application protocols such as HTTP, SMTP, and LDAP to provide public key certificate-based authentication, a secure encrypted communications channel, and data integrity in the form of digital signatures. The Netscape LDAP SDK will support SSL very soon (it is already supported by the Netscape Directory Server and LDAP command line tools).

Figure 13.1

How SSL relates to other protocols.

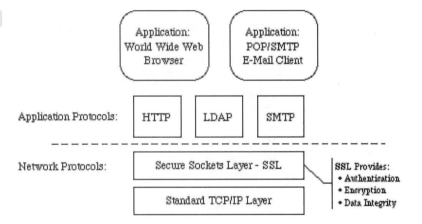

One of the key advantages of SSL is the ease with which it can be layered beneath existing application protocols. Using LDAP over SSL instead of directly over TCP, for example, does not change LDAP's essential characteristics at all: All of the same operations are available, with the stronger authentication, encryption, and data integrity functions provided under the covers by SSL. The main difference is that the standard TCP port used for LDAP over SSL (also called LDAPS) is port 636 instead of LDAP's standard 389.

LDAPv3 Feature: Support for an extensible authentication framework called Simple Authentication and Security Layer (SASL) is being added to LDAPv3 to support SSL and other security options. SASL is already used within a variety of Internet protocols including IMAP4 and POP3. Note that there is no relationship between SASL and SSL, except that the former is a framework that supports the latter (along with many other authentication protocols).

As corporations, government organizations, and universities deploy mission-critical applications that use LDAP, expect to see the use of SSL and other security-enhancing measures to greatly increase. For now though, many people are content to use simple password-based authentication.

Simple Password-Based Authentication (Synchronous)

Example 13.1: Bind to a directory server as manager of the directory and delete a person's entry. Use a simple, clear-text password and the synchronous LDAP functions.

```
1.    #include <stdio.h>
2.    #include <ldap.h>

3.    #define BINDDN      "cn=Directory Manager, o=Ace industry,
      ➡c=US"
4.    #define BINDPWD     "ldap=fun"
5.    #define DELETEDN    "cn=Sam Carter, ou=Accounting, o=Ace
      ➡Industry, c=US"

6.    main()
7.    {
8.            LDAP    *ld;

9.            if ( (ld = ldap_init( "ldap.netscape.com", LDAP_PORT ))
              ➡== NULL ) {
10.                   perror( "ldap_init" );
11.                   exit( 1 );
12.           }

13.           if ( ldap_simple_bind_s( ld, BINDDN, BINDPWD ) !=
              ➡LDAP_SUCCESS ) {
14.                   ldap_perror( ld, "ldap_simple_bind" );
15.                   ldap_unbind( ld );
16.                   exit( 1 );
17.           }
```

```
18.          if ( ldap_delete_s( ld, DELETEDN ) != LDAP_SUCCESS ) {
19.                      ldap_perror( ld, "ldap_delete" );
20.                      ldap_unbind( ld );
21.                      exit( 1 );
22.          }

23.          ldap_unbind( ld );
24.          exit( 0 );
25.  }
```

On line 13, the ldap_simple_bind_s() call that was introduced in Chapter 6 is called with a non-NULL name and password to bind as the directory manager. The ldap_delete_s() call used on line 18 is covered in detail in Chapter 14.

The ldap_simple_bind_s() call is summarized below.

Synopsis:

```
int ldap_simple_bind_s( LDAP *ld, char *dn, char *passwd );
```

Synchronously identifies, or authenticates, your application to the directory server using a DN and password. If successful, the authentication is in effect for the life of the LDAP session (or until another bind call is made).

Return Value:

Type: int

An LDAP error code (equal to LDAP_SUCCESS if the operation succeeds). Error handling is discussed in more detail in Chapter 8.

Parameters:

LDAP *ld: A handle to an LDAP session as returned by ldap_init() or ldap_open().

char *dn: The distinguished name of the entry that is binding to the directory. If this parameter is NULL or a zero-length string, an unauthenticated bind is performed (that is, you will be bound anonymously).

char *passwd*: The password associated with *dn*. If this is NULL or a zero-length string, an unauthenticated bind is performed (that is, you will be bound anonymously).

Tip

> By calling `ldap_simple_bind_s()` with a NULL DN and a NULL password, you can make the server forget your identity. This is useful when you want to discard authentication credentials and server privileges without ending your LDAP session.

Tip

> By design, LDAP servers will accept a NULL (or zero-length) password even if the DN is not NULL. No special privileges will be granted, but the DN will probably be recorded in the server's access log file. By assigning a unique DN but no password to your application and using that DN in the `ldap_simple_bind_s()` call, you can help server administrators track how often your application is used.

Example 13.2: An LDAP-enabled application identifies itself to the server for statistical purposes by using an unauthenticated bind (no password) with a DN that identifies the application itself.

```
1.    #include <stdio.h>
2.    #include <ldap.h>

3.    #define LOGDN          "cn=Search Utility, ou=Applications,
      ➡o=ACME Inc., c=US"

4.    main()
5.    {
6.           LDAP    *ld;

7.           if ((ld = ldap_init( "ldap.netscape.com", LDAP_PORT ))
             ➡== NULL ) {
8.                   perror( "ldap_init" );
9.                   exit( 1 );
10.          }
```

```
11.          if ( ldap_simple_bind_s( ld, LOGDN, NULL ) !=
             ➥LDAP_SUCCESS ) {
12.                  ldap_perror( ld, "bind" );
13.                  ldap_unbind( ld );
14.                  exit( 1 );
15.          }

16.          /* do some real work here: LDAP search, etc. */

17.          ldap_unbind( ld );
18.          exit( 0 );
19.     }
```

The only difference between this example and a completely unauthenticated one is the use of the LOGDN parameter in the
ldap_simple_bind_s() call on line 11. The LOGDN is defined on line 3.

Tip

Some server implementations unfortunately require that the DN specified on the bind operation name an entry that exists in the directory,
even if you are binding anonymously with a NULL password. If possible, it's best to have your application bind as the DN of an existing
entry.

Simple Password-Based Authentication (Asynchronous)

Like all of the LDAP operation functions, the ldap_simple_bind_s()
call has an asynchronous cousin. The asynchronous call can be used to
limit the amount of time spent waiting for an operation to complete, or
to perform other tasks within your application while waiting.

Example 13.3: Bind to a directory server as manager of the directory
and delete a person's entry. Use a simple, clear-text password. Use the
asynchronous LDAP API functions to limit the amount of time the
bind and delete operations can take to 30 seconds each.

```
1.   #include <stdio.h>
2.   #include <ldap.h>
3.   #include <time.h>
```

```
4.   #define BINDDN              "cn=Directory Manager, o=Ace industry,
     ➥c=US"
5.   #define BINDPWD             "ldap=fun"
6.   #define DELETEDN            "cn=Sam Carter, ou=Accounting, o=Ace
     ➥Industry, c=US"
7.   #define TIMELIMIT    30       /* seconds per operation */

8.   int
9.   wait4result( LDAP *ld, char *msg, int limit, int msgid )
10.  {
11.            int                rc;
12.            struct timeval     tv;
13.            LDAPMessage        *result;

14.            tv.tv_sec = limit;
15.            tv.tv_usec = 0;

16.            rc = ldap_result( ld, msgid, 0, &tv, &result );

17.            if ( rc == -1 ) {
18.                    ldap_perror( ld, msg );
19.                    return( -1 );
20.            } else if ( rc == 0 ) {
21.                    fprintf( stderr, "The %s took too long!\n",
                       ➥msg );
22.                    ldap_abandon( ld, msgid );
23.                    return( -1 );
24.            }

25.            if ( ldap_result2error( ld, result, 1 ) !=
               ➥LDAP_SUCCESS ) {
26.                    ldap_perror( ld, msg );
27.                    return( -1 );
28.            }

29.            return( 0 );
30.  }


31.  main()
32.  {
33.            LDAP               *ld;
34.            int                    msgid;
```

```
35.                 /* get an LDAP session handle */
36.                 if ( (ld = ldap_init( "ldap.netscape.com", LDAP_PORT ))
37.                         == NULL ) {
38.                             perror( "ldap_init" );
39.                             exit( 1 );
40.                 }

41.                 /* send the bind request */
42.                 if ( (msgid = ldap_simple_bind( ld, BINDDN, BINDPWD
        ➥)) == -1 ) {
43.                             ldap_perror( ld, "LDAP bind" );
44.                             ldap_unbind( ld );
45.                             exit( 1 );
46.                 }

47.                 /* wait up to TIMELIMIT seconds for the bind to
                    ➥complete */
48.                 if ( wait4result( ld, "LDAP bind", TIMELIMIT, msgid )
        ➥!= 0 ) {
49.                             ldap_unbind( ld );
50.                             exit( 1 );
51.                 }

52.                 /* send the delete request */
53.                 if ( (msgid = ldap_delete( ld, DELETEDN )) == -1 ) {
54.                             ldap_perror( ld, "LDAP delete" );
55.                             ldap_unbind( ld );
56.                             exit( 1 );
57.                 }

58.                 /* wait up to TIMELIMIT seconds for the delete to
                    ➥complete */
59.                 if ( wait4result( ld, "LDAP delete", TIMELIMIT, msgid
        ➥) != 0 ) {
60.                             ldap_unbind( ld );
61.                             exit( 1 );
62.                 }

63.             ldap_unbind( ld );
64.             exit( 0 );
65.     }
```

This example is fairly long, but we have seen most of these calls before.

A utility function called wait4result() is used to enforce our desired 30 second LDAP operation time limit. See Chapter 9 for more information on the ldap_result() call (used on line 16).

The asynchronous ldap_simple_bind() call (line 42) is called just like its synchronous cousin but it returns an LDAP message id instead of an LDAP result code. The asynchronous ldap_delete() function is also used; it is covered in detail in Chapter 14.

The next section examines the parameters of the ldap_simple_bind() call in more detail.

Synopsis:

```
int ldap_simple_bind( LDAP *ld, char *dn, char *passwd );
```

Initiates an LDAP bind operation to identify, or authenticate, your application to the directory server using a DN and password. If successful, the authentication is in effect for the life of the LDAP session (or until another bind call is made). The ldap_result() call must be used to retrieve the result of the bind operation.

Return Value:

Type: int

An LDAP message id, suitable for use in the ldap_result() and ldap_abandon() calls is returned.

Parameters:

LDAP *ld: A handle to an LDAP session as returned by ldap_init() or ldap_open().

char *dn: A string representation of the Distinguished Name of the entry that is binding to the directory. If this parameter is NULL or a zero-length string, an unauthenticated bind is performed.

char *passwd: The password associated with dn. If this is NULL or a zero-length string, an unauthenticated bind is performed.

The General Authentication Functions

Another pair of bind functions that take an authentication method parameter is included in the LDAP API. If your application supports more than one authentication method (such as Kerberos—see previous note), it may be convenient to use these more general functions. First we look at the synchronous, general purpose bind function, `ldap_bind_s()`.

Synopsis:

```
int ldap_bind_s( LDAP *ld, char *dn, char *creds, int
method, );
```

Synchronously identifies, or authenticates, your application to the directory server using a DN and some arbitrary credentials. If successful, the authentication is in effect for the life of the LDAP session (or until another bind call is made).

Return Value:

Type: `int`

An LDAP error code (equal to `LDAP_SUCCESS` if the operation succeeds). Error handling is discussed in more detail in Chapter 8.

Parameters:

`LDAP *ld`: A handle to an LDAP session as returned by `ldap_init()` or `ldap_open()`.

`char *dn`: The distinguished name of the entry that is binding to the directory. If this parameter is `NULL` or a zero-length string, an unauthenticated bind is performed.

`char *creds`: A pointer to the authentication credentials. For simple password binds, this is a pointer to the password.

`int method`: This parameter specifies which authentication method to use. For simple password-based authentication, pass `LDAP_AUTH_SIMPLE` (defined in the `ldap.h` header file).

You may notice that the *creds* parameter is a `char *`, suggesting that it points to credentials that are either `NULL`-terminated or self-describing. This is actually a bug in the API. A future version will likely let you pass arbitrary credentials and their length. For now, it doesn't make much difference since the only accepted credentials are a password (which is `NULL`-terminated) or Kerberos credentials (which are self-describing).

Example 13.4: Bind to a directory server as manager of the directory and delete a person's entry. Use a simple, clear-text password and the general, synchronous LDAP bind function.

```
1.      #include <stdio.h>
2.      #include <ldap.h>

3.      #define BINDDN       "cn=Directory Manager, o=Ace industry,
        ➥c=US"
4.      #define BINDPWD      "ldap=fun"
5.      #define DELETEDN     "cn=Sam Carter, ou=Accounting, o=Ace
        ➥Industry, c=US"


6.      main()
7.      {
8.              LDAP       *ld;

9.              if ( (ld = ldap_init( "ldap.netscape.com", LDAP_PORT
                ➥)) == NULL ) {
10.                     perror( "ldap_init" );
11.                     exit( 1 );
12.             }

13.             if ( ldap_bind_s( ld, BINDDN, BINDPWD,
                ➥LDAP_AUTH_SIMPLE )
14.                     != LDAP_SUCCESS ) {
15.                     ldap_perror( ld, "ldap_simple_bind"
        );
16.                     ldap_unbind( ld );
17.                     exit( 1 );
18.             }
```

```
19.                 if ( ldap_delete_s( ld, DELETEDN ) != LDAP_SUCCESS )
                    {
20.                         ldap_perror( ld, "ldap_delete" );
21.                         ldap_unbind( ld );
22.                         exit( 1 );
23.                 }

24.             ldap_unbind( ld );
25.             exit( 0 );
26.     }
```

The only difference between the code in this example and that in example 13.1 is the use of `ldap_bind_s()` instead of `ldap_simple_bind_s()` on line 13. In this case, there is no real advantage of one call over the other. There is also an asynchronous general purpose bind call available. It is detailed next.

Synopsis:

```
int ldap_bind( LDAP *ld, char *dn, char *creds, int method );
```

Initiates an LDAP bind operation to identify, or authenticate, your application to the directory server using a DN and some arbitrary credentials. If successful, the authentication is in effect for the life of the LDAP session (or until another bind call is made). The `ldap_result()` call must be used to retrieve the result of the bind operation.

Return Value:

Type: `int`

An LDAP message id, suitable for use in the `ldap_result()` and `ldap_abandon()` calls is returned.

Parameters:

`LDAP *ld`: A handle to an LDAP session as returned by `ldap_init()` or `ldap_open()`.

char `*dn`: The distinguished name of the entry that is binding to the directory. If this parameter is NULL or a zero-length string, an unauthenticated bind is performed.

char `*creds`: A pointer to the authentication credentials. For simple password binds, this is a pointer to the password.

int `method`: This parameter specifies which authentication method to use. For simple password-based authentication, pass LDAP_AUTH_SIMPLE (defined in the `ldap.h` header file).

Handling LDAP Re-Binds

Sometimes the LDAP library needs to perform a bind operation behind the scenes, that is, at some other time than when you have made an explicit call to one of the LDAP bind functions covered earlier in this chapter. This is called a *re-bind*, and it happens most often when additional LDAP servers need to be contacted in the course of following one or more referrals. Because the LDAP library does not save the DN and password or other authentication credentials that were used in the last bind call (this is for security purposes), by default it performs an unauthenticated re-bind. You can override this behavior by installing a re-bind function.

The re-bind function works like this: when the LDAP library is about to perform a "behind the scenes" bind on your behalf, it calls your re-bind function to obtain the DN and password or other credentials to use in the bind operation. When it is done using the credentials, it calls the re-bind function again to give you a chance to dispose of any memory or other resources allocated in the first call.

An outline of how the re-bind function is used when the LDAP library is following a referral to another server is shown in Figure 13.2. Referrals are not discussed in a lot of detail in this book, but they serve well to show how the re-bind function is used by the LDAP library.

Figure 13.2

How the re-bind function is used when following referrals. Arrows indicate LDAP exchanges between client and server.

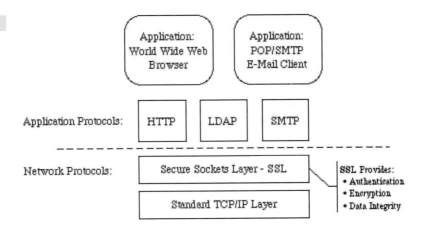

Note that the re-bind function is inside your application and can be called by the LDAP library any time it is handling an LDAP operation such as search, modify, or delete. The ldap_set_rebind_proc() API call is the preferred method for installing your re-bind function.

Example 13.5: Installing an LDAP re-bind function (Netscape SDK).

```
1.    #include <ldap.h>

2.    char    *binddn;
3.    char    *bindpasswd;

4.    int
5.    get_rebind_credentials( LDAP *ld, char **dnp, char **pwp,
6.            int *authmethodp, int freeit, void *arg )
7.    {
8.            if ( freeit == 0 ) {
9.            /* first time called: return a copy of the DN and
               ➥password */
10.                    *authmethodp = LDAP_AUTH_SIMPLE;
11.                    if ( binddn == NULL ) {
12.                            *dnp = *pwp = NULL;
13.                    } else {
14.                            *dnp = strdup( binddn );
15.                            *pwp = strdup( bindpasswd );
16.                    }

17.            } else {
18.            /* second time called: free the DN and password
               ➥copies */
```

```
19.                              if ( *dnp != NULL ) {
20.                                      free( *dnp );
21.                                      free( *pwp );
22.                              }
23.                      }

24.                      return( LDAP_SUCCESS );
25.      }

26.      void
27.      install_rebind_proc( LDAP *ld )
28.      {
29.              ldap_set_rebind_proc( ld, get_rebind_credentials,
                 ➡NULL );
30.      }
```

Lines 4–25 define a re-bind function called get_rebind_credentials().
It is installed by the function shown on lines 26–30. The re-bind function assumes that two global variables called binddn and bindpasswd are
maintained by the application, and that these variables contain the DN
and password used on the last bind. The first time the re-bind function
is called, the freeit parameter is zero. On this call, the re-bind function will return a copy of the DN and password to the LDAP library.
The second time the re-bind function is called, freeit is non-zero. On
this call, the re-bind function frees the memory allocated last time.

Note that in the University of Michigan SDK, the
ldap_set_rebind_proc() takes only two parameters and the re-bind
function itself should only have five. The last argument to both is an
application-defined argument that is passed as the last parameter to the
re-bind function. This parameter is not used in Example 13.5. The re-
bind function is described below.

Synopsis:

Netscape SDK:

int ldap_set_rebind_proc(LDAP *ld,

(int (*rebindproc)(LDAP *ld, char **dnp, char **pwp,

```
int *authmethodp, int freeit, void *arg )),
```

```
void *arg );
```

University of Michigan SDK:

```
int ldap_set_rebind_proc( LDAP *ld,
```

```
(int (*rebindproc)( LDAP *ld, char **dnp, char **pwp,
```

```
int *authmethodp, int freeit )));
```

Installs an application-defined function to be called by the LDAP library when it needs to obtain authentication credentials. Note that in the Netscape SDK, ldap_set_rebind_proc() takes three parameters and in the U-M SDK it only takes two. The re-bind function itself also gains an additional parameter in the Netscape SDK.

Return Value:

Type: int

An LDAP error code (equal to LDAP_SUCCESS if function installation succeeds). Error handling is discussed in more detail in Chapter 8.

Parameters:

LDAP *ld: A handle to an LDAP session as returned by ldap_init() or ldap_open().

rebindproc: A pointer to the re-bind function to install. This is described in more detail later.

void *arg: A parameter that will be passed intact to the re-bind function. This parameter does not exist in the University of Michigan SDK.

Tip

In the Netscape SDK, the `ldap_set_option()` call can also be used to install a re-bind function. The option name is `LDAP_OPT_REBIND_FN`.

The application-defined LDAP re-bind function is summarized below.

Synopsis:

Netscape SDK:

```
int rebindproc( LDAP *ld, char **dnp, char **pwp,
int *authmethodp, int freeit, void *arg ));
```

University of Michigan SDK:

```
int rebindproc( LDAP *ld, char **dnp, char **pwp,
int *authmethodp, int freeit ));
```

Application-defined function that is called by the LDAP library when it needs to obtain authentication credentials in the course of performing a "behind-the-scenes" bind operation. Note that in the Netscape SDK this function takes an extra `void *arg` parameter.

Return Value:

Type: `int`

An LDAP error code. Return `LDAP_SUCCESS` to let the bind continue and any other error that is defined in the `ldap.h` header file to abort the bind.

Parameters:

`LDAP *ld`: The LDAP session handle.

`char **dnp`: A pointer to the location where a pointer to the bind Distinguished Name should be stored.

char **pwp*: A pointer to the location where a pointer to the bind password or other credentials should be stored.

int **authmethodp*: A pointer to the location where the bind method should be stored. Set *authmethodp to LDAP_AUTH_SIMPLE for simple password authentication.

int *freeit:* If this parameter is zero, bind credentials are being requested and the *dnp*, *pwp*, and *authmethodp* pointers should be set. Otherwise, the re-bind function is being called a second time to give you the opportunity to dispose of any memory or other resources that you used when returning the authentication credentials.

void **arg*: The *arg* parameter that was passed to ldap_set_rebind_proc(). You can use this in whatever way you desire; typically, it is used to pass an application-specific piece of data to the re-bind function. This parameter does not exist in the University of Michigan SDK.

Summary

The following table summarizes the routines described in this chapter.

Name	Description
ldap_simple_bind_s()	Synchronously authenticates to the directory server using a DN and password.
ldap_simple_bind()	Asynchronously authenticates to the directory server using a DN and password.
ldap_bind_s()	Synchronously authenticates to the directory server (general interface).
ldap_bind()	Asynchronously authenticates to the directory server (general interface)
ldap_set_rebind_proc()	Installs an application-defined function to be called by the LDAP library when it needs to obtain authentication credentials.
rebindproc()	User-defined re-bind procedure.

Looking Ahead

Now that you know how to authenticate to the directory server, you are prepared to learn about an entirely new dimension of the Lightweight Directory Access Protocol: how to make changes to the information that is stored in LDAP servers. Turn the page and read the next chapter to learn how to update directory information.

CHAPTER 14

Update

S everal of the previous chapters have talked about how to search for and retrieve information from an LDAP directory and how to authenticate to an LDAP directory. This chapter shows you how you can update information in an LDAP directory, providing an easy way to create and delete directory entries, or to change the contents of existing directory entries.

You might want to update the directory for many reasons. If you are writing an e-mail application, you may want to allow users to store their address book information in the directory so they can access it from work or home. If you are writing a network management application, you may need to store network configuration information in the directory. Of course, if you are writing a directory application, you may want to allow your users to edit information about themselves in the directory. And just about any kind of application may benefit from storing user preference information in the LDAP directory. All of these functions are possible using LDAP's update capability.

There are four LDAP operations you can use to update the contents of the directory. They are modify, add, delete, and modify RDN. Each operation is described below, along with the LDAP API calls that execute it. As with other LDAP operations, both synchronous and asynchronous forms of each API call are available. And as we did with search and compare, we will begin each operation section by talking about the simpler synchronous interface and then talk about the asynchronous interface.

Modifying Entries (Synchronous)

The following example illustrates a simple application of the LDAP modify operation.

Example 14.1: The goal of the program shown below is to change the e-mail address of one Babs Jensen, an employee of Ace Industry, to the value babs@ace.com. We don't care what the existing value of Babs's e-mail address is (if any exists). We just want the value after the modification to be babs@ace.com.

```
1.    #include <stdio.h>
2.    #include <ldap.h>

3.    #define ENTRYDN "cn=Barbara Jensen, o=Ace Industry, c=US"
4.    #define ENTRYPW "hifalutin"

5.    main( int argc, char **argv )
6.    {
7.    LDAP      *ld;
8.    char      *mailvals[2];
9.    LDAPMod   mod;
10.   LDAPMod   *mods[2];

11.   /* initialize the LDAP session */
12.   if ( (ld = ldap_init( "ldap.netscape.com", LDAP_PORT ))
13.   == NULL) {
14.   perror( "ldap_init" );
15.   exit( 1 );
16.   }

17.   /* authenticate to the LDAP server */
18.   if ( ldap_simple_bind_s( ld, ENTRYDN, ENTRYPW )
19.   != LDAP_SUCCESS ) {
20.   ldap_perror( ld, "ldap_simple_bind_s" );
21.   exit( 1 );
22.   }

23.   /* construct the modification to make */
24.   mailvals[0] = "babs@ace.com";
25.   mailvals[1] = NULL;
26.   mod.mod_op = LDAP_MOD_REPLACE;
```

```
27.   mod.mod_type = "mail";
28.   mod.mod_values = mailvals;
29.   mods[0] = &mod;
30.   mods[1] = NULL;

31.   /* make the modification */
32.   if ( ldap_modify_s( ld, ENTRYDN, mods ) != LDAP_SUCCESS ) {
33.   ldap_perror( ld, "ldap_modify_s" );
34.   exit( 1 );
35.   }

36.   /* clean up */
37.   ldap_unbind( ld );
38.   return( 0 );
39.   }
```

There are several things to notice about this example. First, the initialization and cleanup parts at lines 11–16 and 36–38 are exactly the same as the initialization and cleanup parts in the search examples and indeed nearly all the other examples in this book. The first difference is encountered at line 17, when authenticating to the directory. The search example passed NULL for the name and password arguments to ldap_bind_s(), where our modify example passes two #defined constants identifying Babs's entry and giving her password. Since we are planning to make a change to the directory, it is very likely that the directory server will have access control in place that requires us to prove our identify before the change will be accepted.

| Tip |

> When updating the contents of the directory, authentication is almost always required. Make sure each call to the ldap_modify() or ldap_modify_s() routine is preceded by a successful LDAP Bind operation that proves your identity to the directory as a user who has the necessary privileges to perform the update.

The really interesting part of this example occurs on lines 23–30 and 31–35. The first set of lines construct the modification we want to make to Babs's entry. The second set of lines actually perform the modification, contacting the directory and waiting for the result.

The parameter passed to `ldap_modify_s()` that describes the modification is actually an array. In this example, the array has only one element indicating that all the values of the "mail" attribute, if any, should be replaced with the single value "babs@ace.com". In more complicated situations the array might have many elements, with each element describing a change to be made to the entry. A more complicated example later in this chapter illustrates just such a situation.

The `mod_values` field in the `LDAPMod` structure is also an array. In this simple example we've chosen to replace whatever values currently exist with only a single value. We could have easily replaced the existing values with two or more values, simply by including more elements in the `mod_values` array.

The next sections examine the parameters of `ldap_modify_s()` in more detail.

Synopsis:

```
int ldap_modify_s( LDAP *ld, char *entrydn, LDAPMod **mods );
```

Modifies an existing LDAP directory entry. The caller is blocked until the modification is complete.

Return Value:

Type: `int`

The `ldap_modify_s()` routine returns an indication of the success or failure of the modification operation. `LDAP_SUCCESS` will be returned if the operation was successful (that is, the entry was modified as requested). Any other return value indicates that an error occurred. The error can be interpreted by calling one of the LDAP error handling routines, such as `ldap_perror()` or `ldap_err2string()`, described more fully in Chapter 8.

Parameters:

`LDAP *ld`: This parameter is a handle to an LDAP session, as returned by a successful call to `ldap_init()` or `ldap_open()`. In the Netscape

LDAP SDK, this handle references an opaque data type. In the University of Michigan SDK, this handle is a pointer to a structure that is exposed to your program.

`char *entrydn`: This parameter specifies the name of the directory entry whose contents are to be modified. The entry must exist in the directory already. To create new entries in the LDAP directory, use the LDAP add operation, described in the next section.

`LDAPMod **mods`: This parameter specifies the modifications to make to the directory entry named by the `entrydn` parameter. It is a NULL-terminated array of pointers to `LDAPMod` structures. Each `LDAPMod` structure describes one sub-modification to make to the entry. The `LDAPMod` structure is described more fully in the next section.

Tip

> Each call to `ldap_modify()` or `ldap_modify_s()` performs one LDAP protocol Modify operation. The Modify operation may consist of several actual changes to the entry (for example, by including multiple elements in the `LDAPMod` array). All of the changes must either succeed or fail as a group. It is not possible for some of the changes to have been applied to the entry but not others.

The LDAPMod Structure

The `LDAPMod` structure is what you use to specify the changes you want made to an LDAP entry. The structure is defined as follows.

```
typedef struct ldapmod {
        int     mod_op;
        char    *mod_type;
        union {
                char            *modv_strvals;
                struct berval   **modv_bvals;
        } mod_vals;
#define mod_values      mod_vals.modv_strvals
#define mod_bvalues     mod_vals.modv_bvals
} LDAPMod;
```

The structure definition is a little messy, what with the union and all, but your use of it is pretty straightforward. There are three fields of interest. You fill in the mod_op field with the type of modification, the mod_type field with the name of the attribute type to which the modification applies, and either the mod_values or mod_bvalues field with the set of values to add, delete, or replace. In addition, the mod_op field is used to select either the mod_values or mod_bvalues member of the discriminated union in the structure. Each field is described in more detail below.

mod_op: This field specifies the type of modification to perform. It can have one of three values: LDAP_MOD_ADD, LDAP_MOD_DELETE, or LDAP_MOD_REPLACE. In addition, each of these values may be logically ANDed with the value LDAP_MOD_BVALUES, to select the mod_bvalues, rather than mod_values field. The meaning of each mod_op value is given below.

LDAP_MOD_ADD: This value of mod_op indicates that the values contained in the mod_values or mod_bvalues field should be added to the attribute given in the mod_type field. If the attribute does not already exist within the entry (that is, have one or more values), it will be created. If any of the values supplied in an LDAP_MOD_ADD operation already exist in the entry, you can expect the LDAP_TYPE_OR_VALUE_EXISTS error to be returned to you, and none of the modifications will have been performed.

LDAP_MOD_DELETE: This value of mod_op indicates that the values contained in the mod_values or mod_bvalues field should be removed from the attribute given in the mod_type. If all of the attribute's values are removed in this way, the attribute itself is deleted. (Recall that an attribute with zero values is not allowed in the LDAP model.) If one or more of the attribute values specified does not exist in the attribute, you can expect the LDAP_NO_SUCH_ATTRIBUTE error to be returned to you, and none of the modifications will have been performed. If the mod_values or mod_bvalues field is NULL, the entire attribute will be deleted from the entry.

LDAP_MOD_REPLACE: This value of mod_op indicates that any and all existing values of the attribute given in the mod_type parameter should be removed and replaced by the values contained in the `mod_values` or `mod_bvalues` field. If the given attribute does not already exist in the entry, it is created. If the `mod_values` or `mod_bvalues` field is `NULL`, the replace operation acts like a delete operation, and the entire attribute is deleted from the entry. A replace with `NULL` values will always succeed, while a delete may fail if the attribute does not exist.

`LDAP_MOD_BVALUES`: This value is only logically `OR`ed with one of the other three values given above. It is used to select the `mod_bvalues` field instead of the `mod_values` field in the `mod_un` union portion of the `LDAPMod` structure. This is because the `mod_op` field has been overloaded and is used to select both the type of modification to perform, and as the discriminating tag for the `mod_vals` union.

`mod_type`: This field specifies the attribute type in the given entry to which the modification applies. It is simply a string indicating the attribute type name, for example, `mail`, `cn`, etc.

`mod_values`: Only one of this field or the `mod_bvalues` field should be filled in. The `mod_values` field specifies the attribute values to add, delete, or replace as a `NULL`-terminated array of `NULL`-terminated strings. This field is useful and convenient for specifying simple textual values that can be represented as C strings. If binary data must be represented, the `mod_bvalues` field should be used instead.

`mod_bvalues`: Only one of this field or the `mod_values` field should be filled in. The `mod_bvalues` field is selected by logically `OR`ing the `mod_op` field with the constant `LDAP_MOD_BVALUES`, and specifies the attribute values to add, delete, or replace as a `NULL`-terminated array of pointers to struct berval structures. Each struct berval is defined as follows.

```
struct berval {
        unsigned long       bv_len;
        char                *bv_val;
};
```

The struct berval is a simple structure used to represent arbitrary data of arbitrary length. The `bv_len` field holds the length of the data pointed to by the `bv_val` field. The following code fragment illustrates the use of the `mod_bvalues` field and struct bervals to add a JPEG photograph attribute to an entry.

```
char            *buf;
struct berval   bv;
struct berval   bvals[2];
LDAPMod         mod;
...
/* fill in buf with jpegPhoto data of length len */
bv.bv_val = buf;
bv.bv_len = len;
bvals[0] = &bv;
bvals[0] = NULL;
mod.mod_op = LDAP_MOD_ADD | LDAP_MOD_BVALUES;
mod.mod_type = "jpegphoto"
mod.mod_bvalues = bvals;
/* call ldap_modify_s() as above */
...
```

Tip

> If your attribute values can be represented as C strings, you can use the simpler `mod_values` field in the `LDAPMod` structure. If you need to represent non-text data such as a photograph or sound attribute, use the `mod_bvalues` field instead, and be sure to logically `OR` the `mod_op` field with `LDAP_MOD_BVALUES`.

Modifying Entries (Asynchronous)

As with the other core LDAP API calls, the LDAP modify operation has both a synchronous and an asynchronous interface. The synchronous interface was discussed above. This section describes the asynchronous interface. Although an asynchronous interface is most important for the search operation (which may take a long time and return many entries) it is also useful on modifies. When performing a large number of modifications to a single entry or performing modifications against a busy server, the modify operation can take longer than you might be willing to wait synchronously. In such situations, you may want to use the asynchronous interface provided by `ldap_modify()`.

The ldap_modify() routine uses the same basic approach to asynchronous operation that ldap_search() and the other LDAP API routines use. ldap_modify() is called to initiate an LDAP modify operation. It takes the parameters you provide, packages them up and actually sends them off in a modify request to the LDAP server. Assuming that all goes well, ldap_modify() then returns to the caller a message ID identifying the request. This message ID can be used in subsequent calls to ldap_result() to retrieve the success or failure of the modify operation.

ldap_result() is at the heart of all asynchronous use of the LDAP API. The LDAP server returns the results of operations, including the modify operation, in separate packets, or protocol data units, delivered over the network. ldap_result() is essentially an interface to retrieving these packets as they come in. ldap_result() lets you specify how long you're willing to wait for a packet to show up, whether you want a particular packet (for example, the result of a given modify operation) or will accept any result. The details of both ldap_modify() and ldap_result() are given below, followed by an example of their use.

Synopsis:

```
int ldap_modify( LDAP *ld, char *entrydn, LDAPMod **mods );
```

Initiates the modification of an existing LDAP directory entry. The modification is performed asynchronously. The result of the operation may be retrieved by a subsequent call to ldap_result().

Return Value:

Type: int

The ldap_modify() routine returns the greater-than-zero message ID of the operation it initiates, or −1 in case of error. If an error occurs, the LDAP error code is set to indicate the nature of the error.

Parameters:

LDAP *ld: This parameter is a handle to an LDAP session, as returned by a successful call to ldap_init() or ldap_open(). In the Netscape

LDAP SDK, this handle references an opaque data type. In the University of Michigan SDK, this handle is a pointer to a structure that is exposed to your program.

char *entrydn: This parameter specifies the name of the directory entry whose contents are to be modified. The entry must exist in the directory already. To create new entries in the LDAP directory, use the LDAP add operation, described in the next section.

LDAPMod **mods: This parameter specifies the modifications to make to the directory entry named by the entrydn parameter. It is a NULL-terminated array of pointers to LDAPMod structures. Each LDAPMod structure describes one sub-modification to make to the entry. The LDAPMod structure is described more fully in the previous section.

The value returned by ldap_modify() is quite different from the value returned by ldap_modify_s(). While the latter routine returns one of the error codes found in <ldap.h> indicating the ultimate success or failure of the modify operation, ldap_modify() returns the message ID of the request it has initiated. Recall that ldap_modify() only initiates the modification. The result of the modification must be retrieved later by calling ldap_result().

The message ID ldap_modify() returns is unique among other message IDs outstanding on the LDAP session and is used to reference the modify operation on a later call to ldap_result(). It has no other significance. You must call ldap_result() to find out the result of the modification (what the LDAP server has sent back in response to your modify request).

ldap_modify() will return −1 if it was unable to initiate the request, which can happen if the network was down, memory could not be allocated, etc. The LDAP error will be set to indicate the problem if −1 is returned.

Synopsis:

```
int ldap_result( LDAP *ld, int msgid, int all, struct timeval
➡*timeout, LDAPMessage **result );
```

Checks the status or retrieve the result of a previously initiated LDAP operation (for example, that invoked by a call to `ldap_modify()`).

Return Value:

Type: `int`

The return value of `ldap_result()` follows a convention similar to that used by the select() system call. It returns values in one of three categories. A return of –1 indicates that some error has occurred. The LDAP error will be set to indicate the problem. A return of `0` (zero) indicates that a timeout has occurred. The timeout you specified in the *timeout* parameter expired before an appropriate result came in. A greater-than-zero return indicates success, and that a result has been returned in the result parameter. The value of the greater-than-zero return from `ldap_result()` indicates the type of result contained in the result parameter. It will be one of the result type constants declared in the `ldap.h` header file. Possible values and their meanings are described below.

Parameters:

`LDAP *ld`: This parameter is a handle to an LDAP session, as returned by a successful call to `ldap_init()` or `ldap_open()`.

`int msgid`: This parameter specifies the message ID for which results are desired, as returned from a successful call to `ldap_modify()` or any of the other asynchronous operation initiation routines. If the result of any operation is desired, the special value `LDAP_RES_ANY` may be passed for *msgid*.

`int all`: This parameter only has meaning for search operations. Recall that the result of a search operation as sent by the LDAP server consists of zero or more entries followed by a final search outcome packet indicating the ultimate success or failure of the search. The *all* parameter is a Boolean that determines whether `ldap_result()` should return single search entries or the final outcome packets as they come in (zero), or if instead it should wait and return the entire chain of search entries and final outcome only after all the entries and the final outcome has been received (non-zero). If *all* is non-zero `ldap_result()` will always return at most one "packet" per call, either an entry from a search operation, or a final outcome result from any operation. If you are only interested in the outcome of a modify operation, you should set this parameter to zero.

`struct timeval *timeout`: This parameter controls how long `ldap_result()` should wait for results if none have already come in and are waiting to be returned. A value of NULL for `timeout` indicates that `ldap_result()` should block indefinitely, until the requested results come in. A non-NULL value of `timeout` with the `timeout` set to zero indicates that `ldap_result()` should effect a polling behavior. If results are available immediately, they will be returned. If not, `ldap_result()` will not wait for them.

`LDAPMessage **result`: This parameter is a pointer to an LDAPMessage * used to hold the result of a successful call to `ldap_result()`. If the `ldap_result()` call returns a value greater than zero, the `result` parameter will be filled in with the result, which in the case of a modify result, is a simple packet indicating success or failure of the operation. This result can be interpreted by calling `ldap_result2error()`. The `result` parameter should be freed by the caller by calling `ldap_msgfree()` when it is no longer in use.

The possible greater-than-zero returns from `ldap_result()` are described below. Only the first one has significance for the LDAP modify operation, but the others are described for completeness.

LDAP_RES_MODIFY_RESULT	The result of a previously initiated modify operation.
LDAP_RES_ADD_RESULT	The result of a previously initiated add operation.
LDAP_RES_DELETE_RESULT	The result of a previously initiated delete operation.
LDAP_RES_MODRDN_RESULT	The result of a previously initiated modify RDN operation.

LDAP_RES_SEARCH_ENTRY	A single entry matching a previously initiated search request.
LDAP_RES_SEARCH_RESULT	Either a result indicating the final outcome of a previously initiated search operation or an entire chain of entries matching a previously initiated search request, along with the final outcome.
LDAP_RES_BIND_RESULT	The result of a previously initaited bind operation.
LDAP_RES_COMPARE_RESULT	The result of a previously initiated compare operation.

If you have specified LDAP_RES_ANY in the call to ldap_result(), it may be useful to know the message ID of the result finally returned. ldap_result() returns the type of the result, but not its message ID. In the University of Michigan SDK, the message ID of the result is available in the following field of the LDAPMessage structure.

```
int          msgid;
LDAPMessage  *result;
/* successful call to ldap_result() fills in result */
msgid = result->lm_msgid;
```

In the Netscape SDK, the LDAPMessage holding results is an opaque data type. The message ID associated with a result can be obtained by calling the following accessor function.

```
int          msgid;
LDAPMessage  *result;
/* successful call to ldap_result() fills in result */
msgid = ldap_msgid( ld, result );
```

Asynchronous Programming Example

Having described the asynchronous modify routine in detail, we now present a complete example illustrating its use.

Example 14.2: This example is basically a rewrite of our previous example that changed the e-mail address of Barbara Jensen. We've made two changes to help illustrate the power of the asynchronous LDAP API and the use of the mod_bvalues field in the LDAPMod structure.

First, instead of waiting for the modification to complete by calling ldap_modify_s(), we call ldap_modify() and then loop while waiting for the result, printing out an indication of our status. Though our example may be somewhat unrealistic, imagine your own application doing something other than printing a message while waiting. It might spin the cursor, display a progress bar, respond to user-driven events, or do other useful work, all while the server is off working away on modifying Barbara's entry.

Second, we've chosen to replace Barbara's photograph with one we read from a file, in addition to the simple e-mail address replacement of our previous example. This helps illustrate the use of the mod_bvalues and LDAP_MOD_BVALUES features of the ldap_modify() call, and the use of multiple changes within a single modify operation.

```
1.    #include <stdio.h>
2.    #include <sys/stat.h>
3.    #include <ldap.h>

4.    #define ENTRYDN    "cn=Barbara Jensen, o=Ace Industry, c=US"
5.    #define ENTRYPW    "hifalutin"
6.    #define PHOTOFILE  "/tmp/babs.jpg"

7.    main( int argc, char **argv )
8.    {
9.    LDAP            *ld;
10.   LDAPMessage     *result;
11.   LDAPMod         photomod, mailmod;
12.   LDAPMod         *mods[3];
13.   char            *buf;
```

```
14.   struct berval      photobv;
15.   struct berval      *photobvals[2];
16.   char               *mailvals[2];
17.   struct stat        st;
18.   FILE               *fp;
19.   int                msgid, rc;
20.   struct timeval     tv;

21.   if ( (ld = ldap_init( "ldap.netscape.com", LDAP_PORT ))
22.   == NULL) {
23.   perror( "ldap_init" );
24.   exit( 1 );
25.   }

26.   if ( ldap_simple_bind_s( ld, ENTRYDN, ENTRYPW )
27.   != LDAP_SUCCESS ) {
28.   ldap_perror( ld, "ldap_simple_bind_s" );
29.   exit( 1 );
30.   }

31.   if ( stat( PHOTOFILE, &st ) != 0
32.   || (fp = fopen( PHOTOFILE, "rb" )) == NULL ) {
33.   perror( PHOTOFILE );
34.   exit( 1 );
35.   }
36.   if ( (buf = (char *) malloc( st.st_size )) == NULL
37.   || fread( buf, st.st_size, 1, fp ) != 1 ) {
38.   perror( buf ? "fread" : "malloc" );
39.   exit( 1 );
40.   }
41.   fclose( fp );

42.   /* photograph modification */
43.   photobv.bv_len = st.st_size;
44.   photobv.bv_val = buf;
45.   photobvals[0] = &photobv;
46.   photobvals[1] = NULL;
47.   photomod.mod_op = LDAP_MOD_REPLACE | LDAP_MOD_BVALUES;
48.   photomod.mod_type = "jpegphoto";
49.   photomod.mod_bvalues = photobvals;
50.   /* email modification */
51.   mailvals[0] = "babs@ace.com";
52.   mailvals[1] = NULL;
```

```
53.    mailmod.mod_op = LDAP_MOD_REPLACE;
54.    mailmod.mod_type = "mail";
55.    mailmod.mod_values = mailvals;
56.    /* make the list of mods */
57.    mods[0] = &photomod;
58.    mods[1] = &mailmod;
59.    mods[2] = NULL;

60.    /* initiate the modification */
61.    if ( (msgid = ldap_modify( ld, ENTRYDN, mods )) == -1 ) {
62.    ldap_perror( ld, "ldap_modify" );
63.    exit( 1 );
64.    }
65.    free( buf );

66.    tv.tv_sec = 0;
67.    tv.tv_usec = 100;
68.    while ( (rc = ldap_result( ld, msgid, 0, &tv, &result ))
69.    == 0 ) {
70.    printf( "waiting...\n" );
71.    }
72.    ldap_result2error( ld, result, 1 );
73.    ldap_perror( ld, "ldap_modify" );

74.    ldap_unbind( ld );
75.    return( 0 );
76.    }
```

This example strings together a series of two modifications to be performed within a single LDAP Modify operation. Both modifications (the mail replacement and the jpegphoto replacement) must succeed for the entire operation to succeed. After initiating the modify operation, the example loops, calling ldap_result() every tenth of a second, printing out a message indicating that it is still waiting after each timed out call to ldap_result().

Lines 21–30 contain the usual calls to initialize an LDAP session and authenticate us to the LDAP server, in preparation for the modification. The next set of statements on lines 31–41 are only concerned with reading in the JPEG photograph that we are planning to add to Barbara's entry.

Interesting things start to happen on lines 42–59, which construct the modifications to make to Barbara's entry. Notice the use of the LDAP_MOD_BVALUES constant logically ORed with the mod_op field, to indicate that the mod_bvalues field contains the photograph value. Notice also that in this example, we've strung together two changes to the entry to be performed in a single modify operation.

The modify operation is initiated by the call to ldap_modify() on line 61. Notice that as soon as we've initiated the operation, all necessary data has been transferred to the server and we can free the buffer we allocated to hold the photograph value. This happens on line 65.

The while loop on lines 68–71 calls ldap_result() result repeatedly with a 1/10 second timeout value. ldap_result() will return 0 (zero) if this timeout is exceeded before the result we have requested arrives, in which case we print the "waiting..." message and call ldap_result() again. The result of the modify operation is eventually returned in the *result* parameter, which we interpret by calling ldap_result2error() and then display by calling ldap_perror(). Both of these functions are described in more detail in Chapter 8 on error handling.

Adding Entries (Synchronous)

The LDAP Add operation is used to create new entries in the LDAP directory. Typically, you would want to do this less often than you might want to modify existing entries, but there are plenty of applications that require adding entries to the directory. For example, you might write a tool for use by system administrators that adds a new user to the directory. Or you might write a user application that allows users to create entries representing electronic mailing lists in the LDAP directory. Both applications require the ability to add entries to the directory. The LDAP API provides both synchronous and asynchronous interfaces to this functionality.

As with other operations, we will begin by describing the synchronous interface to the LDAP Add operation, ldap_add_s(). The synchronous interface is somewhat simpler. We will discuss the asynchronous interface, ldap_add() and ldap_result(), next.

Synchronous Add Example

Example 14.3: First, an example. The purpose of this example is to add an entry to the directory for a new user named Bjorn Jensen. Bjorn has just started working at Ace Industry and needs an entry in the corporate directory.

```
1.    #include <stdio.h>
2.    #include <ldap.h>

3.    #define ADMINDN    "cn=Directory Admin, o=Ace Industry, c=US"
4.    #define ADMINPW    "secret"
5.    #define ENTRYDN    "cn=Bjorn Jensen, o=Ace Industry, c=US"

6.    main( int argc, char **argv )
7.    {
8.    LDAP       *ld;
9.    char       *cnvals[2], *snvals[2], *ocvals[2];
10.   LDAPMod    cnmod, snmod, ocmod;
11.   LDAPMod    *mods[4];

12.   /* initialize the LDAP session */
13.   if ( (ld = ldap_init( "ldap.netscape.com", LDAP_PORT ))
14.   == NULL) {
15.   perror( "ldap_init" );
16.   exit( 1 );
17.   }

18.   /* authenticate to the LDAP server */
19.   if ( ldap_simple_bind_s( ld, ADMINDN, ADMINPW )
20.   != LDAP_SUCCESS ) {
21.   ldap_perror( ld, "ldap_simple_bind_s" );
22.   exit( 1 );
23.   }

24.   /* construct the entry to add */
25.   cnvals[0] = "Bjorn Jensen";
26.   cnvals[1] = NULL;
27.   cnmod.mod_op = 0;
28.   cnmod.mod_type = "cn";
29.   cnmod.mod_values = cnvals;
30.   snvals[0] = "Jensen";
31.   snvals[1] = NULL;
```

```
32.   snmod.mod_op = 0;
33.   snmod.mod_type = "sn";
34.   snmod.mod_values = snvals;
35.   ocvals[0] = "top";
36.   ocvals[1] = "person";
37.   ocvals[2] = NULL;
38.   ocmod.mod_op = 0;
39.   ocmod.mod_type = "objectclass";
40.   ocmod.mod_values = ocvals;
41.   mods[0] = &cnmod;
42.   mods[1] = &snmod;
43.   mods[2] = &ocmod;
44.   mods[3] = NULL;

45.   /* make the modification */
46.   if ( ldap_add_s( ld, ENTRYDN, mods ) != LDAP_SUCCESS ) {
47.   ldap_perror( ld, "ldap_add_s" );
48.   exit( 1 );
49.   }

50.   /* clean up */
51.   ldap_unbind( ld );
52.   return( 0 );
53.   }
```

The first thing to notice about this example is how similar it is to the modify example at the beginning of the previous section. The same LDAPMod structure is used to represent the attributes of the entry to add as was used to represent the changes to make to an existing entry's attributes.

The usual initialization and authentication is performed on lines 12–23. Notice, however, that this time we authenticate as the directory administrator. (There's nothing special about the name of this entry—we're just assuming for the purposes of this example that an entry with this name exists and is allowed to add entries to the directory.) Since Bjorn's entry does not yet exist in the directory, we can't very well authenticate as him.

Next, lines 24–44 construct the attributes of the entry we're going to add. The same LDAPMod structure used to modify entries is used to represent the attributes of a new entry. Of course, if this were a real example, we would probably not hard-code in the name of the entry and the values of its attributes.

One interesting thing we have not seen before is the `objectClass` attribute, set in lines 35–40. Recall from Chapter 3 on the LDAP information model that the `objectClass` attribute serves two purposes. First, it tells what kind of entry is being added (in this case, a person entry). Second, it controls what other attributes are required or allowed to be in the entry. In the case of a person entry, three attributes are required: `cn`, `sn`, and `objectClass`. We've chosen only to fill in the required fields, though other attributes are allowed.

Recall also from Chapter 3 that object classes are hierarchical. That is, one object class can be defined in terms of another, inheriting all of the parent object class's required and allowed attributes. When adding an entry of a derived object class (for example, person), you must also specify the object classes of its parent object classes (for example, top).

Tip

> Some LDAP server implementations may allow you to add an entry without adding all of the parent object classes (for example, just the "person" value for the object class, not "top"). This behavior cannot be counted on, though, so you should always add all the required values for `objectClass`.

The entry is actually added by the call to `ldap_add_s()` on line 46, and then the usual cleanup is done and the LDAP session is terminated before we return.

The next section examines the parameters of the `ldap_add_s()` API call in more detail.

Synopsis:

```
int ldap_add_s( LDAP *ld, char *entrydn, LDAPMod **attrs );
```

Adds a new entry to the LDAP directory. The entry is added synchronously. The parent entry of the entry to be added must already exist in the directory.

Return Value:

Type: `int`

The `ldap_add_s()` routine returns an indication of the success or failure of the add operation. `LDAP_SUCCESS` will be returned if the operation was successful (i.e., the entry was added as requested). Any other return value indicates an error occurred. The error can be interpreted by calling one of the LDAP error handling routines, such as `ldap_perror()` or `ldap_err2string()`, described more fully in Chapter 8.

Parameters:

`LDAP *ld`: This parameter is a handle to an LDAP session, as returned by a successful call to `ldap_init()` or `ldap_open()`. In the Netscape LDAP SDK, this handle references an opaque data type. In the University of Michigan SDK, this handle is a pointer to a structure that is exposed to your program.

`char *entrydn`: This parameter specifies the name of the directory entry to be created.

`LDAPMod **attrs`: This parameter specifies the attributes of the new directory entry named by the `entrydn` parameter. It is a `NULL`-terminated array of pointers to `LDAPMod` structures. Each `LDAPMod` structure describes one attribute of the entry to create. The `LDAPMod` structure is described more fully in the modify section above, and `ldap_add_s()`'s use of the `LDAPMod` structure is described following.

Tip

> The LDAP directory has a hierarchical namespace. In order to add an entry to the directory, the entry above it must already exist. If it does not, you will be returned an `LDAP_NO_SUCH_OBJECT` error, indicating that the parent entry of the object you tried to add does not exist. If this happens, you should either add the parent entry, or perhaps add your entry under a different part of the directory tree.

Using the LDAPMod Structure to Add Entries

The LDAPMod structure is used to specify the attributes you want your new entry to have. This is the same structure used by ldap_modify() and ldap_modify_s() to represent changes to an entry. The ldap_add_s() routine uses the same fields within LDAPMod, with the following restrictions.

mod_op: This field is ignored by ldap_add_s(), except for the setting of LDAP_MOD_BVALUES, which is still used to select between the mod_values and mod_bvalues fields, described below. To select mod_values (a NULL-terminated array of strings) to represent values, set the mod_op field to 0 (zero). To select mod_bvalues (a NULL-terminated array of pointers to struct bervals), set the mod_op field to LDAP_MOD_BVALUES.

mod_type: This field specifies an attribute type within the new entry, whose values are given in the associated mod_values or mod_bvalues field.

mod_values: Only one of this field or the mod_bvalues field should be filled in. The mod_values field specifies the attribute values of the associated attribute as a NULL-terminated array of NULL-terminated strings. This field is useful and convenient for specifying simple textual values that can be represented as C strings. If binary data must be represented, the mod_bvalues field should be used instead.

mod_bvalues: Only one of this field or the mod_values field should be filled in. The mod_bvalues field is selected by setting the mod_op field to the constant LDAP_MOD_BVALUES. mod_bvalues specifies the attribute values of the associated attributes as a NULL-terminated array of pointers to struct berval structures. Each struct berval is defined as follows.

```
struct berval {
        unsigned long    bv_len;
        char             *bv_val;
};
```

The struct berval is a simple structure used to represent arbitrary data of arbitrary length. The bv_len field holds the length of the data pointed to by the bv_val field.

Adding Entries (Asynchronous)

As with modify and the other update operations, adding entries can take longer than you might want to wait. In this situation, you may want to use the asynchronous interface to the LDAP Add operation, given by the ldap_add() API call. ldap_add() works similarly to its modify and search counterparts. It initiates an LDAP Add operation and returns immediately, without waiting for the server to send the result. The result of the add operation can be obtained by a subsequent call to ldap_result().

The next section examines the parameters of ldap_add() in more detail.

Synopsis:

```
int ldap_add( LDAP *ld, char *entrydn, LDAPMod **attrs );
```

Initiates the addition of a new entry to the LDAP directory. The entry is added asynchronously. The result of the add operation may be obtained by a subsequent call to ldap_result(). The parent entry of the entry to be added must already exist in the directory.

Return Value:

Type: int

The value returned by ldap_add() is quite different from the value returned by ldap_add_s(). While the latter routine returns one of the error codes found in the ldap.h header file indicating the ultimate success or failure of the add operation, ldap_add() returns the message ID of the request it has initiated. Recall that ldap_add() only initiates the add operation. The result of the add must be retrieved later by calling ldap_result(). In case of error ldap_add() returns −1 and sets the LDAP error code to indicate the error.

Parameters:

LDAP *ld: This parameter is a handle to an LDAP session, as returned by a successful call to ldap_init() or ldap_open(). In the Netscape LDAP SDK, this handle references an opaque data type. In the University of Michigan SDK, this handle is a pointer to a structure that is exposed to your program.

char *entrydn: This parameter specifies the name of the directory entry to create.

LDAPMod **attrs: This parameter specifies the attributes of the new directory entry named by the entrydn parameter. It is a NULL-terminated array of pointers to LDAPMod structures. Each LDAPMod structure describes one attribute of the new entry.

The message ID ldap_add() returns is unique among other message IDs outstanding on the LDAP session and is used to reference the add operation on a later call to ldap_result(). It has no other significance. You must call ldap_result() to find out the result of the add (what the LDAP server has sent back in response to your add request). The ldap_result() routine is described in detail earlier in this chapter.

ldap_add() will return –1 if it was unable to initiate the request, which can happen if the network was down, memory could not be allocated, etc. The LDAP error will be set to indicate the problem if –1 is returned.

Deleting Entries (Synchronous)

Occasionally, you may want to remove entries from the LDAP directory. For example, you might want to write an application for system administrators allowing them to delete entries for users that have left the company. Or if you are writing an e-mail application that stores its address book information in the LDAP directory, you might want to allow the user to delete entries from the address book that are no longer in use.

The LDAP API provides the ldap_delete_s() and ldap_delete() calls for this purpose. These calls are a general interface to the LDAP protocol Delete operation. As with other operations, the synchronous version of the API is described first, followed by the asynchronous version.

Synchronous Delete Example

Example 14.4: But first, a simple example. The goal of our example below is to delete the entry for Gern Jensen, a former employee of Ace Industry who has recently left the company.

```
1.    #include <stdio.h>
2.    #include <ldap.h>

3.    #define ADMINDN    "cn=Directory Admin, o=Ace Industry, c=US"
4.    #define ADMINPW    "secret"
5.    #define ENTRYDN    "cn=Gern Jensen, o=Ace Industry, c=US"

6.    main( int argc, char **argv )
7.    {
8.    LDAP            *ld;

9.    /* initialize the LDAP session */
10.   if ( (ld = ldap_init( "ldap.netscape.com", LDAP_PORT ))
11.   == NULL) {
12.   perror( "ldap_init" );
13.   exit( 1 );
14.   }

15.   /* authenticate to the LDAP server */
16.   if ( ldap_simple_bind_s( ld, ADMINDN, ADMINPW )
17.   != LDAP_SUCCESS ) {
18.   ldap_perror( ld, "ldap_simple_bind_s" );
19.   exit( 1 );
20.   }

21.   /* delete the entry */
22.   if ( ldap_delete_s( ld, ENTRYDN ) != LDAP_SUCCESS ) {
23.   ldap_perror( ld, "ldap_add_s" );
24.   exit( 1 );
25.   }

26.   /* clean up */
27.   ldap_unbind( ld );
28.   return( 0 );
29.   }
```

As you can see, this is one of our simplest examples so far. That's because there's very little information to provide when deleting an entry. After the usual initialization and setup on lines 9–20, we call `ldap_delete_s()` with the name of the entry we want deleted. `ldap_delete_s()` sends the delete operation to the server and waits for the result, notifying us if any errors occur. All that's left is to clean up and return on lines 26–29.

Again notice that we authenticated as a user different from the one we are deleting. While it would have been possible to authenticate as Gern himself, since his entry does exist in the directory, it's unlikely that you'd want to do this in real life.

The next section examines the `ldap_delete_s()` routine in more detail.

Synopsis:

```
int ldap_delete_s( LDAP *ld, char *entrydn );
```

Deletes an entry from the LDAP directory. The entry is deleted synchronously, meaning the caller is blocked until the entry is deleted or some error occurs.

Return Value:

Type: `int`

The `ldap_delete_s()` routine returns an indication of the success or failure of the delete operation. `LDAP_SUCCESS` will be returned if the operation was successful (i.e., the entry was deleted as requested). Any other return value indicates an error occurred. The error can be interpreted by calling one of the LDAP error handling routines, such as `ldap_perror()` or `ldap_err2string()`, described more fully in Chapter 8.

Parameters:

`LDAP *ld`: This parameter is a handle to an LDAP session, as returned by a successful call to `ldap_init()` or `ldap_open()`. In the Netscape LDAP SDK, this handle references an opaque data type. In the

University of Michigan SDK, this handle is a pointer to a structure that is exposed to your program.

`char *entrydn`: This parameter specifies the name of the directory entry to be removed. This entry must be a leaf in the LDAP directory tree.

Tip

The LDAP directory has a hierarchical namespace, and the LDAP protocol delete operation only allows the deletion of leaf entries, not entire subtrees of the directory. A leaf entry is one that has no children below it in the directory tree. If you attempt to delete a non-leaf entry from the directory (that is, an entry that has one or more child entries below it in the directory tree), you will be returned an `LDAP_NOT_ALLOWED_ON_NONLEAF` error, indicating that non-leaf entries cannot be deleted. The way around this situation is to remove all of the entry's children prior to removing the entry itself.

Deleting Entries (Asynchronous)

The delete operation is likely to be one of the faster update operations, but there may be times when a busy server, or one not optimized for delete may not carry out the operation and return a result to you in the time that you're willing to wait. In this situation, you may want to use the asynchronous `ldap_delete()` LDAP API call.

`ldap_delete()` works just like `ldap_modify()` and `ldap_add()`. It sends a request to the LDAP server, initiating a delete operation and returns the message ID of the request. The result of the delete operation is retrieved by a subsequent call to `ldap_result()`.

The `ldap_delete()` call is examined in more detail below.

Synopsis:

```
int ldap_delete( LDAP *ld, char *entrydn );
```

Initiates the deletion of an entry from the LDAP directory. The entry is deleted asynchronously, meaning the result of the delete operation must be retrieved through a subsequent call to `ldap_result()`.

Return Value:

Type: `int`

The value returned by `ldap_delete()` is quite different from the value returned by `ldap_delete_s()`. While the latter routine returns one of the error codes found in the `ldap.h` header file indicating the ultimate success or failure of the delete operation, `ldap_delete()` returns the message ID of the request it has initiated. Recall that `ldap_delete()` only initiates the add operation. The result of the add must be retrieved later by calling `ldap_result()`. In case of error, −1 is returned and the LDAP error code is set to indicate the problem.

Parameters:

`LDAP *ld`: This parameter is a handle to an LDAP session, as returned by a successful call to `ldap_init()` or `ldap_open()`. In the Netscape LDAP SDK, this handle references an opaque data type. In the University of Michigan SDK, this handle is a pointer to a structure that is exposed to your program.

`char *entrydn`: This parameter specifies the name of the directory entry to be removed. This entry must be a leaf in the LDAP directory tree.

The message ID `ldap_delete()` returns is unique among other message IDs outstanding on the LDAP session and is used to reference the delete operation on a later call to `ldap_result()`. It has no other significance. You must call `ldap_result()` to find out the result of the delete (what the LDAP server has sent back in response to your delete request). The `ldap_result()` routine is described earlier in this chapter.

`ldap_delete()` will return −1 if it was unable to initiate the request, which can happen if the network was down, memory could not be allocated, etc. The LDAP error will be set to indicate the problem if −1 is returned.

Changing the Name of an Entry (Synchronous)

Sometimes it is desirable to change the name of an existing directory entry. For example, if a person changes their name, it may be desirable that their directory entry change names as well. These situations can be handled by the LDAP ModRDN protocol operation. The ldap_modrdn2() and ldap_modrdn2_s() routines provide an interface to the ModRDN operation.

As with other chapters, we examine the synchronous interface, ldap_modrdn2_s() first, followed by the asynchronous interface, ldap_modrdn2().

Tip

You may be wondering why there is a 2 on the end of these function names. The reason is historical, as you might imagine. There was a previous version of the LDAP protocol (version 1) that did not support the deleteoldrdn flag in the protocol. The original ldap_modrdn() and ldap_modrdn_s() routines provided an interface to this protocol, but no way to get at the new features of versions two and later.

Name Change Example

Example 14.5: The following is a short example illustrating the use of the synchronous ldap_modrdn2_s() call. In this example Bjorn Jensen has gotten married, and would like to change his name to Bjorn Jensen-Johansen.

```
1.    #include <stdio.h>
2.    #include <ldap.h>

3.    #define ADMINDN    "cn=Directory Admin, o=Ace Industry, c=US"
4.    #define ADMINPW    "secret"
5.    #define ENTRYDN    "cn=Bjorn Jensen, o=Ace Industry, c=US"
6.    #define NEWRDN     "cn=Bjorn Jensen-Johansen"

7.    main( int argc, char **argv )
8.    {
9.    LDAP           *ld;

10.   /* initialize the LDAP session */
11.   if ( (ld = ldap_init( "ldap.netscape.com", LDAP_PORT ))
12.   == NULL) {
```

```
13.    perror( "ldap_init" );
14.    exit( 1 );
15.    }

16.    /* authenticate to the LDAP server */
17.    if ( ldap_simple_bind_s( ld, ADMINDN, ADMINPW )
18.    != LDAP_SUCCESS ) {
19.    ldap_perror( ld, "ldap_simple_bind_s" );
20.    exit( 1 );
21.    }

22.    /* delete the entry */
23.    if ( ldap_modrdn2_s( ld, ENTRYDN, NEWRDN, 0 )
24.    != LDAP_SUCCESS ) {
25.    ldap_perror( ld, "ldap_modrdn2_s" );
26.    exit( 1 );
27.    }

28.    /* clean up */
29.    ldap_unbind( ld );
30.    return( 0 );
31.    }
```

The usual initialization takes place on lines 10–21. The name change is performed on line 23. In this example, we set the fourth parameter of ldap_modrdn2_s() to 0 (zero) indicating that we wish to keep the attributes comprising the old RDN (in this case, a cn attribute with value "Bjorn Jensen") as an attribute of the entry.

Notice also that while the complete name of the entry must be given in the second parameter, the new RDN alone is given as the third parameter, not the full new DN of the entry.

The ldap_modrdn2_s() routine is described in more detail below.

Synopsis:

```
int ldap_modrdn2_s( LDAP *ld, char *entrydn, char *newrdn, int
deleteoldrdn );
```

Renames the given entry to have the new relative distinguished name. The attributes making up the old relative distinguished name are deleted from the entry or not, according to the setting of the `deleteoldrdn` flag. The rename is done synchronously, meaning the caller is blocked until the operation is complete.

Return Value:

Type: `int`

The `ldap_modrdn2_s()` routine returns an indication of the success or failure of the `ModRDN` operation. `LDAP_SUCCESS` will be returned if the operation was successful (that is, the entry was renamed as you requested). Any other return value indicates an error occurred. The error can be interpreted by calling one of the LDAP error handling routines, such as `ldap_perror()` or `ldap_err2string()`, described more fully in Chapter 8.

Parameters:

`LDAP *ld`: This parameter is a handle to an LDAP session, as returned by a successful call to `ldap_init()` or `ldap_open()`. In the Netscape LDAP SDK, this handle references an opaque data type. In the University of Michigan SDK, this handle is a pointer to a structure that is exposed to your program.

`char *entrydn`: This parameter specifies the name of the directory entry to be renamed. This entry must be a leaf in the LDAP directory tree.

`char *newrdn`: This parameter specifies the new relative distinguished name to give the entry being renamed.

`int deleteoldrdn`: This parameter specifies whether or not the attribute values in the old relative distinguished name should be removed from the entry or retained as non-distinguished values. If `deleteoldrdn` is non-zero, the attributes will be deleted. If `deleteoldrdn` is zero, they will be retained as non-distinguished attributes in the renamed entry.

Tip

> The LDAP directory has a hierarchical namespace, and the LDAP protocol ModRDN operation only allows the renaming of leaf entries, not interior nodes of the directory. If you attempt to rename a non-leaf entry (that is, an entry that has one or more child entries below it in the directory tree), you will be returned an LDAP_NOT_ALLOWED_ON_NONLEAF error, indicating that non-leaf entries cannot be renamed. There is no easy way around this, aside from creating an entry with the new name and then deleting all of the entries under the old node and then re-adding them under the new node.

Changing the Name of an Entry (Asynchronous)

The ModRDN operation, like other update operations, may take longer than you are willing to wait. In this situation, you may want to use the asynchronous ldap_modrdn2() LDAP API call.

ldap_modrdn2() works just like ldap_modify(), ldap_add(), and ldap_delete(). It sends a request to the LDAP server, initiating a ModRDN operation and returns the message ID of the request. The result of the ModRDN operation is retrieved by a subsequent call to ldap_result().

The ldap_modrdn2() call is examined in more detail below.

Synopsis:

```
int ldap_modrdn2_s( LDAP *ld, char *entrydn, char *newrdn, int
deleteoldrdn );
```

Initiates an operation to rename the given entry to have the new relative distinguished name. The attributes making up the old relative distinguished name will be deleted from the entry or not, according to the setting of the deleteoldrdn flag. The rename is done asynchronously, meaning the result of the operation must be retrieved by a subsequent call to ldap_result().

Return Value:

Type: `int`

The value returned by `ldap_modrdn2()` is quite different from the value returned by `ldap_modrdn2_s()`. While the latter routine returns one of the error codes found in `<ldap.h>` indicating the ultimate success or failure of the renaming operation, `ldap_modrdn2()` returns the message ID of the request it has initiated. Recall that `ldap_modrdn2()` only initiates the name change operation. The result of the name change must be retrieved later by calling `ldap_result()`.

Parameters:

`LDAP *ld`: This parameter is a handle to an LDAP session, as returned by a successful call to `ldap_init()` or `ldap_open()`. In the Netscape LDAP SDK, this handle references an opaque data type. In the University of Michigan SDK, this handle is a pointer to a structure that is exposed to your program.

`char *entrydn`: This parameter specifies the name of the directory entry to be renamed. This entry must be a leaf in the LDAP directory tree.

`char *newrdn`: This parameter specifies the new relative distinguished name to give the entry being renamed.

`int deleteoldrdn`: This parameter specifies whether or not the attribute values in the old relative distinguished name should be removed from the entry or retained as non-distinguished values. If `deleteoldrdn` is non-zero, the attributes will be deleted. If `deleteoldrdn` is zero, they will be retained as non-distinguished attributes in the renamed entry.

The message ID `ldap_modrdn2()` returns is unique among other message IDs outstanding on the LDAP session and is used to reference the ModRDN operation on a later call to `ldap_result()`. It has no other significance. You must call `ldap_result()` to find out the result of the name change (what the LDAP server has sent back in response to your ModRDN request).

ldap_modrdn2() will return −1 if it was unable to initiate the request, which can happen if the network was down, memory could not be allocated, etc. The LDAP error will be set to indicate the problem if −1 is returned.

Summary

The following table summarizes the routines described in this chapter.

Name	Description
ldap_modify_s()	Synchronously modifies an existing LDAP directory entry
ldap_modify()	Asynchronously initiates a modification to an existing LDAP directory entry
ldap_add_s()	Synchronously adds a new entry to the LDAP directory
ldap_add()	Asynchronously initiates an add of a new entry to the LDAP directory
ldap_delete_s()	Synchronously deletes an existing entry from the LDAP directory
ldap_delete()	Asynchronously initiates the deletion of an existing entry from the LDAP directory
ldap_modrdn2_s()	Synchronously renames an existing LDAP directory entry
ldap_modrdn2()	Asynchronously initiates the renaming of an existing LDAP directory entry
ldap_result()	Retrieves results of previously initiated operations asynchronously

Looking Ahead

If you've read through to the end of this chapter, you now know all about the core LDAP API functions. In the next chapter, we examine some miscellaneous functions used for handling LDAP URLs, and in the final chapter on the API, we pull together many of the calls we've seen in a more substantial complete example.

15

LDAP URLs

I n the past few years, the Uniform Resource Locator (URL) has moved out of the obscure realm of academia and research laboratories to become part of our mainstream society. URLs (sometimes pronounced as "earls" and sometimes as the letters) are the cryptic addresses that helped launch the World Wide Web, which in turn is fueling the Internet explosion that is taking place today. It is now common to see URLs in magazine ads, newspapers, and on the evening news. During a recent presidential debate, one of the candidates even mentioned his Web site's URL during his closing statement!

Most URLs in use today are for the HyperText Transfer Protocol (HTTP), although FTP and `mailto` URLs are also quite popular. Here are three sample URLs:

```
http://www.umich.edu/
ftp://ftp7.netscape.com/pub/navigator
mailto:bjensen@aceindustry.com
```

The general URL framework and the details of many common schemes are described in RFC-1738, Uniform Resource Locators (URL). Most URLs are used to retrieve information, typically in the form of a file or document (a notable exception is `mailto:` URLs, which initiate the sending of an e-mail message). Not surprisingly, there is also an URL format defined for the Lightweight Directory Access Protocol.

At the time of this writing the LDAP URL format is on the verge of being widely supported in commercial Internet client software. The University of Michigan and Netscape LDAP SDKs both include functions to help you make your own applications aware of LDAP URLs. This chapter explains LDAP URLs and explores the related API functions.

An Introduction to LDAP URLs

The official definition of LDAP URLs can be found in RFC-1959, An LDAP URL Format. They are designed to provide a text-based representation of an LDAP directory search operation. The pieces of an LDAP URL correspond closely to the parameters of the `ldap_search()` API call that was discussed in Chapter 9.

All LDAP URLs must conform to the general format:

```
ldap://hostport/dn[?attributes[?scope[?filter]]]
```

where the parts in square brackets are optional. The parts are as follows:

- `hostport` is the name of the LDAP server (with optional port number) to contact. The `hostport` can be a zero-length string, in which case the choice of host is up to the application. If a port number is included, it is separated from the host name itself by a colon character. If not, the standard port of 389 should be used.

- `dn` is an LDAP distinguished name (name of an entry in the directory) that specifies the base point for the search.

- `attributes` is an optional, comma-separate list of LDAP attribute types to be returned from the server. If there is no `attributes` list or if it is of zero length, all attribute types should be requested when performing the search.

- `scope` is an optional string that indicates the scope of the search. It must be one of these three strings: base, one, or sub to represent a base-object search, a one-level search, or a subtree search.

In order to include a `scope`, an `attributes` list must also be included as well. If the scope is omitted, a base-object search should be done.

- `filter` is an optional LDAP search filter, as described in detail in Chapter 10. If omitted, the filter (`objectClass=*`) should be used. In order to include a filter, the `attributes` and `scope` portions of the URL must be included as well.

As in all types of URLs, blanks and some special characters must appear in escaped form within the URL. This is done by translating a character into its hexadecimal equivalent and preceding it with a percent symbol. For example, space characters are represented by the three-character sequence `%20`. A complete list of special characters that must be escaped within URLs can be found in RFC-1738. Let's look at a few examples of LDAP URLs.

Example 15.1: An LDAP URL that will read a single directory entry, Babs Jensen's, and retrieve all her attributes. Only the LDAP server and a base DN are included. Notice the escaped space characters in the DN.

```
ldap://ldap.netscape.com/cn=Babs%20Jensen,o=Ace%20Industry,c=US
```

Example 15.2: An LDAP URL that will perform a subtree search of an organization and return the `drink` attribute for all people with a surname of "Jensen". This URL includes a host, base DN, attribute list, scope, and filter.

```
ldap://ldap.netscape.com/o=Ace%20Industry,c=US?drink?sub?sn=jensen
```

Example 15.3: An LDAP URL that will perform a one-level search of the United States and return all organizations whose name contains "university". In the URL, two attribute types are requested: o (organization) and `description`.

```
ldap://ldap.itd.umich.edu/c=US?o,description?one?o=*university*
```

As you are probably aware, the great strength of URLs is their unusual combination of power, flexibility, and simplicity. As the preceding examples illustrate, the LDAP URL is no exception.

Using LDAP URLs to Perform Searches

Because LDAP URLs include almost all of the parameters needed to call the `ldap_search()` or `ldap_search_s()` function, it is fairly easy to add support for URLs to an application that already supports search. Naturally, the LDAP API includes functions that perform an LDAP search given an LDAP URL.

Example 15.4: An "urlsearch" program. This example shows a program that accepts one or more LDAP URLs as arguments, performs the search represented by each URL, and prints the information returned.

```
1.     #include <stdio.h>
2.     #include <ldap.h>

3.     main( int argc, char **argv )
4.     {
5.         LDAP            *ld;
6.         LDAPMessage     *result;
7.         int             i;
8.         char            *url;

9.         if ( argc < 2 ) {
10.            fputs( "usage: urlsearch ldapurl...\n", stderr );
11.            exit( 1 );
12.        }

13.        if ( (ld = ldap_init( "ldap.netscape.com", LDAP_PORT )) ==
           ➥NULL ) {
14.            perror( "ldap_init" );
15.            exit( 1 );
16.        }

17.        for ( i = 1; i < argc; ++i ) {
18.            url = argv[ i ];
19.            result = NULL;
20.            printf( "Following LDAP URL %s...\n", url );

21.            if ( ldap_url_search_s( ld, url, 0, &result )
22.                    != LDAP_SUCCESS ) {
```

```
23.                    ldap_perror( ld, url );
24.                }

25.                if ( result != NULL ) {
26.                    print_entries_with_values( ld, result );
27.                    ldap_msgfree( result );
28.                }
29.                putchar( '\n' );
30.            }

31.            ldap_unbind( ld );
32.            exit( 0 );
33.        }
```

Let's look at this program in some detail. Lines 9–12 check to make sure we were given at least one command line argument. Lines 13–16 initialize the LDAP library and obtain a session handle. We pass ldap.netscape.com for the default host, which will be used for any LDAP URLs that do not contain a host name.

On line 17 we begin to loop through all of the URLs given as command line arguments, calling the ldap_url_search_s() function for each one. This function acts just like ldap_search_s() except that most of the search parameters are obtained from the URL itself. The *result* parameter can be used with any of the LDAP API functions that are designed to handle search results. On line 26 we take advantage of that fact to call the general purpose print_entries_with_values() function (defined back in Chapter 9) to print the attribute values contained in each returned entry.

As you can see, supporting LDAP URLs is so easy that every LDAP application should do so. The next section provides a summary of the ldap_url_search_s() function.

Synopsis:

```
int ldap_url_search_s( LDAP *ld, char *url, int attrsonly,
LDAPMessage **res);
```

Synchronously searches the LDAP directory based on the contents of an LDAP URL.

Return Value:

Type: int

An LDAP error code (equal to LDAP_SUCCESS if the operation succeeds). Error handling is discussed in more detail in Chapter 8.

Parameters:

LDAP *ld: A handle to an LDAP session as returned by ldap_init() or ldap_open().

char *url: An LDAP URL. The format of this string should conform to the definition of LDAP URLs given in RFC-1959, An LDAP URL Format. URLs that are surrounded by angle-brackets or preceded by the four characters URL: are also tolerated.

int attrsonly: A Boolean parameter specifying whether both attribute types and values should be returned (zero) or types only should be returned (non-zero).

LDAPMessage **res: A pointer to an LDAPMessage * used to hold the result of a successful URL search. The result parameter should be freed by calling ldap_msgfree() when it is no longer needed. See Chapter 9 for more information on handling search results.

Tip

> If you have a string but are not sure if it is an LDAP URL or not, you can use the ldap_is_ldap_url() function (described later in this chapter) to check.

The ldap_url_search_st() function should be used when you want to limit the time your application will wait for an URL-based search to complete. Except for the addition of a time-out parameter, this function is identical to ldap_url_search_s(). The next section provides a summary of the ldap_url_search_st() function.

Synopsis:

```
int ldap_url_search_st( LDAP *ld, char *url, int
attrsonly, struct timeval *timeout, LDAPMessage **res);
```

Synchronously searches the LDAP directory based on the contents of an LDAP URL, respecting a time-out.

Return Value:

Type: int

An LDAP error code (equal to LDAP_SUCCESS if the operation succeeds). Error handling is discussed in more detail in Chapter 8.

Parameters:

LDAP *ld: A handle to an LDAP session as returned by ldap_init() or ldap_open().

char *url: An LDAP URL. The format of this string should conform to the definition of LDAP URLs given in RFC-1959, An LDAP URL Format. URLs that are surrounded by angle-brackets or preceded by the four characters URL: are also tolerated.

int attrsonly: A Boolean parameter specifying whether both attribute types and values should be returned (zero) or types only should be returned (non-zero).

struct timeval *timeout: A pointer to a timeval structure that limits how long your application will wait for a search to complete. A timeval structure contains two elements, tv_sec (time in seconds) and tv_usec (time in microseconds), which allow for fairly fine-grained time limits.

LDAPMessage **res: A pointer to an LDAPMessage * used to hold the result of a successful URL search. The result parameter should be freed by calling ldap_msgfree() when it is no longer needed. See Chapter 9 for more information on handling search results.

There is also an asynchronous URL search call that parallels the ldap_search() function. It can be used when you want to do other work while waiting for an URL-based search to complete, or when you want to initiate more than one search at a time.

Example 15.5: A version of the "urlsearch" program from Example 15.4 that performs all searches in parallel. This program accepts one or more LDAP URLs as arguments, initiates the search represented by each URL, and then prints the search results as they are returned.

```
1.      #include <stdio.h>
2.      #include <ldap.h>

3.      main( int argc, char **argv )
4.      {
5.          LDAP            *ld;
6.          LDAPMessage     *result;
7.          int             i, id, outstanding_searches;
8.          char            *url;

9.          if ( argc < 2 ) {
10.             fputs( "usage: urlsearch ldapurl...\n", stderr );
11.             exit( 1 );
12.         }

13.         if ( (ld = ldap_init( "ldap.netscape.com", LDAP_PORT )) ==
            ➥NULL ) {
14.             perror( "ldap_init" );
15.             exit( 1 );
16.         }

17.         outstanding_searches = 0;
18.         for ( i = 1; i < argc; ++i ) {
19.             url = argv[ i ];
20.             printf( "Initiating search using URL %s...\n", url );

21.             if ( (id = ldap_url_search( ld, url, 0 )) == -1 ) {
22.                 ldap_perror( ld, url );
23.             } else {
24.                 ++outstanding_searches;
25.                 printf( "\tsearch initiated with id %d\n", id );
26.             }
27.         }

28.         while ( outstanding_searches > 0 ) {
29.             printf( "Waiting for %d searches to finish...\n",
30.                     outstanding_searches );
```

```
31.              if ( ldap_result( ld, LDAP_RES_ANY, 1, NULL, &result )
          ➥> 0 ) {
32.                  printf( "search with id %d has finished.\n",
33.                          ldap_msgid( result ));
34.                  print_entries_with_values( ld, result );
35.                  ldap_msgfree( result );
36.              }
37.              putchar( '\n' );
38.              --outstanding_searches;
39.          }

40.          ldap_unbind( ld );
41.          exit( 0 );
42.      }
```

This program uses the asynchronous LDAP functions in a fairly simple way. After some initialization, ldap_url_search() is called once for each URL given on the command line to fire off all of the search operations. A count of outstanding searches is maintained and used to control the loop on lines 28–39. In the body of this loop we call the ldap_result() function to wait for one search to complete, and then we use the print_entries_with_values() from Chapter 9 to print the actual search results.

Notice that this example prints the LDAP message id for each search as it is initiated (line 25). As searches complete, the message id of each search result is also printed (lines 32 and 33). A simple improvement to this program would be to keep track of which URL corresponds to each message id when ldap_url_search() is called to initiate the searches, and print the URL with its search results when ldap_result() returns. The next section provides a summary of the ldap_url_search() function.

Synopsis:

```
int ldap_url_search( LDAP *ld, char *url, int attrsonly);
```

Initiates an asynchronous search of the LDAP directory based on the contents of an LDAP URL. The ldap_result() function should be used to retrieve the search results.

Return Value:

Type: int

If the operation could not be successfully initiated, −1 is returned and a specific error can be obtained from the LDAP session handle. If the search operation was successfully initiated, the message id of the LDAP operation is returned. This message id is suitable for use in a call to ldap_result() or ldap_abandon().

Parameters:

LDAP *ld: A handle to an LDAP session as returned by ldap_init() or ldap_open().

char *url: An LDAP URL. The format of this string should conform to the definition of LDAP URLs given in RFC-1959, An LDAP URL Format. URLs that are surrounded by angle-brackets or preceded by the four characters URL: are also tolerated.

int attrsonly: A Boolean specifying whether both attribute types and values should be returned (zero) or types only should be returned (non-zero).

Tip

Because the ldap_url_search(), ldap_url_search_st(), and ldap_url_search() functions are all implemented on top of the ldap_search() function, the search parameters that you can set that affect ldap_search() also affect the URL search functions. For example, a size limit that is set using ldap_set_option() will be used by the URL search calls. See Chapter 9 for more information.

Breaking Up an LDAP URL into Its Component Pieces

While the LDAP URL search functions we just examined provide a simple way to perform URL-based searches, sometimes you may want to examine the pieces of an LDAP URL. Perhaps you want to implement your own version of the ldap_url_search() call or make a change to one or more components of the URL.

Example 15.6: A program that reads a series of URLs from standard input (one URL per line) and writes them to standard output, changing the attribute list of all LDAP URLs. The resulting LDAP URLs all have an attribute list that consists of the common name (cn) and favorite drink (drink) attributes. Any non-LDAP URLs are left untouched.

```
1.    #include <stdio.h>
2.    #include <ldap.h>
3.    #include <ctype.h>

4.    void write_escaped( char *s );

5.    main()
6.    {
7.        char          url[ 2048 ];
8.        int           err;
9.        LDAPURLDesc   *ludp;

10.       while ( gets( url ) != NULL ) {
11.           if ( !ldap_is_ldap_url( url )) {
12.               puts( url );     /* echo non-LDAP URLs unchanged */
13.               continue;
14.           }

15.           if (( err = ldap_url_parse( url, &ludp )) != 0 ) {
16.               fprintf( stderr, "Unable to parse LDAP URL
                  ➥(error %d)\n",
17.                       url, err );
18.               exit( 1 );
19.           }

20.           fputs( "ldap://", stdout );
21.           write_escaped( ludp->lud_host );
22.           if ( ludp->lud_port != 0 ) {
23.               printf( ":%d", ludp->lud_port );
24.           }
25.           putchar( '/' );
```

```
26.               write_escaped( ludp->lud_dn );
27.               fputs( "?cn,drink", stdout );

28.               if ( ludp->lud_scope == LDAP_SCOPE_SUBTREE) {
29.                   fputs( "?sub", stdout );
30.               } else if ( ludp->lud_scope == LDAP_SCOPE_ONELEVEL ) {
31.                   fputs( "?one", stdout );
32.               } else if ( ludp->lud_filter != NULL ) {
33.                   fputs( "?base", stdout );
34.               }

35.               if ( ludp->lud_filter != NULL ) {
36.                   putchar( '?' );
37.                   write_escaped( ludp->lud_filter );
38.               }
39.               putchar( '\n' );

40.               ldap_free_urldesc( ludp );
41.           }

42.       exit( 0 );
43.
44.   }

45.   #define IS_URL_SAFE( c )    ( isalpha(c) || isdigit(c) || (c)
      == '.' || \
46.                       (c) == '=' || (c) == ',' )

47.   void
48.   write_escaped( char *s )
49.   {
50.       if ( s == NULL ) {
51.           return;
52.       }

53.       while ( *s != '\0' ) {
54.           if ( IS_URL_SAFE( *s )) {
55.               putchar( *s );
56.           } else {
57.               printf( "%%2x", *s );
58.           }
59.           ++s;
60.       }
61.   }
```

This example is fairly long. Lines 10–41 form a while loop that reads a series of URLs from standard input and processes them. On line 11, we use the `ldap_is_ldap_url()` function to test an URL to see if it is an LDAP URL. If not, lines 12 and 13 just write it back to standard output unchanged and continue the read loop.

Around line 15 things really get interesting. The `ldap_url_parse()` function takes a string and tries to interpret it as an LDAP URL, parsing it and setting the second function parameter to point to an `LDAPURLDesc` structure that contains the component pieces of the URL. It returns one of a handful or error codes (zero if it succeeds in parsing the URL).

Most of the rest of the code in this example is concerned with writing out our revised LDAP URLs (we replaced the attribute list with "`cn,drink`"). Unfortunately, the LDAP API does not include a function that builds an LDAP URL for us, so we have to do this ourselves. The code on lines 20–39 and the `write_escaped()` utility function accomplish this mundane task. Finally, on line 40 we free the `LDAPURLDesc` structure that was returned during the call to `ldap_url_parse()`.

Assuming a file called `someurls` exists and contains these URLs:

```
mailto:ldap-request@umich.edu
ldap://ldap.netscape.com:4000/o=Ace%20Industry,%20c=US
http://www.umich.edu/~rsug/ldap/
ldap:///c=US?o,description?one?o=*university*
```

The result of feeding this file into the program presented in Example 15.6 would be this output:

```
mailto:ldap-request@umich.edu
ldap://ldap.netscape.com:4000/
↦o=Ace%20Industry,%20c=US?cn,drink?base?%28objectClass=%2a%29
http://www.umich.edu/~rsug/ldap/
ldap:///c=US?cn,drink?one?o=%2auniversity%2a
```

The next section provides a summary of the `ldap_is_ldap_url()` function.

Synopsis:

```
int ldap_is_ldap_url( char *url);
```

Checks a string to see if it looks like an LDAP URL.

Return Value:

Type: `int`

If the `url` parameter looks like an LDAP URL (that is, if it begins with the characters `ldap://`), a non-zero number is returned. Otherwise, zero is returned.

Parameters:

`char *url`: A string that may (or may not) be an LDAP URL. URLs that are surrounded by angle-brackets or preceded by the four characters `URL:` are also tolerated.

Tip

> The `ldap_is_ldap_url()` function only does a quick check to see if a string is likely to contain an LDAP URL as opposed to some other kind of data. If you need to know if a string conforms to the exact syntax required for LDAP URLs, use the `ldap_url_parse()` function instead.

The next section provides a summary of the `ldap_url_parse()` function.

Synopsis:

```
int ldap_url_parse( char *url, LDAPURLDesc **ludpp);
```

Breaks up an LDAP URL into its component pieces.

Return Value:

Type: `int`

If the URL is a valid LDAP URL and it was successfully parsed, zero is returned. If an error occurs, one of these constants is returned:

LDAP_URL_ERR_NOTLDAP	URL doesn't begin with `ldap://`
LDAP_URL_ERR_NODN	URL is missing the required base DN
LDAP_URL_ERR_BADSCOPE	URL scope string was invalid
LDAP_URL_ERR_MEM	memory allocation failed

Parameters:

> `char *url`: A string that may (or may not) be an LDAP URL. URLs that are surrounded by angle-brackets or preceded by the four characters URL: are also tolerated.

> `LDAPURLDesc **ludpp`: A pointer to an `LDAPURLDesc *` structure pointer that, if this function returns zero, is set to point to a newly allocated URL description structure. The `LDAPURLDesc` structure contains the component pieces of the URL and is described in detail next.

The `LDAPURLDesc` structure contains the following elements that you may access:

> `char *lud_host`: The name of the LDAP directory server to contact. This may be NULL, in which case the application should choose a default directory server to use.

> `int lud_port`: The TCP port of the directory server. If this value is zero, the default LDAP port of 389 should be used.

> `char *lud_dn`: The Distinguished Name that was included in the URL. This will usually serve as the base point for an LDAP search operation.

> `char **lud_attrs`: A NULL-terminated array of attributes to retrieve from the directory server. If this element is NULL, the URL did not contain a list of attributes, which indicates that all attributes should be retrieved.

int *lud_scope*: The scope of the search, either LDAP_SCOPE_BASE, LDAP_SCOPE_ONELEVEL, or LDAP_SCOPE_SUBTREE. If no scope was included in the URL, this structure element is set to the default scope of LDAP_SCOPE_BASE.

int *lud_filter*: The LDAP search filter to be used. If no filter was included in the URL, this field will be set to the default filter of (objectClass=*).

The next section provides a summary of the ldap_free_urldesc() function.

Synopsis:

```
void ldap_free_urldesc( LDAPURLDesc *ludp);
```

Frees an URL description structure that was allocated by ldap_url_parse(). Call this function when you are done using an LDAPURLDesc structure.

Return Value:

None.

Parameter:

LDAPURLDesc *ludp: An URL description pointer that was returned in the second parameter of a successful call to ldap_url_parse().

Summary

The following table summarizes the routines and structures described in this chapter.

Name	Description
ldap_url_search_s()	Synchronously searches the LDAP directory based on the contents of an LDAP URL.
ldap_url_search_st()	Synchronously searches the LDAP directory based on the contents of an LDAP URL, respecting a time-out.
ldap_url_search()	Initiates an asynchronous search of the LDAP directory based on the contents of an LDAP URL.
ldap_is_ldap_url()	Checks a string to see if it looks like an LDAP URL.
ldap_url_parse()	Breaks up an LDAP URL into its component pieces.
ldap_free_urldesc()	Frees an URL description structure that was allocated by ldap_url_parse().
LDAPURLDesc	Structure that holds the components of an LDAP URL.

Looking Ahead

Our journey through the LDAP API is nearly complete! We have covered all of the important functions included in the University of Michigan and Netscape LDAP SDKs. If you have skipped any chapters, this is a good time to consider going back and reading them. Although nearly every chapter has included some small example programs and functions, each of them only used a handful of the LDAP API calls. In the next chapter, we take a broader look at LDAP programming by constructing a larger example application.

16

Using the LDAP API to Build an Application

The previous chapters have introduced you to various aspects of LDAP and the LDAP API. So far, we've presented many small examples that, though complete, have been designed to focus on specific aspects of the API. Now it's time to present a larger example that weaves together many of the concepts explained in the previous chapters. Our goal is to produce an example that is useful on its own and illustrates as many LDAP API calls as possible.

We've chosen a simple yet functional command-line directory client for our example. The program provides access to the basic LDAP operations, allowing you to add, delete, and search for entries. We've also implemented read and list commands. The implementation of modify, compare, and other functions has been left as an exercise to the reader.

The following sections present pieces of our example, starting with the main program, which contains the command interpreter defining our program's interface with the user. Next, we present the routines that implement each command. We also present, but do not go into great detail about, various utility routines used to parse commands and perform other functions. Each section includes code for the function and an explanation of what it does.

The Main Program

The following code implements the command interpreter for our example. It also includes the necessary global declarations and initialization.

```c
1.    #include <stdio.h>
2.    #include <string.h>
3.    #include <ldap.h>

4.    /* prototypes for command functions */
5.    typedef void (CMD_FUNC)( LDAP *, int, char ** );
6.    CMD_FUNC add, auth, delete, list, dread, first;
7.    void init( LDAP **, int, char ** );
8.    void next( LDAP * );
9.    /* prototypes for utility functons */
10.   int parse_command( char *, int *, char ** );
11.   char *strtok_quote( char *line, char *sep );
12.   void help( void );
13.   void print_entry( LDAP *ld, LDAPMessage *e );

14.   #define MAXARGS 20

15.   main( int argc, char **argv )
16.   {
17.           char     line[BUFSIZ];        /* command line */
18.           int      cargc;               /* command argument
              ➥count */
19.           char     *cargv[MAXARGS];     /* command argument
              ➥vector */
20.           LDAP     *ld;                 /* LDAP session handle */
21.           int      cmd;

22.           ld = NULL;
23.           printf( "cmd: " );
24.           while ( fgets( line, sizeof(line), stdin ) != NULL ) {
25.                   cmd = parse_command( line, &cargc, cargv );
26.                   if ( ld == NULL && (cmd == 'a' || cmd == 'b' ||
                      ➥cmd == 'd'
27.                       || cmd == 'f' || cmd == 'n' || cmd == 'u') ) {
28.                           printf( "LDAP session must be initial-
                              ➥ized first\n" );
```

```
29.                              help();
30.                  } else {
31.                      switch ( cmd ) {
32.                      case 'a':        /* synchronous add */
33.                          add( ld, cargc, cargv );
34.                          break;
35.                      case 'b':        /* synchronous bind */
36.                          auth( ld, cargc, cargv );
37.                          break;
38.                      case 'd':        /* synchronous delete */
39.                          delete( ld, cargc, cargv );
40.                          break;
41.                      case 'f':        /* first search entry */
42.                          first( ld, cargc, cargv );
43.                          break;
44.                      case 'I':        /* initialize */
45.                          init( &ld, cargc, cargv );
46.                          break;
47.                      case 'l':        /* list children of an
                     ➡entry */
48.                          list( ld, cargc, cargv );
49.                          break;
50.                      case 'n':        /* next search entry */
51.                          next( ld );
52.                          break;
53.                      case 'r':        /* read an entry */
54.                          dread( ld, cargc, cargv );
55.                          break;
56.                      case 'u':        /* unbind */
57.                          ldap_unbind( ld );
58.                          ld = NULL;
59.                          break;
60.                      default:
61.                          help();
62.                          break;
63.                      }
64.                  }
65.                  printf( "cmd: " );
66.          }
67. }
```

There's not much LDAP-specific about this part of the example. It includes the header files we'll need and defines some prototypes for the command and other functions implementing the core part of the example.

Initialization

The 'i' command is used to initialize the LDAP session. This function is implemented by the code below.

```
1.    void
2.    init( LDAP **ld, int cargc, char **cargv )
3.    {
4.            if ( cargc != 3 ) {
5.                    printf( "usage: i host port\n" );
6.                    return;
7.            }
8.            if ( (*ld = ldap_init( cargv[1], atoi( cargv[2] ) )) ==
      ➡NULL ) {
9.                    perror( "ldap_init" );
10.           }
11.  }
```

The init() function must be called before any of the other commands are used. It initializes the LDAP session, complaining if anything goes wrong. Because we called ldap_init() instead of ldap_open(), we have the opportunity to change various settings global to the LDAP connection before actually connecting to the server.

Add

The preceding main program calls the add() routine in response to the user giving an add command. We want to allow the user to add entries contained in files in LDIF format, so we've included in this section an ldif2entry() routine that converts a file containing an LDIF entry into the format expected by the ldap_add_s() routine. LDIF is a simple text format for representing LDAP entries. It is described in Chapter 17.

```
1.    void
2.    add( LDAP *ld, int cargc, char **cargv )
3.    {
4.            LDAPMod     **attrs;
5.            char        *dn;

6.            if ( cargc != 2 ) {
7.                    printf( "usage: a ldiffile\n" );
8.                    return;
9.            }
10.           if ( ldif2entry( cargv[1], &dn, &attrs ) != 0 ) {
11.                   printf( "Could not convert ldif file %s to
                      ⮥entry\n",
12.                       cargv[1] );
13.                   return;
14.           }
15.           if ( ldap_add_s( ld, dn, attrs ) != LDAP_SUCCESS ) {
16.                   ldap_perror( ld, "ldap_add_s" );
17.           }
18.           ldap_mods_free( attrs, 1 );
19.           free( dn );
20.    }
```

The add() function itself is pretty simple. After checking its arguments, it calls the ldif2entry() routine to convert the given file containing an LDIF representation of an entry into the LDAPMod array expected by ldap_add_s(). The ldif2entry() routine is shown and explained next.

```
1.    int
2.    ldif2entry( char *fname, char **dn, LDAPMod ***attrs )
3.    {
4.            FILE        *fp;
5.            char        line[BUFSIZ];
6.            char        *type, *value;
7.            int         lineno;

8.            /* open the ldif file */
9.            if ( (fp = fopen( fname, "r" )) == NULL ) {
10.                   printf( "Could not open ldif file %s\n", fname );
11.                   return( -1 );
12.           }
13.           lineno = 0;
14.           /* first line should be "dn: distinguished name\n" */
```

```
15.         if ( fgets( line, sizeof(line), fp ) == NULL ) {
16.             printf( "LDIF file %s is empty\n", fname );
17.             fclose( fp );
18.             return( -1 );
19.         }
20.         lineno++;
21.         line[ strlen(line) - 1 ] = '\0';
22.         if ( ldif2typeval( line, &type, &value ) != 0 ) {
23.             printf( "Bad LDIF in %s: line %d\n", fname,
                ➥lineno );
24.             return( -1 );
25.         }
26.         if ( (*dn = strdup( value )) == NULL ) {
27.             printf( "No more memory\n" );
28.             fclose( fp );
29.             return( -1 );
30.         }
31.         /* following lines are "type: value\n" */
32.         *attrs = NULL;
33.         while ( fgets( line, sizeof(line), fp ) != NULL ) {
34.             lineno++;
35.             line[ strlen(line) - 1 ] = '\0';
36.             /* parse the ldif line into type and value */
37.             if ( ldif2typeval( line, &type, &value ) != 0 ) {
38.                 printf( "Bad LDIF line in %s: line
                    ➥%d\n", fname,
39.                     lineno );
40.                 free( *dn );
41.                 ldap_mods_free( *attrs, 1 );
42.                 return( -1 );
43.             }
44.             /* merge the type and value into our attr list */
45.             if ( merge_typeval( attrs, type, value ) != 0 ) {
46.                 printf( "Cannot add LDIF from file
                    ➥%s\n",
47.                     fname );
48.                 free( *dn );
49.                 ldap_mods_free( *attrs, 1 );
50.                 return( -1 );
```

```
51.                        }
52.            }
53.            return( 0 );
54.    }
```

This routine is not too exciting, because it mostly contains rather grungy parsing code. But it is necessary to our example. There are a couple of things to notice about it, mostly areas where it could stand improvement. First, this example does not handle continued lines in an LDIF file. Not hard, but in the interest of conserving space, we've left this as an exercise for the reader.

Second, the example does not handle base 64-encoded LDIF, which you might need to include binary values such as a JPEG photo or audio attribute. Again, this is not hard, but it involves some slightly messy parsing and base 64 conversion code.

The ldif2entry() routine calls the ldif2typeval() routine to parse each line of LDIF it reads. It then calls the merge_typeval() to add the given type and value to the list of entry attributes being built in preparation for the add operation itself. These routines are presented and explained next.

```
1.    int
2.    ldif2typeval( char *ldif, char **type, char **value )
3.    {
4.            /* the line looks like "type: value" */
5.            if ( (*value = strchr( ldif, ':' )) == NULL ) {
6.                    return( -1 );
7.            }
8.            *(*value)++ = '\0';
9.            while ( isspace( **value ) ) {
10.                    (*value)++;
11.            }
12.            *type = ldif;
13.            return( 0 );
14.    }

15.    int
16.    merge_typeval( LDAPMod ***attrs, char *type, char *value )
17.    {
```

```
18.            int     i, j;

19.            /* find the attribute in the LDAPMod array to merge with */
20.            for ( i = 0; *attrs != NULL && (*attrs)[i] != NULL; i++ ){
21.                    if ( strcasecmp( (*attrs)[i]->mod_type, type )
                       ➥== 0 ) {
22.                            break;
23.                    }
24.            }

25.            /* not found - create slot for the first one */
26.            if ( *attrs == NULL ) {
27.                    if ( (*attrs = (LDAPMod **) calloc( 1, 2 *
                       ➥sizeof(LDAPMod *)) )
28.                        == NULL ) {
29.                            return( -1 );
30.                    }
31.                    i = 0;
32.            /* not found - create slot for the new one */
33.            } else if ( (*attrs)[i] == NULL ) {
34.                    if ( (*attrs = (LDAPMod **) realloc( *attrs,
35.                        (i + 2) * sizeof(LDAPMod *) )) == NULL ) {
36.                            return( -1 );
37.                    }
38.            }

39.            /* we've got a new slot - create the new mod */
40.            if ( (*attrs)[i] == NULL ) {
41.                    if ( ((*attrs)[i] = (LDAPMod *) malloc(
                       ➥sizeof(LDAPMod) ))
42.                        == NULL ) {
43.                            return( -1 );
44.                    }
45.                    (*attrs)[i]->mod_op = 0;
46.                    (*attrs)[i]->mod_type = strdup( type );
47.                    if ( ((*attrs)[i]->mod_values = (char **)
                       ➥malloc(
48.                        * sizeof(char *) )) == NULL ) {
49.                            return( -1 );
50.                    }
51.                    (*attrs)[i]->mod_values[0] = strdup( value );
52.                    (*attrs)[i]->mod_values[1] = NULL;
53.                    (*attrs)[i + 1] = NULL;
```

```
54.                    return( 0 );
55.              }

56.              /* found an existing attribute - add a value to it */
57.              for ( j = 0; (*attrs)[i]->mod_values[j] != NULL; j++ ) {
58.                      /* NULL */
59.              }
60.              (*attrs)[i]->mod_values = (char **) realloc(
                 ➥(*attrs)[i]->mod_values,
61.                   (j + 2) * sizeof(char *) );
62.              (*attrs)[i]->mod_values[j] = strdup( value );
63.              (*attrs)[i]->mod_values[j+1] = NULL;

64.              return( 0 );
65.      }
```

As you can see, this code is a bit ugly and tedious, but it gets the job done. The ldif2typeval() routine simply looks for the colon in a line of LDIF and splits the line into type and value accordingly.

The merge_typeval() routine takes this type and value combination and merges it with a growing list of attributes for the entry. merge_typeval() first looks through the list to see if an existing type matches, meaning that a previous line of LDIF already mentioned that type, and that the current value should be added to this type's list of values. If no existing type is found, a new LDAPMod structure is allocated and added to the list of attributes.

The messiest part of this example is the memory (re)allocation that needs to happen for the list of attributes and their values. We've cut a few corners by not checking all the return values from these allocations. This is only in the interest of saving space, and of course you should check these returns in your programs.

Bind

The next piece of our example implements the bind command, which a user of our application can use prior to an add or delete operation (or a search for that matter), to authenticate him or herself to the directory.

```
1.   void
2.   auth( LDAP *ld, int cargc, char **cargv )
3.   {
4.         if ( cargc != 3 ) {
5.               printf( "usage: b dn passwd\n" );
6.               return;
7.         }
8.         if ( ldap_simple_bind_s( ld, cargv[1], cargv[2] )
9.              != LDAP_SUCCESS ) {
10.              ldap_perror( ld, "ldap_simple_bind_s" );
11.              return;
12.        }
13.  }
```

At last, a short and simple piece of code! No parsing or other nastiness, the auth() routine simply checks to make sure the command was invoked with the proper number of arguments and then calls ldap_simple_bind_s() to do the actual authentication.

Delete

The delete() function is shown next, and its goal is to delete an entry from the directory whose distinguished name is given by the user.

```
1.   void
2.   delete( LDAP *ld, int cargc, char **cargv )
3.   {
4.         if ( cargc != 2 ) {
5.               printf( "usage: d dn\n" );
6.               return;
7.         }
8.         if ( ldap_delete_s( ld, cargv[1] ) != LDAP_SUCCESS ) {
9.               ldap_perror( ld, "ldap_delete_s" );
10.              return;
11.        }
12.  }
```

Again, this example is very simple. It checks its number of arguments and then calls the synchronous ldap_delete_s() routine.

List

The list() routine prints out the RDNs of entries directly below a given entry in the directory tree. This part of the example demonstrates both how to emulate a list operation using the search operation, and how to use the ldap_explode_dn() routine to parse distinguished names.

```
1.    void
2.    list( LDAP *ld, int cargc, char **cargv )
3.    {
4.         LDAPMessage      *res, *e;
5.         char             *dn;
6.         char             *attrs[2];
7.         char             **rdns;
8.         if ( cargc != 2 ) {
9.              printf( "usage: l dn\n" );
10.             return;
11.        }
12.        attrs[0] = "c";
13.        attrs[1] = NULL;
14.        if ( ldap_search_s( ld, cargv[1], LDAP_SCOPE_ONELEVEL,
15.            "(objectclass=*)", attrs, 0, &res ) != LDAP_SUCCESS ) {
16.             ldap_perror( ld, "ldap_search_s" );
17.             return;
18.        }
19.        for ( e = ldap_first_entry( ld, res ); e != NULL;
20.            e = ldap_next_entry( ld, e ) ) {
21.             if ( (dn = ldap_get_dn( ld, e )) == NULL ) {
22.                  printf( "ldap_get_dn failed\n" );
23.                  continue;
24.             }
25.             if ( (rdns = ldap_explode_dn( dn, 0 )) != NULL ) {
26.                  printf( "%s\n", rdns[0] );
27.                  ldap_value_free( rdns );
28.             }
29.             ldap_memfree( dn );
30.        }
31.        ldap_msgfree( res );
32.    }
```

The first part of the list() routine is a simple synchronous LDAP search to retrieve all of the entries one level below the given DN. We ask for the "c" attribute and that types only (no values) be returned because we really don't want anything but the distinguished names of the entries.

The second part of the list() routine steps through the entries that were returned, retrieving each entry's distinguished name. The DN is then parsed into its RDN components by ldap_explode_dn(), and the first component, the RDN, is printed. Notice the use of ldap_memfree(), ldap_value_free(), and ldap_msgfree() to free memory allocated by the LDAP library.

Read

The dread() routine is called to read and display the attributes of a single entry from the directory. This part of the example consists of two parts. There is the dread() routine that actually does the LDAP search. If a single entry is matched this routine calls the print_entry() routine to print the attributes of the entry.

```
1.    void
2.    dread( LDAP *ld, int cargc, char **cargv )
3.    {
4.            LDAPMessage        *res, *e;

5.            if ( cargc != 2 ) {
6.                    printf( "usage: r dn\n" );
7.                    return;
8.            }
9.            if ( ldap_search_s( ld, cargv[1], LDAP_SCOPE_BASE,
10.               "(objectclass=*)", NULL, 0, &res ) != LDAP_SUCCESS ) {
11.                    ldap_perror( ld, "ldap_search_s" );
12.                    return;
13.            }
14.            if ( (e = ldap_first_entry( ld, res )) == NULL ) {
15.                    printf( "Could not retrieve entry %s\n", cargv[1] );
16.                    return;
17.            }
18.            print_entry( ld, e );
```

```
19.          ldap_msgfree( res );
20.  }

21.  void
22.  print_entry( LDAP *ld, LDAPMessage *e )
23.  {
24.          BerElement      *ber;
25.          char            *dn, *a;
26.          char            **vals;
27.          int             i;

28.          if ( (dn = ldap_get_dn( ld, e )) != NULL ) {
29.                  printf( "dn: %s\n", dn );
30.                  ldap_memfree( dn );
31.          }
32.          for ( a = ldap_first_attribute( ld, e, &ber ); a != NULL;
33.            a = ldap_next_attribute( ld, e, ber ) ) {
34.              if ( (vals = ldap_get_values( ld, e, a )) != NULL ) {
35.                      for ( i = 0; vals[i] != NULL; i++ ) {
36.                              printf( "%s: %s\n", a, vals[i] );
37.                      }
38.                      ldap_value_free( vals );
39.              }
40.              ldap_memfree( a );
41.          }
42.          if ( ber != NULL ) {
43.                  ber_free( ber, 0 );
44.          }
45.  }
```

This code starts out very similar to the list example, except that the LDAP search that's done is a base object search, and we ask for all attributes to be returned to us. If we get something back, we print the entry's DN and then step through the entry's attributes, printing out each one in LDIF format.

Notice the use of ldap_memfree() to dispose of memory allocated for the entry's DN and the name of each attribute. Notice also the use of ber_free() to free up memory used by ldap_first_attribute() and ldap_next_attribute() to keep track of their position in the entry.

Search

To make the search portion of our example interesting, we've implemented it as two commands. The "first entry" command initiates the search and retrieves the first entry. The "next entry" command retrieves subsequent entries, one at a time. The first() and next() routines implementing these two commands are presented and described next.

```
1.    static int          srchid;

2.    void
3.    first( LDAP *ld, int cargc, char **cargv )
4.    {
5.          char        *attrs[20];      /* max of 20 attributes by
                  ➥name */
6.          int         i, scope;

7.          if ( cargc < 4 ) {
8.                printf( "usage: f dn scope filter [attr ...]\n" );
9.                return;
10.         }
11.         /* determine scope */
12.         if ( strcasecmp( cargv[2], "sub" ) == 0 ) {
13.               scope = LDAP_SCOPE_SUBTREE;
14.         } else if ( strcasecmp( cargv[2], "one" ) == 0 ) {
15.               scope = LDAP_SCOPE_ONELEVEL;
16.         } else {
17.               printf( "Invalid scope %s\n", cargv[2] );
18.               return;
19.         }
20.         /* collect attributes to retrieve */
21.         for ( i = 4; i < cargc && i < 24; i++ ) {
22.               attrs[ i - 4 ] = cargv[i];
23.         }
24.         attrs[ i - 4 ] = NULL;
25.         /* initiate the search */
26.         if ( (srchid = ldap_search( ld, cargv[1], scope,
                  ➥cargv[3],
27.            attrs[0] == NULL ? NULL : attrs, 0 )) < 0 ) {
28.               ldap_perror( ld, "ldap_search_s" );
29.               return;
30.         }
```

```
31.          next( ld );
32.  }

33.  void
34.  next( LDAP *ld )
35.  {
36.          LDAPMessage        *result, *e;

37.          if ( srchid == -1 ) {
38.          return;
39.          }
40.          if ( ldap_result( ld, srchid, 0, NULL, &result ) <= 0 ) {
41.                  ldap_perror( ld, "ldap_result" );
42.                  return;
43.          }
44.          if ( (e = ldap_first_entry( ld, result )) != NULL ) {
45.                  print_entry( ld, e );
46.          } else {
47.                  srchid = -1;
48.          }
49.          ldap_msgfree( result );
50.  }
```

There are two parts to this search interface. The first routine, `first()`, is used to initialize the search and print out the first entry in the result, which it does by calling the `next()` routine. The `next()` routine keeps track of its current position in the result through the global variables `result` and `lastentry`. It calls the `print_entry()` routine to actually do the printing. This is the same routine we devised earlier for the read part of our example.

Notice the use of `ldap_result()` in this routine to retrieve one entry from the search at a time. Our results are restricted to only search operations initiated by the `first()` routine through the use of the `srchid` parameter. `first()` sets `srchid` to the id of the search it initiates.

Miscellaneous Routines

The following routines implement various miscellaneous functions auxiliary to our program. The functions don't teach us much new about LDAP, but they are necessary for the application to work.

```
1.    void
2.    help( void )

3.    {
4.            printf( "Commands:\n" );
5.            printf( "\ta\tadd an entry\n" );
6.            printf( "\tb\tbind to the directory\n" );
7.            printf( "\td\tdelete an entry\n" );
8.            printf( "\tf\tfirst search entry\n" );
9.            printf( "\ti\tinitialize an LDAP session\n" );
10.           printf( "\tl\tlist children of entry\n" );
11.           printf( "\tn\tnext search entry\n" );
12.           printf( "\tr\tread entry\n" );
13.           printf( "\tu\tunbind\n" );
14.   }

15.   int
16.   parse_command( char *line, int *argcp, char **argv )
17.   {
18.           char *      token;

19.           line[strlen(line)-1] = '\0';
20.           *argcp = 0;
21.           for ( token = strtok_quote( line, " \t" ); token !=
              ➥NULL;
22.               token = strtok_quote( NULL, " \t" ) ) {

23.                   if ( *argcp == MAXARGS ) {
24.                           printf( "Too many arguments (max %d)\n",
                              ➥MAXARGS );
25.                           exit( 1 );
26.                   }
27.                   argv[(*argcp)++] = token;
28.           }
29.           argv[*argcp] = NULL;
30.           return( *argcp == 0 ? -1 : *argv[0] );
31.   }

32.   char *
33.   strtok_quote( char *line, char *sep )
34.   {
35.           int             inquote;
```

```
36.          char         *tmp, *d;
37.          static char  *next;
38.          if ( line != NULL ) {
39.                  next = line;
40.          }
41.          while ( *next && strchr( sep, *next ) ) {
42.                  next++;
43.          }

44.          if ( *next == '\0' ) {
45.                  next = NULL;
46.                  return( NULL );
47.          }

48.          d = tmp = next;
49.          for ( inquote = 0; *next; next++ ) {
50.                  switch ( *next ) {
51.                  case '"':
52.                          if ( inquote ) {
53.                                  inquote = 0;
54.                          } else {
55.                                  inquote = 1;
56.                          }
57.                          break;
58.                  case '\\':
59.                          + = *++next;
60.                          break;
61.                  default:
62.                          if ( ! inquote ) {
63.                                  if ( strchr( sep, *next ) != NULL ) {
64.                                          + = '\0';
65.                                          next++;
66.                                          return( tmp );
67.                                  }
68.                          }
69.                          + = *next;
70.                          break;
71.                  }
72.          }
73.          *d = '\0';

74.          return( tmp );
75.  }
```

These routines have nothing new to teach us about LDAP. They just do some simple but rather tedious parsing of commands, and print the help menu (such as it is). The only thing of interest to note is that the parse_command() function breaks the command line up into tokens. It allows tokens that contain spaces to be input inside double quotes, a handy feature for typing in distinguished names, which often contain spaces.

Sample Session

Once we've put together our entire application, a sample session might look something like this.

```
cmd: h
Commands:
a       add
b       bind
d       delete
r       read
l       list
f       first search entry
n       next search entry
h       help
cmd: i ldap.host.name 389
cmd: b "cn=directory manager, o=Ace Industry, c=US" "secret"
cmd: a /tmp/ldif.file
cmd: r "cn=Barbara Jensen, o=Ace Industry, c=US"
dn: cn=Barbara Jensen, o=Ace Industry, c=US
cn: Barbara Jensen
cn: Babs Jensen
sn: Jensen
objectclass: top
objectclass: person
cmd: l "o=Ace Industry, c=US"
cn=Aaron Jensen
cn=Barbara Jensen
cn=Bjorn Jensen
cn=Gern Jensen
cmd: f "o=Ace Industry, c=US" sub "(sn=Jensen)" mail
dn: cn= Aaron Jensen, o=Ace Industry, c=US
mail: ajensen@ace.com
```

```
cmd: n
dn: cn=Barbara Jensen, o=Ace Industry, c=US
mail: babs@ace.com
cmd: n
dn: cn=Bjorn Jensen, o=Ace Industry, c=US
mail: bjorn@ace.com
cmd: n
dn: cn=Gern Jensen, o=Ace Industry, c=US
mail: gern@ace.com
cmd: n
cmd: <end-of-file>
```

The data, of course, is made up, as is the host name. But the preceding session should give you an idea of what the capabilities of this example are and how you might make use of it.

Summary

As this example has shown, it's relatively easy to use the LDAP API to write real applications. While this example is not much to look at in the way of user interface, it does demonstrate much of the functionality of the LDAP API. Some good exercises for you might be the following:

UI Improvement: While mostly not LDAP-related, improving the UI in this example will give you experience using LDAP in a different environment. For example, you could modify the example to run in a windowed, GUI environment such as MS Windows, X Windows, or MacOS.

Getfilter routines: By making use of the `getfilter` routines, a user of our example would not have to know anything about LDAP search filters. Instead, they could just type in a general query string and have the getfilter routines do the work of converting to a search filter. See Chapter 10 for details.

Modify support: The current example provides a way to add, delete, and search for entries, but no way to modify existing entries. Adding a new command that implements this functionality would give you experience with `ldap_modify()` and friends. See Chapter 14 for details.

ModRDN support: By adding a new command enabling users to change the name of an entry, you will gain experience with `ldap_modrdn2()` and friends. See Chapter 14 for details.

And, of course, you no doubt have your own ideas about how to improve this example. The best way to learn is by doing, so dive right in and start improving!

Looking Ahead

Now that we've covered the entire LDAP API in detail and tied many of the calls together into a complete example, it's time to turn our attention to the LDAP command line tools. The next two chapters introduce the tools and present several examples of their use.

CHAPTER 17

LDAP Command Line Tools

At this point we are going to turn away from the LDAP C API and look at a different way to use LDAP. A set of five command line tools that can be used to access LDAP directory servers is included in both the University of Michigan and Netscape LDAP Software Development Kits. Each of these tools is a pre-built utility application that supports one or more LDAP functions. In this chapter you will learn how to use these tools by themselves and within the context of an interpreted scripting language such as Perl.

Overview

The five LDAP command line tools are:

ldapsearch Searches for directory entries; display attributes and values found

ldapmodify Modifies, add, delete, or rename directory entries

ldapadd   Adds new directory entries

ldapdelete Deletes existing directory entries

ldapmodrdn Renames existing directory entries

These tools were all built using the LDAP API functions. All of these tools are designed to be executed from the UNIX shell prompt or the MS-DOS prompt (while running Microsoft Windows). These tools are not available for the Macintosh. The tools can also be used easily from within one of the many simple scripting languages that are supported by the various command shells (for example, Bourne shell scripts, C shell scripts, MS-DOS batch files). For more complex applications, they can be used from a complete scripting language such as Perl. When compared to traditional compiled languages such as C/C++ and Pascal, these interpreted languages tend to simplify the task of constructing programs and are a favorite of advanced users and system administrators.

These five tools correspond to the operations that can be performed using the LDAP protocol (and LDAP programmers' API) itself, although there is no ldapcompare tool. Note that the actual filenames of the Microsoft Windows versions of these tools end in ".exe" like all MS-DOS executables. On UNIX the names are as shown above. Each tool supports a common set of options, including authentication/bind parameters. The ldapsearch, ldapadd, and ldapmodify tools support a common text-based format for representing directory information called the LDAP Data Interchange Format (LDIF).

	Tip

> Some of the command line parameters used with the LDAP tools tend to contain blanks and other characters that may be interpreted in a special way by your command line interpreter or shell. You will need to quote such parameters—usually enclosing an argument in double quotes is sufficient. With most UNIX shells, single quote marks are even more effective in ensuring that special characters are not interpreted by the shell. The examples in this chapter use double quotes around parameters where necessary.

The ldapsearch Tool

The ldapsearch tool is a command line interface to the `ldap_search()` API function. ldapsearch opens a connection to an LDAP directory server, binds, and performs a search. One or more entries may be returned as a result of the search.

Example 17.1: Find all the people with a last name of Smith and display all attributes.

```
command: ldapsearch -L -b "o=ACME Inc., c=US" "(sn=smith)"

result:   dn: cn=Joe Smith, o=ACME Inc., c=US
       objectclass: top
       objectclass: person
       cn: Joe Smith
       cn: Joseph Smith
       sn: Smith
       mail: jsmith@acme.com

       dn: cn=Amy Smith, o=ACME Inc., c=US
       objectclass: top
       objectclass: person
       cn: Amy Smith
       sn: Smith
       mail: amys@acme.com
```

In this example two "smith" entries were returned, each of which has values for the `objectclass`, `cn`, `sn`, and `mail` attributes. Notice that if any attribute has more than one value, each value is printed on a separate line.

Example 17.2: Given a colleague's e-mail address, retrieve her favorite drink.

```
command: ldapsearch -L -b "o=ACME Inc., c=US"
➥"(mail=bjensen@acme.com)" drink

result:    dn: cn=Barbara Jensen, o=ACME Inc., c=US
       drink: orange juice
```

The `drink` on the end of the command line (after the LDAP filter) says "only retrieve the favorite drink attribute values." Barbara seems to have a very healthy drinking habit.

Detailed Explanation of ldapsearch Command Line Parameters

The ldapsearch tool is invoked like this:

```
ldapsearch [options] -b searchbase filter [attrs...]
```

where:

> *options* includes zero or more ldapsearch command line options (see below)

> *searchbase* is the LDAP Distinguished Name (DN) at which to base the search

> *filter* is an LDAP search filter as defined in RFC-1960 (see Chapter 10)

> *attrs* is an optional space-separated list of attributes to retrieve during the search

ldapsearch will exit with a number that corresponds to the LDAP result code returned by the server (see Chapter 8 for a complete list of these codes). An exit code of zero corresponds to LDAP_SUCCESS and means that no errors occurred; if an error does occur a message is written to standard error. The output produced by ldapsearch and written to standard output is a sequence of zero or more entries, separated by empty lines. This output is in the LDAP Data Interchange Format (LDIF), which is described later in this chapter.

Many optional command-line flags can be used with ldapsearch. UNIX fans can think of ldapsearch as LDAP's answer to the ls command because it has so many options:

-a *deref*   Indicates how alias dereferencing should be done by the server. *deref* should be one of these strings: never, always, search, or find to specify that aliases are never dereferenced, always dereferenced, dereferenced while searching, or dereferenced only when locating the base entry for the search. The default is to never dereference aliases.

-A   Retrieves the names of attributes only, not their values. This is useful if you want to see if an attribute is present in an entry but are not interested in the specific values.

-D *binddn*   When binding (authenticating) to the LDAP server, use *binddn* (a full LDAP Distinguished Name as described in Chapter 3). This is normally used in conjunction with the -w option (see below). By default, an unauthenticated ("null") bind is performed.

-f *filename* Reads a series of lines from the disk file named *filename*, performing one LDAP search for each line. In this case, the *filter* parameter on the command line is treated as a pattern where the first occurrence of %s is replaced with a line from the file. If the *filename* is a single '-' character, the filter lines are read from standard input. Note that Netscape's version of ldapsearch allows you to omit the filter on the command line if you like, in which case the lines in the file are used directly as filters.

-h *ldaphost* Connects to the LDAP directory server on the server named by *ldaphost* (this can also be an IP address in dotted form, for example, 141.211.164.13). If this option is not used, ldapsearch tries to connect to a server on the same computer ldapsearch is running on. Also see the -p option.

-l *timelimit* Instructs the server to spend at most *timelimit* seconds processing the search.

-L Always produces LDIF output.

-n Shows what would be done, but doesn't actually perform a search. This option is useful in conjunction with -v for debugging purposes.

-p *ldapport* Connects to the LDAP directory server on TCP port *ldapport*. If this option is not used, ldapsearch connects to the standard LDAP TCP port of 389. Also see the -h option.

-R Does not follow referrals to additional LDAP servers while searching. Instead, display an LDAP_PARTIAL_RESULTS error message that includes the unfollowed referrals.

-s *scope* Specifies the scope of the search; that is, the set of entries relative to the *searchbase* that will be examined to see if they match the *filter*. *scope* should be one of these strings: base, one, or sub to specify a base-object search (only check the searchbase entry itself), one-level search (check all entries that are one level below the searchbase entry), or subtree search (check the searchbase and all of its descendants). If this option is not given, a subtree search is done.

-S *attribute* Sorts the list of entries returned based on their values for *attribute*. If *attribute* is a zero-length string (for example, ""), the entries are sorted using the components of their distinguished names. Note that ldapsearch normally outputs entries as they are returned by the server and that use of this option causes all entries to be received before any are output. If this option is not used, entries are displayed in the order sent by the server (not guaranteed to be sorted in any way).

-t   Instead of outputting values directly, writes each value to a temporary file. This can be useful when retrieving non-text values such as those stored in the jpegPhoto, audio, or userCertificate;binary attributes.

-u   Includes the so-called user friendly form of each entry's distinguished name in the output as the ufn attribute.

-v   Runs in verbose mode (output diagnostic information). This option is useful for debugging purposes.

-w *bindpasswd*   When binding (authenticating) to the LDAP server, present *bindpasswd* as the password. This is normally used in conjunction with the -D option (see above). By default, an unauthenticated ("null") bind is performed.

-z *sizelimit*   Instruct the LDAP server to return at most sizelimit entries. Note that the server may elect to return fewer entries for security or load-related reasons.

Example 17.3: Return the phone and fax numbers for all the organizational unit entries that are listed directly below o=ACME Inc., c=US. Connect to the LDAP server on the host ldap.acme.com and sort the entries using their distinguished names.

```
command: ldapsearch -L -s one -h ldap.acme.com -S "" -b "o=ACME Inc.,
c=US" "objectClass=organizationalUnit"
telephoneNumber facsimileTelephoneNumber
```

```
result:    dn: ou=Engineering, o=ACME Inc., c=US"
           telephonenumber: +1 555 555-5500
           facsimiletelephonenumber: +1 555 555-5511

           dn: ou=Finance, o=ACME Inc., c=US
           telephonenumber: +1 555 555-4400
           facsimiletelephonenumber: +1 555 555-4411

           dn: ou=Marketing, o=ACME Inc., c=US
```

In this example, no telephone numbers were returned for the Marketing entry.

The LDAP Data Interchange Format (LDIF)

It is often convenient to be able to represent directory information using a text-based format. The LDAP Data Interchange Format (LDIF) is one such representation, and it was created to provide a simple, versatile way for directory information to be transferred between applications and operating system platforms. LDIF is the format produced by the ldapsearch tool, the format accepted by the ldapadd tool, and is the basis for the change information format that the ldapmodify tool uses.

An LDIF file contains one or more entries. Each entry is separated by an empty line. The basic form of an entry in an LDIF file is:

```
[id]
dn: entryDN
attrtype: attrvalue
...
```

where:

id is an optional numeric entry id (this is not used by the LDAP tools)

entryDN is the LDAP Distinguished Name (DN) of the directory entry *attrtype* is an LDAP attribute type, for example, `cn` or `telephoneNumber`

attrvalue is a value for *attrtype*

Note that the *attrtype: attrvalue* line may be repeated as many times as necessary to list all of the attribute values present in an entry, and that any line may be continued by using a single space or horizontal tab character at the start of the next line.

Example 17.4: An LDIF file that contains Babs Jensen's entry that includes six attributes (`cn` and `objectclass` each have two values).

```
dn: cn=Barbara Jensen, o=ACME Inc., c=US
cn: Barbara Jensen
cn: Babs Jensen
sn: Jensen
drink: orange juice
mail: bjensen@acme.com
seeAlso: cn=Babs Jensen, ou=Info Tech Division, o=Peo
 ple, o=University of Michigan, c=US
objectClass: top
objectClass: person
```

Note that the value for `seeAlso` is split across two lines by using a single space character at the start of line that begins with " `ple, ...`".

If an attribute value contains a non-printing character or begins with a space or horizontal tab character, the value must be represented using base-64 encoding. In the University of Michigan SDK, horizontal tab characters within values are also encoded using base-64. When this encoding is used, two colon characters are used after the attribute type. base-64 encoding was invented for use in Internet E-Mail and is documented in RFC-2045 "Multipurpose Internet Mail Extension (MIME) Part One: Format of Internet Message Bodies."

Tip

The Netscape and University of Michigan distributions both contain a program called ldif that is useful in producing base 64-encoded values.

Example 17.5: An LDIF file that contains four entries—one organization, two people, and one group.

```
dn: o=ACME Inc., c=US
o: ACME Inc.
description: maker of many fine products
objectClass: top
objectClass: organization

dn: cn=Fred Flintstone, o=ACME Inc., c=US
cn: Fred Flintstone
sn: Flintstone
 description:: IGJlZ2lucyB3aXRoIGEgc3BhY2U=
postalAddress: 1234 Bedrock Lane $ Bedrock, Stone Age 00000
objectClass: top
objectClass: person

dn: cn=Yogi Bear, o=ACME Inc., c=US
cn: Yogi Bear
sn: Bear
postalAddress: In The Woods $ Somewhere
jpegPhoto:: /9j/4AAQSkZJRgABAAAAAQABAAD/2wBDABALDA4MChAAODQ4
SERATGC...
objectClass: top
objectClass: person

dn: Animated Characters
member: cn=Fred Flintstone, o=ACME Inc., c=US
member: cn=Yogi Bear, o=ACME Inc., c=US
objectClass: top
objectClass: groupOfNames
```

Note that Fred's description is the value "begins with a space" and so it is base-64 encoded. Yogi's JPEG photo is also base-64 encoded (truncated to keep this example short).

The ldapmodify and ldapadd Tools

The ldapmodify tool is a command line interface to the ldap_modify(), ldap_add(), ldap_delete(), and ldap_modrdn() API functions. ldapmodify opens a connection to an LDAP directory server, binds, and performs a sequence of LDAP modify operations. The ldapadd tool is identical to the ldapmodify tool except that by default it adds entries to the directory. Note that ldapmodify can also be used to add entries; the ldapadd tool is only provided as a convenience to make adding entries as straightforward as possible.

Example 17.6: Bind as the directory manager (password "secret") and add an e-mail address to an entry.

```
command: ldapmodify -D "cn=Manager, o=ACME Inc., c=US" -w secret <
➥modfile

contents
of modfile: dn: cn=Joe Smith, o=ACME Inc., c=US
            changetype: modify
            add: mail
            mail: jsmith@acme.com

result: (nothing if successful; otherwise, an error message will be
➥printed)
```

Example 17.7: Bind as Amy Smith (password "ldap=fun") and delete the value "water" from the "drink" attribute value in her entry.

```
command: ldapmodify -D "cn=Amy Smith, o=ACME Inc., c=US" -w
➥"ldap=fun" < modfile

contents
of modfile: dn: cn=Amy Smith, o=ACME Inc., c=US
            changetype: modify
            delete: drink
            drink: water
result: (nothing if successful; otherwise, an error message will be
➥printed)
```

Example 17.8: Bind as the directory manager (password "secret") and delete the entries for Joe Smith and Amy Smith.

```
command: ldapmodify -D "cn=Manager, o=ACME Inc., c=US" -w secret <
➥modfile

contents
of modfile:  dn: cn=Joe Smith, o=ACME Inc., c=US
             changetype: delete
```

```
              dn: cn=Amy Smith, o=ACME Inc., c=US
              changetype: delete
```

result: (nothing if successful; otherwise, an error message will be
➥printed)

Example 17.9: Bind as the directory manager (password "secret") and
add an entry for Amy Smith.

command: ldapadd -D "cn=Manager, o=ACME Inc., c=US" -w secret <
➥addfile

```
contents
of addfile: dn: cn=Amy Smith, o=ACME Inc., c=US
            objectclass: top
            objectclass: person
            objectclass: inetOrgPerson
            cn: Amy Smith
            sn: Smith
            mail: amys@acme.com
```

result: (nothing if successful; otherwise, an error message will be
➥printed)

Example 17.10: Bind as the directory manager (password "secret")
and change the name of a group entry from "User Interface" to "User
Experience". Completely remove the old name from the entry.

command: ldapmodify -D "cn=Manager, o=ACME Inc., c=US" -w secret -f
➥modfile

```
contents
of modfile: dn: cn=User Interface, ou=Groups, o=ACME Inc., c=US
            changetype: modrdn
            newrdn: cn=User Experience
            deleteoldrdn: 1
```

result: (nothing if successful; otherwise, an error message will be
➥printed)

Detailed Explanation of ldapmodify and ldapadd Command Line Parameters

The ldapmodify and ldapadd tools are invoked like this:

```
ldapmodify [options] [ < changefile ]
ldapadd [options] [ < addfile ]
```

where:

> *options* includes zero or more command line options (see below)
>
> *changefile* contains the list of changes to be performed (format described below)
>
> *addfile* contains entries to be added (LDIF format)

ldapmodify will exit with a number that corresponds to the LDAP result code returned by the server (see Chapter 8 for a complete list of these codes). An exit code of zero corresponds to LDAP_SUCCESS and means that no errors occurred; if an error does occur a message is written to standard error. ldapmodify does not write anything to standard output unless the -v flag is used. The changes to be performed are read from *changefile* (if *changefile* is omitted and the -f option is not used, ldapmodify reads change information from standard input). The format of the change information is a modified form of LDIF, and is described in the section "Format of Change Information." Note that when using ldapadd, the entry information is standard LDIF.

Several optional command-line flags can be used with ldapmodify and ldapadd:

-a	Adds new entries (implied if the ldapadd tool is being used). If this flag is used, the input format for the new entries is standard LDIF.
-b	Assumes that values that begin with a '/' character are binary values that should be read from a file. The value itself is assumed to be the name of the file to read the value from.

-c   Uses continuous operation mode: reports errors, but continues with the next change. If this option is not used, ldapmodify and ldapadd exit as soon as an error occurs.

-D *binddn*   When binding (authenticating) to the LDAP server, use *binddn* (a full LDAP Distinguished Name as described in Chapter 3). This is normally used in conjunction with the -w option (see below). Before carrying out any modify operations, most LDAP directory servers will require you to bind using a DN and password. By default, an unauthenticated ("null") bind is performed.

-f *filename*   Reads the change information from the disk file *filename* instead of from standard input.

-h *ldaphost*   Connects to the LDAP directory server on the server named by *ldaphost* (this can also be an IP address in dotted form, for example, 141.211.164.13). If this option is not used, ldapmodify and ldapadd try to connect to a server on the same computer they are running on. Also see the -p option.

-n   Shows what would be done, but doesn't actually perform any LDAP operations. This option is useful in conjunction with -v for debugging purposes

-p *ldapport*   Connects to the LDAP directory server on TCP port *ldapport*. If this option is not used, ldapmodify and ldapadd connect to the standard LDAP TCP port of 389. Also see the -h option.

-v   Runs in verbose mode (output diagnostic information). This option is useful for debugging purposes.

-w *bindpasswd* When binding (authenticating) to the LDAP server, present *bindpasswd* as the password. This is normally used in conjunction with the -D option (see above). By default, an unauthenticated ("null") bind is performed.

Format of Change Information

When adding entries, standard LDIF text (as described earlier in this chapter) is used. This is the format to use with ldapadd and with ldapmodify when invoked with the -a option. For the other kinds of changes (modify, delete, and modifyrdn) a modified form of LDIF is used. As in standard LDIF, entries are separated by a single blank line. We will call each "entry" in the modified format an LDIF change record.

As in standard LDIF, the first line of an LDIF change record must be a dn: line that contains the distinguished name of the entry to add, change, or delete. For example:

```
dn: cn=Joe Smith, o=ACME Inc., c=US
```

The next line indicates the kind of change being made and is one of these four lines:

```
changetype: add
changetype: delete
changetype: modrdn
changetype: modify
```

The format used for the remainder of the change record depends on which of the four types of changes is being made.

changetype: add

For a changetype of add, the remainder of the change record consists of attributes and values in standard LDIF format.

changetype: modify

For a changetype of modify, the rest of the change record is a list of one or more attribute modify records, separated by lines that contain a single hyphen (-) character. There are three kinds of attribute modify records. The first kind is used to add new attribute values to an entry:

```
add: attribute
attribute: value1
```

```
[ attribute: value2 … ]
-
```

The second is used to delete values:

```
delete: attribute
[ attribute: value1 … ]
-
```

Note that if only the delete: attribute line is given, all values for the attribute will be deleted. This will fail with a "no such attribute" error if no values are present for that attribute.

The third kind of attribute modify record is used to replace all of the values for an attribute with a new set of values:

```
replace: attribute
[ attribute: value1 … ]
-
```

Note that if only the replace: attribute line is given, the attribute has an empty set of values that the server will interpret as a request to delete the attribute. This operation will succeed even if there are no existing values for the attribute, and can be used to ensure that an attribute is completely removed without knowing ahead of time whether it exists.

changetype: delete

For a changetype of delete, there is no additional information in the change record.

changetype: modrdn

For a changetype of modrdn, the next line gives the new Relative Distinguished Name for the entry, and is in the form:

```
newrdn: RDN
```

for example,

```
newrdn: cn=Joseph Smith
```

The final line in a modrdn change record is one of these two lines:

```
deleteoldrdn: 0
deleteoldrdn: 1
```

to indicate that the attribute value(s) in the current RDN should be retained or removed, respectively.

Example 17.11: Connect and bind to the directory server running on TCP port 9000 on the server named ldap.acme.com. Replace the favorite drink attribute with a new value and add the JPEG image that is in a local disk file to the same entry.

```
command: ldapmodify -h ldap.acme.com -p 9000 -b -D "cn=Barbara
➥Jensen, o=ACME Inc., c=US" -w "secret" < modfile


contents
of modfile: dn: cn=Barbara Jensen, o=ACME Inc., c=US
           changetype: modify
           replace: drink
           drink: orange juice, fresh squeezed
           -
           add: jpegPhoto
           jpegPhoto: /usr/local/images/babs.jpg


result: (nothing if successful; otherwise, an error message will be
➥printed)
```

The ldapdelete Tool

The ldapdelete tool is a command line interface to the `ldap_delete()` API function. ldapdelete opens a connection to an LDAP directory server, binds, and performs one or more LDAP delete entry operations. Note that the ldapmodify tool can also be used to delete entries.

Example 17.12: Bind as the directory manager (password "secret") and delete the entries for Joe Smith and Amy Smith.

```
command: ldapdelete -D "cn=Manager, o=ACME Inc., c=US" -w secret
➥"cn=Joe Smith, o=ACME Inc., c=US" "cn=Amy Smith, o=ACME Inc., c=US"

result: (nothing if deletion is successful; otherwise, an error mes-
➥sage will be printed)
```

Detailed Explanation of the ldapdelete Command Line Parameters

The ldapdelete tool is invoked like this:

```
ldapdelete [options] [dn...]
```

where:

> *options* includes zero or more ldapdelete command line options (see below)

> *dn* is the distinguished name of an entry to delete

ldapdelete will exit with a number that corresponds to the LDAP result code returned by the server (see Chapter 8 for a complete list of these codes). An exit code of zero corresponds to LDAP_SUCCESS means that no errors occurred; if an error does occur, a message is written to standard error. ldapdelete does not write anything to standard output unless the -v flag is used. The names of the entries to be deleted are given either directly on the command line or in a file using the -f option. If no dns are included on the command line and the -f option is not used, the entry names are read from standard input.

Several optional command line flags can be used with ldapdelete:

-c	Uses continuous operation mode: reports errors, but continues with the next change. If this option is not used, ldapdelete exits as soon as an error occurs.
-D binddn	When binding (authenticating) to the LDAP server, use *binddn* (a full LDAP distinguished name as

described in Chapter 3). This is normally used in conjunction with the -w option (see below). Before carrying out a delete operation, most LDAP directory servers will require you to bind using a DN and password. By default, an unauthenticated ("null") bind is performed.

-f *filename*   Reads the distinguished names of a list of entries to be deleted from the disk file *filename*.

-h *ldaphost*   Connects to the LDAP directory server on the server named by *ldaphost* (this can also be an IP address in dotted form, for example, 141.211.164.13). If this option is not used, ldapdelete tries to connect to a server on the same computer it is running on. Also see the -p option.

-n   Shows what would be done, but doesn't actually perform any LDAP delete operations. This option is useful in conjunction with -v for debugging purposes

-p *ldapport*   Connects to the LDAP directory server on TCP port *ldapport*. If this option is not used, ldapdelete connects to the standard LDAP TCP port of 389. Also see the -h option.

-v   Runs in verbose mode (output diagnostic information). This option is useful for debugging purposes.

-w *bindpasswd*   When binding (authenticating) to the LDAP server, present *bindpasswd* as the password. This is normally used in conjunction with the -D option (see previous page). By default, an unauthenticated ("null") bind is performed.

Example 17.13: Bind as the directory manager (password "secret") and delete the entries for Homer Simpson, Yogi Bear, and Fred Flintstone.

```
command: ldapdelete -D "cn=Manager, o=ACME Inc., c=US" -w secret <
➥delfile

contents
of delfile:    dn: cn=Homer Simpson, o=ACME Inc., c=US
               dn: cn=Yogi Bear, o=ACME Inc., c=US
               dn: cn=Fred Flintstone, o=ACME Inc., c=US

result: (nothing if deletion is successful; otherwise, an error mes-
➥sage will be printed)
```

The ldapmodrdn Tool

The ldapmodrdn tool is a command line interface to the `ldap_modrdn()` API function. ldapmodrdn opens a connection to an LDAP directory server, binds, and performs one or more LDAP modify RDN (rename) operations. Note that the ldapmodify tool can also be used to rename entries.

Example 17.14: Bind as the directory manager (password "secret") and change the name of a group entry from "User Interface" to "User Experience". Completely remove the old name.

```
command: ldapmodrdn -r -D "cn=Manager, o=ACME Inc., c=US" -w secret
"cn=User Interface, ou=Groups, o=ACME Inc., c=US" "cn=User Experi-
ence"

result: (nothing if successful; otherwise, an error message will be
printed)
```

Detailed Explanation of the ldapmodrdn Command Line Parameters

The ldapmodrdn tool is invoked like this:

```
ldapmodrdn [options] [dn rdn]
```

where:

options includes zero or more ldapmodrdn command line options (see below)

dn is the distinguished name of an entry to rename

rdn is the new (relative distinguished) name for the entry

ldapmodrdn will exit with a number that corresponds to the LDAP result code returned by the server (see Chapter 8 for a complete list of these codes). An exit code of zero corresponds to LDAP_SUCCESS and means that no errors occurred. If an error does occur a message is written to standard error. ldapmodrdn does not write anything to standard output unless the -v flag is used. The DN and new RDN of an entry to be renamed is either given directly on the command line or in a file using the -f option. If these parameters are not included on the command line and the -f option is not used, a sequence of DNs and RDN are read from standard input.

Several optional command line flags can be used with ldapmodrdn:

-c	Uses continuous operation mode: reports errors, but continues with the next change. If this option is not used, ldapmodrdn exits as soon as an error occurs.
-D *binddn*	When binding (authenticating) to the LDAP server, use *binddn* (a full LDAP distinguished name as described in Chapter 3). This is normally used in conjunction with the -w option (see below). Before carrying out a ModRDN operation, most LDAP directory servers will require you to bind using a DN and password. By default, an unauthenticated ("null") bind is performed.
-f *filename*	Reads the distinguished names of a list of entries to be deleted from the disk file *filename*.
-h *ldaphost*	Connects to the LDAP directory server on the server named by *ldaphost* (this can also be an IP address in dotted form, for example, 11.21.31.41). If this option is not used, ldapmodrdn tries to

connect to a server on the same computer it is running on. Also see the -p option.

-n   Shows what would be done, but doesn't actually perform any LDAP ModRDN operations. This option is useful in conjunction with -v for debugging purposes

-p *ldapport*   Connects to the LDAP directory server on TCP port *ldapport*. If this option is not used, ldapmodrdn connects to the standard LDAP TCP port of 389. Also see the -h option.

-r   Removes the attribute values contained in the old RDN from the entry. By default, these values are retained.

-v   Runs in verbose mode (output diagnostic information). This option is useful for debugging purposes.

-w *bindpasswd* When binding (authenticating) to the LDAP server, present *bindpasswd* as the password. This is normally used in conjunction with the -D option (see previous page). By default, an unauthenticated ("null") bind is performed.

Example 17.15: Bind as the directory manager (password "secret") and rename the entries for Homer Simpson, Yogi Bear, and Fred Flintstone. Keep the old RDN values. If any errors occur, keep going.

```
command: ldapmodrdn -c -D "cn=Manager, o=ACME Inc., c=US" -w secret <
➥modrfile

contents
of modrfile: cn=Homer Simpson, o=ACME Inc., c=US
        cn=Homer J Simpson

        cn=Yogi Bear, o=ACME Inc., c=US
        cn=Not Your Average Bear
```

```
cn=Fred Flintstone, o=ACME Inc., c=US
cn=Freddy Flintstone
```

```
result: (nothing if deletion is successful; otherwise, an error
➦message will be printed)
```

Using the LDAP Tools over SSL

The Netscape LDAP command line tools support LDAP over the Secure Sockets Layer (SSL). (See Chapter 13 for some basic information on SSL.) Two additional flags are accepted by the ldapadd, ldapmodify, ldapmodrdn, and ldapdelete tools to support SSL. These options are described below.

-z   Connect to the LDAP server using SSL. Note that use of this option also changes the default TCP port used from 389 to 636. Port 636 is the standard port for LDAP over SSL.

-P *directory*   Specify the path to the directory where your certificate database can be found.

Example 17.16: Perform the same e-mail address addition as in Example 17.6 over SSL. The certificate database used is in the /certdb directory.

```
command: ldapmodify -D "cn=Manager, o=ACME Inc., c=US" -w secret -Z -
➦P /certdb < modfile
```

```
contents
of modfile: dn: cn=Joe Smith, o=ACME Inc., c=US
            changetype: modify
            add: mail
            mail: jsmith@acme.com
```

```
result: (nothing if successful; otherwise, an error message will be
➦printed)
```

Summary

The following table summarizes the command line tools described in this chapter.

Name	Description
ldapsearch	Searches for directory entries; display attributes and values found
ldapmodify	Modifies, add, delete, or rename directory entries
ldapadd	Adds new directory entries
ldapdelete	Deletes existing directory entries
ldapmodrdn	Renames existing directory entries

Looking Ahead

These tools support many options, only some of which were used in the examples in this chapter. The next chapter presents a complete example application that is built using several of the LDAP command line tools presented in this chapter.

18

Using the Command Line Tools to Build Applications

In the previous chapter, the LDAP command line tools were introduced. While each of the tools can do useful work by itself, more complex tasks may require additional logic or that you use more than one tool together. For example, if you want to find a set of entries and make a similar change to all of them, you will need to use both the `ldapsearch` and `ldapmodify` command line tools. To tie the tools together, you will probably find it convenient to use a scripting language of some kind.

In this chapter we focus on using the command line tools together to accomplish fairly complex tasks. Several complete utility applications are presented that are written using the UNIX Bourne shell scripting language and Perl. Scripting languages have become a favorite of system administrators and "power users" who want to perform complex tasks without the pain associated with using a compiled language such as C or C++. Even if you eventually plan to build the final version of an application using a compiled language, you may want to use the techniques presented in this chapter to develop a working prototype.

Note that not all of the examples applications presented in this chapter will run on all platforms. If you do not have access to a UNIX system, you probably won't be able to run the Bourne shell examples. The Perl example should run on both Microsoft Windows and UNIX systems, assuming you have a Perl language interpreter installed on your system.

The first three examples in this chapter are written using the Bourne shell's language. The Bourne shell (sh) is the original command line interpreter and scripting language for UNIX and it was written at Bell Labs in the late 1970s by Steve Bourne. While it is no longer very popular as an interactive shell, the Bourne shell is still a favorite for writing shell scripts.

Example 18.1: The lfinger utility—a UNIX Bourne shell script that finds one or more persons in an LDAP directory and "fingers" them using the e-mail address values stored in their directory entries. This program uses the ldapsearch utility and does some fairly simple parsing of the output.

```
1.   #!/bin/sh
2.   #
3.   # lfinger - UNIX Bourne shell script
4.   #
5.   # Search for one or more person entries in the LDAP directory
     ↪and
6.   # 'finger' them using their e-mail address.
7.   #
8.   # e.g.,  lfinger Daniel Smith
9.   #
10.  # set server and search base information
11.  LDAPHOST=ldap.netscape.com
12.  LDAPPORT=389
13.  LDAPBASE="o=Ace Industry, c=US"
14.  # set path to include the directory that contains LDAP command
     ↪line tools
15.  LDAPTOOLDIR=/usr/local/bin
16.  PATH=$LDAPTOOLDIR:$PATH; export PATH
17.  # check for at least one argument
18.  if [ $# -lt 1 ]; then
19.          echo "usage: $0 name"
20.  exit 1
21.  fi
22.  # initialize a few variables
23.  SRCHFILE=/tmp/lf-srch.$$
24.  EMAILFILE=/tmp/lf-mail.$$
```

```
25.   # find the entry and retrieve the e-mail address (mail
       ➥attribute)
26.   echo Searching $LDAPBASE...
27.   ldapsearch -L -h $LDAPHOST -p $LDAPPORT -b "$LDAPBASE" \
28.           "(|(cn=$*)(sn=$*)(uid=$*))" mail > $SRCHFILE
29.   STATUS=$?
30.   if [ $STATUS -ne 0 ]; then
31.           rm $SRCHFILE
32.           exit $STATUS
33.   fi
34.   # Use grep and wc to count entries
35.   echo "Found " `grep '^dn:' $SRCHFILE | wc -l` "entry(ies)..."
36.   # Use grep to pull out all of the e-mail addresses
37.   grep '^mail: ' $SRCHFILE | sed -e 's/^mail: //' > $EMAILFILE
38.   if [ $? -ne 0 ]; then
39.           echo 'No e-mail addresses found.'
40.           rm $SRCHFILE $EMAILFILE
41.           exit 1
42.   fi
43.   # Finger each e-mail address
44.   for mail in 'cat $EMAILFILE'; do
45.           echo "*** finger $mail:"
46.           finger $mail
47.           echo
48.   done
49.   rm $SRCHFILE $EMAILFILE
50.   exit $STATUS
```

This script is fairly straightforward, but let's examine it piece-by-piece. On lines 11–13 some shell variables are set to hold the LDAP server, port, and search base we will use. Lines 15 and 16 set up our path to ensure that the LDAP command line tools can be found and executed. Lines 18–21 check to make sure that at least one command line argument was given to lfinger (a usage message is displayed and the program exits if not).

On lines 27–33 the ldapsearch tool is invoked to contact the directory server and perform a search:

```
ldapsearch -L -h $LDAPHOST -p $LDAPPORT -b "$LDAPBASE" \
           "(|(cn=$*)(sn=$*)(uid=$*))" mail > $SRCHFILE
STATUS=$?
```

```
if [ $STATUS -ne 0 ]; then
            rm $SRCHFILE
            exit $STATUS
fi
```

We use the command line arguments passed to lfinger to search for entries that exactly match values within the common name (cn), surname (sn), or userid (uid) attributes. The -L option is included to ensure that LDIF will be produced, and the output of the search command is redirected to a temporary file. The only attribute we ask to be returned is the mail attribute. Since ldapsearch exits with an LDAP error code, an exit code of zero corresponds to the LDAP_SUCCESS error code included in the LDAP C API. We check the exit status of ldapsearch and exit our entire script if it is not zero. By assigning the shell's $? variable to a temporary STATUS variable of our own, we can pass ldapsearch's exit code out of our lfinger script so it can be checked by whoever executed the lfinger program.

Line 35 uses the grep and wc (word count) utilities to print a count of entries returned:

```
echo "Found " `grep '^dn:' $SRCHFILE | wc -l` "entry(ies)..."
```

Because each entry in ldapsearch's output includes a single line that begins with the three characters dn:, counting the entries is a straightforward matter.

The code on lines 37–42 uses a similar technique to pull out all the e-mail addresses contained in the returned entries:

```
grep '^mail: ' $SRCHFILE | sed -e 's/^mail: //' > $EMAILFILE
if [ $? -ne 0 ]; then
            echo 'No e-mail addresses found.'
            rm $SRCHFILE $EMAILFILE
            exit 1
fi
```

We grep for lines that begin with the tag mail: and use the sed utility to strip off the attribute name and colon, redirecting the output to a second temporary file. An LDIF line with a really long value on it would be continued onto a second line, but we ignore this possibility.

We also check the exit status of the grep command to see if any e-mail addresses were returned (grep exits with zero if it succeeds in finding one or more lines that match the input pattern).

Finally, lines 44–48 invoke the UNIX finger command for each e-mail address value. The output from finger is not redirected anywhere, so it goes directly to standard output (usually the user's terminal). Cleanup of our temporary files is done by lines 49 and 50.

That's it—we now have a utility that is more useful than ldapsearch by itself because it does something with the results returned. Assuming that an entry's e-mail address is "finger-able" we can use this utility application to find out more information about the person, perhaps including whether they are logged onto their system right now and when they last read their e-mail.

Here's an example that shows how to use the lfinger utility.

```
% lfinger babs jensen
Searching o=Ace Industry, c=US...
Found 1 entry(ies)...
*** finger bjensen@aceindustry.com:
Login name: bjensen           In real life: Barbara Jensen
Directory: /u/bjensen          Shell: /bin/csh
On since Oct 4 20:21:41 on pts/0 from dialup1.acindustry.com
No unread mail
Plan:
  Title:  Development Team Manager
  E-Mail:  bjensen@aceindustry.com
  Phone:  +1 101 555-1234
  Location: Building Seven - Cube 5000
```

One entry was found that matched "babs jensen." All of the output after the line that begins with *** finger was of course produced by the UNIX finger command.

Example 18.2: The mventry utility is a UNIX Bourne shell script that moves an entry from one location in the directory to another. It accomplishes this task by using ldapsearch to read all of the information contained in the entry, adding a new entry at the destination using ldapadd, and finally deleting the original entry using the ldapdelete tool. Recall that the LDAP modify RDN operation can only rename entries within the same container; this utility can move entries between arbitrary directory subtrees. With a few minor changes, it could be used to move entries between servers as well.

```
1.   #!/bin/sh
2.   #
3.   # mventry - UNIX Bourne shell script
4.   #
5.   # Move an entry from one location in the LDAP directory to
     ➥another. Unlike
6.   # the LDAP modify RDN operation, this utility can move entries
     ➥from one
7.   # subtree to another. It does this by adding a new entry and
     ➥deleting the
8.   # old one.
9.   #
10.  # e.g., mventry 'cn=Daniel Smith, ou=Accounting, o=ACME Inc.,
     ➥c=US' \
11.  #           'cn=Daniel Smith, ou=Payroll, o=ACME, c=US'
12.  #
13.  # set server and authentication information
14.  LDAPHOST=ldap.netscape.com
15.  LDAPPORT=389
16.  BINDDN="cn=Directory Manager, o=Ace Industry, c=US"
17.  BINDPWD=secret
18.  # set path to include the directory that contains LDAP command
     ➥line tools
19.  LDAPTOOLDIR=/usr/local/bin
20.  PATH=$LDAPTOOLDIR:$PATH; export PATH
21.  # check for exactly two arguments
22.  if [ $# -ne 2 ]; then
23.      echo "usage: $0 srcdn destdn"
24.      exit 1
25.  fi
26.  # initialize a few variables
27.  SRCDN=$1
28.  DESTDN=$2
29.  SRCENTRYFILE=/tmp/mvsrc.$$
30.  DESTENTRYFILE=/tmp/mvdest.$$
```

```
31.  # read the existing entry into a temporary file
32.  echo Reading entry: $SRCDN
33.  ldapsearch -L -h $LDAPHOST -p $LDAPPORT -D "$BINDDN" -w
     ➥"$BINDPWD" \
34.      -b "$SRCDN" -s base 'objectclass=*' > $SRCENTRYFILE
35.  STATUS=$?
36.  if [ $STATUS -ne 0 ]; then
37.      rm $SRCENTRYFILE
38.      exit $STATUS;
39.  fi
40.  # add the entry in the new location
41.  echo
42.  echo "dn: $DESTDN" > $DESTENTRYFILE
43.  tail +2 $SRCENTRYFILE >> $DESTENTRYFILE
44.  ldapadd -h $LDAPHOST -p $LDAPPORT -D "$BINDDN" -w "$BINDPWD" <
     ➥$DESTENTRYFILE
45.  STATUS=$?
46.  if [ $STATUS -ne 0 ]; then
47.      rm $SRCENTRYFILE $DESTENTRYFILE
48.      exit $STATUS;
49.  fi
50.  # remove the original entry
51.  echo Removing entry: $SRCDN
52.  ldapdelete -h $LDAPHOST -p $LDAPPORT -D "$BINDDN" -w "$BINDPWD"
     ➥"$SRCDN"
53.  STATUS=$?
54.  rm $SRCENTRYFILE $DESTENTRYFILE
55.  exit $STATUS
```

The mventry script is a bit longer than the lfinger script and it uses three of the LDAP command line tools. Let's examine this script in detail.

Lines 14–17 set some shell variables that we use later when we connect and bind to the LDAP server. The bind password is included in the script on line 17; it would of course be more secure not to embed the password in plain text inside a script. Lines 19 and 20 set up our path to ensure that the LDAP command line tools can be found and executed. Lines 22–25 check to make sure that exactly two command line arguments were given, displaying a usage message and exiting if not. Lines 27–30 set a few more shell variables.

The code on lines 32–39 reads and stores the entire LDIF representation of the source entry (the one we are going to move) into a temporary file:

```
ldapsearch -L -h $LDAPHOST -p $LDAPPORT -D "$BINDDN" -w "$BINDPWD" \
           -b "$SRCDN" -s base 'objectclass=*' > $SRCENTRYFILE
STATUS=$?
if [ $STATUS -ne 0 ]; then
               rm $SRCENTRYFILE
               exit $STATUS;
fi
```

There are a couple of interesting things to notice here. First, because we have the complete Distinguished Name of the source entry we read the entry by using a base object search with an objectclass=* filter. Second, since we want to move the entire entry we do not limit the attributes returned by including any specific attributes on the ldapsearch command line—we hope to get them all.

Next, we want to create a copy of this entry at the destination location. This is accomplished by the code on lines 42–49 using the ldapadd tool:

```
echo "dn: $DESTDN" > $DESTENTRYFILE
tail +2 $SRCENTRYFILE >> $DESTENTRYFILE
ldapadd -h $LDAPHOST -p $LDAPPORT -D "$BINDDN" -w "$BINDPWD"
➥<$DESTENTRYFILE
STATUS=$?
if [ $STATUS -ne 0 ]; then
               rm $SRCENTRYFILE $DESTENTRYFILE
               exit $STATUS;
fi
```

The first two lines of this sequence create a temporary file that contains an LDIF representation of the new entry. The first line is constructed using the destination DN and the rest of the file is copied from lines 2 on of the source entry. A simple ldapadd command is used to actually add the entry. We carefully check for any errors during the add operation, since lines 51–53 call upon ldapdelete to remove the old entry:

```
echo Removing entry: $SRCDN
ldapdelete -h $LDAPHOST -p $LDAPPORT -D "$BINDDN" -w "$BINDPWD"
```

```
➥"$SRCDN"
STATUS=$?
```

Finally, our temporary files are removed by line 54 and line 55 exits with the STATUS code returned by the ldapdelete command.

Here's an example that shows how to use the mventry utility. Commands entered by the user are presented in boldface type.

```
% ./mventry.sh 'cn=Daniel Smith, ou=Human Resources, o=Ace Industry,
➥c=US \
'cn=Daniel Smith, ou=Accounting, o=Ace Industry, c=US'
Reading entry: cn=Daniel Smith, ou=Human Resources, o=Ace Industry,
➥c=US

adding new entry cn=Daniel Smith, ou=Accounting, o=Ace Industry, c=US

Removing entry: cn=Daniel Smith, ou=Human Resources, o=Ace Industry,
➥c=US
```

Here we have moved Dan Smith's entry from the Human Resources department to the Accounting Department. Notice that two complete Distinguished Names (source and destination for the entry move) must be entered on the command line. This is kind of painful, and it would be fairly simple to enhance the mventry utility to use the ldapsearch command to find the source entry and destination location based on common name, userid, or some other attribute.

Example 18.3: The chgvalue utility application is a UNIX Bourne shell script that does a selective replace of values within a collection of entries. This program uses the ldapsearch and ldapmodify tools. It also takes advantage of UNIX command pipes to avoid the use of any temporary files. This can be important when processing a large number of entries.

```
1.    #!/bin/sh
2.    #
3.    # chgvalue - UNIX Bourne shell script
4.    #
5.    # Find all entries in an LDAP directory subtree that include a
      ➥particular
```

```
6.   # attribute value that ends with a given string and replace that
     ➥value with
7.   # a new string. This can be used to change everyone's e-mail
     ➥address when
8.   # a mail host is renamed, etc.
9.   #
10.  # e.g., chgvalue mail @aceindustry.com @ace.com
11.  #
12.  # set server, search base, and authentication information
13.  LDAPHOST=ldap.netscape.com
14.  LDAPPORT=389
15.  LDAPBASE="o=Ace Industry, c=US"
16.  BINDDN="cn=Directory Manager, o=Ace Industry, c=US"
17.  BINDPWD=secret
18.  # set path to include the directory that contains LDAP command
     ➥line tools
19.  LDAPTOOLDIR=/usr/local-local/bin
20.  PATH=$LDAPTOOLDIR:$PATH; export PATH
21.  # check for exactly three arguments
22.  if [ $# -ne 3 ]; then
23.      echo "usage: $0 attribute old-suffix new-suffix"
24.      exit 1
25.  fi
26.  # initialize a few variables
27.  ATTR=$1
28.  OLDSUFFIX=$2
29.  NEWSUFFIX=$3
30.  # find all the entries that contain values we need to change
31.  ldapsearch -L -h $LDAPHOST -p $LDAPPORT -D "$BINDDN" -w
     ➥"$BINDPWD" \
32.    -b "$LDAPBASE" "$ATTR=*$OLDSUFFIX" $ATTR | \
33.    ( while [ 1 ]; do
34.      read DN
35.      if [ -z "$DN" ]; then
36.          break
37.      fi
38.
39.      echo "$DN"
40.      echo "changetype: modify"
41.
42.      while [ 1 ]; do
43.        read VALUE
44.        VALUE=`echo $VALUE | sed -e s/$ATTR:.//`
```

```
45.        if [ -z "$VALUE" ]; then
46.              break
47.        fi
48.        NEWVALUE='echo $VALUE | sed -e s/$OLDSUFFIX\$/$NEWSUFFIX/'
49.            if [ "$NEWVALUE" != "$VALUE" ]; then
50.            echo "delete: $ATTR"
51.            echo "$ATTR: $VALUE"
52.            echo "-"
53.            echo "add: $ATTR"
54.            echo "$ATTR: $NEWVALUE"
55.            echo "-"
56.          fi
57.      done
58.      echo ""
59.  done ) | ldapmodify -v -D "$BINDDN" -w "$BINDPWD"
```

This script does more extensive parsing of the output of the ldapsearch tool and it uses pipes instead of relying on temporary files, so it may appear more complex than the previous two examples.

Lines 12–29 are similar to the other Bourne shell scripts we have examined: set some variables, set up our path, and check to make sure the script was invoked with the correct number of arguments. Things begin to get interesting with the ldapsearch invocation on lines 31 and 32:

```
ldapsearch -L -h $LDAPHOST -p $LDAPPORT -D "$BINDDN" -w "$BINDPWD" \
          -b "$LDAPBASE" "$ATTR=*$OLDSUFFIX" $ATTR | \
```

The search filter is constructed from the script's command line arguments. The ATTR variable contains the attribute name that was given as the first argument, and the OLDSUFFIX variable contains the value we want to find and replace. If we were invoked like this:

```
chgvalue mail @aceindustry.com @ace.com
```

the search filter would look like this:

```
mail=*@aceindustry.com
```

Our goal is to find all the entries that have mail attributes with values ending in @aceindustry.com, and this search filter does the job nicely.

Another thing to note about the ldapsearch command is that the output is piped into a sub-shell (enclosed in parentheses) that encompasses lines 33–58. The purpose of the sub-shell is to combine the reading of the ldapsearch output with generation of LDIF update statements that we plan to feed to the ldapmodify command. The first portion of the code that is contained in the sub-shell is shown below:

```
( while [ 1 ]; do
                read DN
                if [ -z "$DN" ]; then
                                break
                fi

                echo "$DN"
                echo "changetype: modify"
```

Here in lines 33–40 we begin the outer of two nested Bourne shell while loops that are exited using a break statement. This portion of the chgvalue script reads the first line of an entry and produces the start of a change record to be used as input for the ldapmodify command. We break out of the loop when no more dn: *Distinguished Name* lines can be read.

Lines 42–57 make up the inner while loop:

```
while [ 1 ]; do
                read VALUE
                VALUE=`echo $VALUE | sed -e s/$ATTR:.//`
                if [ -z "$VALUE" ]; then
                        break
                fi
                NEWVALUE=`echo $VALUE | sed -e s/$OLDSUFFIX\$/
$NEWSUFFIX/`
                        if [ "$NEWVALUE" != "$VALUE" ]; then
                echo "delete: $ATTR"
                echo "$ATTR: $VALUE"
                echo "-"
                echo "add: $ATTR"
                        echo "$ATTR: $NEWVALUE"
```

```
                    echo "-"
                    fi
    done
```

This loop is nested within the outer loop, and its mission in life is to read lines until it sees a blank one (marking the end of an entry). Each line contains a VALUE we want to change. We use the UNIX sed utility to compute our NEWVALUE by replacing the OLDSUFFIX portion of each value with our NEWSUFFIX (this is the third command line argument passed to chgvalue). Finally, we output a sequence of LDIF update statements to remove the old attribute value and add the new one.

We complete our pipeline on line 59 by ending the outer while loop, closing off the sub-shell, and feeding the output to the ldapmodify tool:

```
done ) | ldapmodify -v -D "$BINDDN" -w "$BINDPWD"
```

ldapmodify is invoked with the -v (verbose) flag so the user can see what changes are made. That's our entire script, and it's a long one! It does quite a bit, though, and is not hard to understand if you break it into pieces.

Here is an example that shows one way to use the chgvalue utility. Suppose Ace Industry changes its company domain name and wants to change all of the e-mail addresses in their LDAP directory to end in @ace.com instead of @aceindustry.com.

```
% chgvalue.sh mail @aceindustry.com @ace.com
delete mail:
    scarter@aceindustry.com
add mail:
    scarter@ace.com
modifying entry cn=Sam Carter, ou=Accounting, o=Ace Industry, c=US
modify complete

delete mail:
    tmorris@aceindustry.com
```

```
add mail:
    tmorris@ace.com
modifying entry cn=Ted Morris, ou=Accounting, o=Ace Industry, c=US
modify complete

delete mail:
    kvaughan@aceindustry.com
add mail:
    kvaughan@ace.com
modifying entry cn=Kirsten Vaughan, ou=Human Resources, o=Ace Indus-
try, c=US
modify complete
etc...
```

Notice that all of the output is produced by the ldapmodify command line tool, which was invoked by the chgvalue script with the -v flag. To make chgvalue work silently, we could just remove the -v flag from the ldapmodify command.

The next example program is written in the increasingly popular Perl interpreted scripting language. Perl is an acronym for Practical Extraction and Report Language or Pathologically Eclectic Rubbish Lister (the answer depends on who you ask). Perl was created by Larry Wall, and has been ported to most popular computing platforms, including MS-DOS/Windows, many flavors of UNIX, and Macintosh. It is beyond the scope of this book to teach you Perl, but a number of good books and online resources are available. We did try to avoid the more obscure corners of the Perl language in our example code.

This next example also happens to be Web-based. It is a Common Gateway Interface (CGI) program that runs on a Web server and responds to LDAP queries entered through a HyperText Markup Language (HTML) form. It is also beyond the scope of this book to teach CGI programming and HTML, but there are many online and printed resources available on these topics as well.

Example 18.4: The lookup CGI program is a Common Gateway Interface program written in Perl that responds to simple queries and presents HTML-formatted results. This program uses the ldapsearch tool and its behavior is driven by HTML form variables. The form variables used are shown in Table 18.1.

Table 18.1

HTML Form Variables Accepted by the lookup CGI Program

Name	Description	Format	Example
attrlist *	List of attributes to retrieve and display	attr/attr/...	sn/cn/mail
directory *	LDAP server, port, and search base	host:port/ base	ldap.acme. com:389/ o=ACME Inc,c=US
display names	Labels for attributes in the attrlist variable	label/label/...	Surname/ Full Name /E-Mail Address
search- string *	Value to search for	any string	babs jensen
sortattr	Attribute used to order the entries if more than one is found	attr	sn

* this variable is required by the lookup program

Here is the Perl source code for the lookup program itself:

```
1.   #!/usr/local/bin/perl
2.   #
3.   # lookup -- Perl 4/5 script
4.   #
5.   # A simple HTML interface to an LDAP directory
6.   #
7.   # Notes:
8.   #         should handle continued lines produced by ldapsearch
9.   #         should display multiple values if present
10.  # location of ldapsearch command
11.  $ldapsearch = "/usr/local/bin/ldapsearch";
12.  # begin CGI output
13.  print("Content-type: text/html\n\n");
14.  print( "<HTML><HEAD><TITLE>LDAP Search Results</TITLE>
     ⮡</HEAD><BODY>\n" );
```

```perl
15.    print( "<CENTER><H2>LDAP Search Results</H2></CENTER>\n" );
16.    # build an associative array from the values contained in the
       ➥URL's
17.    # query string
18.    @cgiQueryPairs = split( "&", $ENV{ 'QUERY_STRING' } );
19.    foreach $p ( @cgiQueryPairs ) {
20.        ( $var, $val ) = split( "=", $p );
21.        $val =~ s/\+/ /g;                # translate '+' to space
22.        $val =~ s/%(..)/pack("c",hex($1))/ge;  # undo '%HH' URL-
           ➥encoding
23.        $cgiValues{ "$var" } = "$val";
24.    }
25.    # pull out required form variables
26.    $searchString = $cgiValues{ "searchstring" };
27.    if ( $searchString eq "" ) {
28.        &formVarMissingError( "searchstring" );
29.    }
30.    $directory = $cgiValues{ "directory" };
31.    if ( $directory eq "" ) {
32.        &formVarMissingError( "directory" );
33.    }
34.    ( $var, $base ) = split( '/', $directory );
35.    ( $host, $port ) = split( ':', $var );
36.    if ( $port eq "" ) {
37.        $port = "389";
38.    }
39.    $tmp = $cgiValues{ "attrlist" };
40.    if ( $tmp eq "" ) {
41.        &formVarMissingError( "attrlist" );
42.    }
43.    @attrList = split( "/", $tmp );
44.    # pull out optional form variables
45.    $sortAttr = $cgiValues{ "sortattr" };
46.    $tmp = $cgiValues{ "displaynames" };
47.    if ( $tmp eq "" ) {
48.        @displayNames = @attrList;
49.    } else {
50.        @displayNames = split( "/", $tmp );
51.    }
52.    for ( $i=0; $i < scalar( @attrList ); $i++ ) {
53.        $attr2Name{ $attrList[ $i ] } = $displayNames[ $i ];
54.    }
55.    # build ldapsearch command
```

```
56.  $searchcmd = join( " ", ( $ldapsearch, "-h $host -p $port",
57.       "-b \"$base\"", "-S \"$sortAttr\"",
58.  "\"(||(cn=$searchString)(sn=$searchString)(uid=$searchString))\"",
59.       @attrList ));
60.  # fire off ldapsearch command
61.  if ( !open( SRCHOUT, "$searchcmd|" )) {
62.       &reportError( "Unable to execute search" );
63.  }
64.  $count = 0;
65.  $inEntry = 0;
66.  while ( $line = <SRCHOUT> ) {
67.       chop( $line );
68.       if ( length( $line ) == 0 ) {
69.            &displayEntry( $sortAttr, $attrVals );
70.            $inEntry = 0;
71.            $count++;
72.       }
73.       ($tag,$val) = split( ':', $line );
74.       if ( ! $inEntry && $tag eq "dn" ) {
75.            $inEntry = 1;
76.       }
77.       $attrVals{ "$tag" } = "$val";
78.  }
79.  if ( $inEntry ) {
80.       &displayEntry( $sortAttr, $attrVals );
81.       $count++;
82.  }
83.  print( "<HR><H3>Found ", $count, " entries that matched \"" ,
     ➡$searchString,
84.       "\".</H3>\n" );
85.  $rc = close( SRCHOUT );
86.  print( "</BODY></HTML>\n" );
87.  exit( 0 );
88.  # subroutine to report an error and exit
89.  sub
90.  reportError {
91.       print( "<B>Error:<B> ", @_, "\n</BODY></HTML>\n" );
92.       exit( 0 );
93.  }
94.  # report "required form variable missing" error and exit
95.  sub
96.  formVarMissingError {
```

```
97.      &reportError( join( " ", ( "Missing required form variable",
         ➥@_ )));
98.  }
99.  # subroutine to display an LDAP entry as HTML
100. sub
101. displayEntry {
102.     $attrVals = @_[0];
103.     $sortAttr = @_[1];
104.     print( "<HR>\n<H3>", $attrVals{ "dn" }, "</H3>\n" );
105.     print( "<DL>\n" );
106.     if ( $sortAttr ne "" ) {
107.         &displayAttr( $attrVals, $sortAttr );
108.     }
109.     foreach $attr ( @attrList ) {
110.         if ( $attr ne $sortAttr ) {
111.             &displayAttr( $attrVals, $attr );
112.         }
113.     }
114.     print( "</DL>\n" );
115. # remove the evidence
116.     foreach $key ( keys(%attrVals)) {
117.         delete( $attrVals{ $key } );
118.     }
119. }
120. sub
121. displayAttr {
122.     $attrVals = @_[0];
123.     $attr = @_[1];
124.     $displayName = $attr2Name{ $attr };
125.     $val = $attrVals{ $attr };
126.     if ( $val ne "" ) {
127.         print( "<DT>", $displayName, ":\n<DD>" );
128.         if ( $attr eq "mail" ) {
129.             print( "<A HREF=\"mailto:$val\">$val</A>" );
130.         } else {
131.             print( $val );
132.         }
133.         print( "</DT>\n" );
134.     }
135. }
```

Let's examine this program in some detail. Lines 10–15 set the stage by assigning a variable to hold the path to the ldapsearch command line tool and outputting the start of the HTML results document we will generate. This is very straightforward.

The lookup program is designed to be started in response to an HTTP GET request. This means that the form variables we receive are encoded in the QUERY_STRING CGI environment variable. The query string looks like this:

```
var1=value1&var2=value2…
```

Spaces within the form variable values are replaced by a plus sign character and other special characters may be encoded using the %HH hexadecimal encoding that is commonly used within URLs. This section of code on lines 18–24:

```
@cgiQueryPairs = split( "&", $ENV{ 'QUERY_STRING' } );
foreach $p ( @cgiQueryPairs ) {
    ( $var, $val ) = split( "=", $p );
              $val =~ s/\+/ /g;                # translate '+' to space
              $val =~ s/%(..)/pack("c",hex($1))/ge;  # undo '%HH'
URL-encoding
              $cgiValues{ "$var" } = "$val";
}
```

parses the contents of the query string and creates a Perl associative array called cgiValues that contains all of the form variables. This array is indexed by the variable name.

The code on lines 26–54 accesses the cgiValues array to pull out all of the required and optional form variables the lookup CGI program supports. If a required form variable is missing, the formVarMissingError subroutine is called to report the error and terminate the program. Most of the code that pulls out the HTML form variable values is fairly simple. Let's examine the section that deals with the displaynames form variable in more detail. The displaynames form variable is optional. If present, it contains a list of labels, separated by a foward-slash (/), to be displayed next to the attribute values contained in the entries we find. The relevant code is on lines 46–54:

```
$tmp = $cgiValues{ "displaynames" };
if ( $tmp eq "" ) {
    @displayNames = @attrList;
} else {
    @displayNames = split( "/", $tmp );
}
for ( $i=0; $i < scalar( @attrList ); $i++ ) {
    $attr2Name{ $attrList[ $i ] } = $displayNames[ $i ];
}
```

First, we use our cgiValues array to retrieve the value of the HTML form variable and assign it to a Perl variable called tmp. Next, we create a Perl array called displayNames that contains all of the attribute display names. This is done either by copying the attribute names themselves from the attrList array (if no value was given for the displaynames form variable) or by splitting the tmp variable at each forward-slash character. Finally, we construct an associative array called attr2Name that can be used to map each LDAP attribute name to the display name that should be used to label its values.

Lines 55–59 use all of the information that has been gathered so far to construct an appropriate ldapsearch command:

```
$searchcmd = join( " ", ( $ldapsearch, "-h $host -p $port",
    "-b \"$base\"", "-S \"$sortAttr\"",
    "\"(|(cn=$searchString)(sn=$searchString)(uid=$searchString))\"",
    @attrList ));
```

The only really interesting thing to notice is the use of the sort option (-S). If no sortAttr is defined, ldapsearch will be passed -S "" so the results are sorted based on the Distinguished Names of the entries found; otherwise, they will be sorted by the LDAP attribute contained in sortAttr, which was taken from the sortattr HTML form variable.

Lines 60–82 execute the ldapsearch command and parse the output returned. The rich string manipulation functions that Perl supports make parsing the LDIF produced by ldapsearch relatively easy. As the attribute: value lines are processed, an associative array called attrVals is built. When we come to the end of an entry, the displayEntry subroutine is called to produce an HTML formatted version of the entry. We also maintain a count of entries found and display the count (lines 83 and 84) after the entries themselves have all been displayed. Lines 85–87 take care of cleanup and finish off our HTML document.

The `displayEntry` subroutine fills lines 100–119, but it is very simple. The basic strategy is to first display the entry's DN and then display the attribute we have sorted the results by, followed by all of the other requested attributes. The work to actually display an attribute is done in another subroutine called `displayAttr`. The code appears on lines 120–135 and is repeated below:

```
sub
displayAttr {
    $attrVals = @_[0];
    $attr = @_[1];
    $displayName = $attr2Name{ $attr };

    $val = $attrVals{ $attr };
    if ( $val ne "" ) {
        print( "<DT>", $displayName, ":\n<DD>" );
        if ( $attr eq "mail" ) {
            print( "<A HREF=\"mailto:$val\">$val</A>" );
        } else {
            print( $val );
        }
        print( "</DT>\n" );
    }
}
```

A few things to notice: the attribute values array (@attrVals) and LDAP attribute name itself ($attr) are passed in as parameters to this subroutine. The `attr2Name` associative array is used to get the label that goes with the attribute. Finally, if there are any attribute values, they are displayed as HTML definition list items (<DT> and <DD>). The surrounding <DL> tags for the definition list itself are output by the `displayEntry` routine. A final note: The value output code has a special case so that `mailto:` links are generated for the `mail` attribute. This makes addressing an e-mail message to a person found as simple as clicking on the address value that is displayed.

The HTML source for a sample lookup form is listed below:

```
<HTML>
<HEAD>
<TITLE>LDAP Directory Lookup</TITLE>
</HEAD>
<BODY>

<CENTER>
<H2>LDAP Directory Lookup</H2>
</CENTER>

<FORM METHOD=GET ACTION="/cgitest/lookup.pl">

Directory to search:
<SELECT NAME="directory">
<OPTION VALUE="ldap.netscape.com:389/o=Ace Industry, c=US">
Ace Industry
<OPTION VALUE="ldap.itd.umich.edu/o=University of Michigan, c=US">
University of Michigan
</SELECT>

Sort results by:
<SELECT NAME="sortattr">
<OPTION VALUE="">Entry Name
<OPTION VALUE="cn">Full Name
<OPTION VALUE="sn">Last Name
<OPTION VALUE="telephoneNumber">Phone Number
</SELECT>

<INPUT TYPE="hidden" NAME="attrlist"
    VALUE="sn/cn/mail/telephoneNumber/drink">
<INPUT TYPE="hidden" NAME="displaynames"
    VALUE="Surname/Full Name/E-Mail Address/Phone Number/Favorite
    ⇒Drink">

<BR>

Name to find: <INPUT TYPE="input" NAME="searchstring">

<INPUT TYPE="submit">
</FORM>

</BODY>
</HTML>
```

The form contains a <SELECT> form element (displayed by most Web browsers as a pop-up menu) that contains two options for the LDAP directory to search. A second <SELECT> element is included to allow the user to choose which attribute will be used to sort the entries that are returned. Finally, a standard text <INPUT> form element is used for the search string and of course a "Submit Query" button is provided.

The sample form as it appears in a Web browser is shown in figure 18.1. The user has chosen to search the Ace Industry LDAP server for the name "jensen." The results will come back sorted by Full Name (that is, by the cn attribute values).

Figure 18.1

HTML search form for submitting a search.

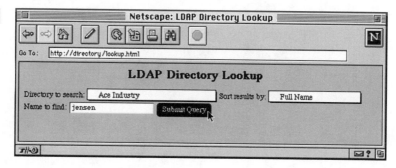

An example of the output produced by the lookup program is shown in figure 18.2.

Figure 18.2

Search results.

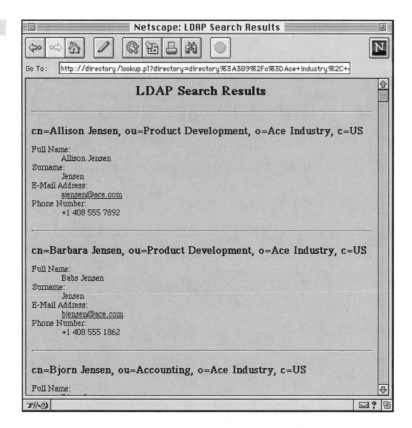

There are many things that could be done to improve the lookup program. The current program only displays one value for an attribute even if many are present. Tables, frames, and other fancier HTML features could be used to spruce up the output. It would be nice to avoid showing Distinguished Names in their raw form—showing just the first part of the DN without the cn= part would be a nice improvement.

Looking Ahead

As this chapter has shown, the LDAP command line tools are very flexible. While not as glamorous, they provide all of the basic functionality that the full LDAP C API does. Since the command line tools are not tied to any particular scripting language, they can easily be used to make an existing script directory-aware. They can also be used to build standalone directory applications ranging from quick-and-dirty utilities that you use once and throw away, to complex directory-centric applications that you deploy across your enterprise. The sky is the limit!

CHAPTER 19

Future Directions

B y now, you should be familiar with LDAP programming, well
on your way to becoming an expert, and more than ready to
begin writing new LDAP applications, or enabling your existing
applications to use LDAP. As you gain experience with LDAP, you will
no doubt find yourself encountering some of LDAP's limitations and
wishing in some cases for more features than it provides.

Throughout this book, we've pointed out various features likely to
be included in LDAP version 3, where they address omissions or
deficiencies with the current version 2 LDAP protocol. This chapter
summarizes the features likely to be provided by LDAPv3, giving you a
preview of what's coming up. We go on to discuss more generally the
future of directory service on the Internet. We cover both potential
protocol extensions beyond LDAPv3 and how we see the use of directories evolving and expanding on the Internet.

LDAP Version 3

At the time of this writing, the IETF was still working on finalizing version 3 of the LDAP protocol. However, as the drafts of the RFCs defining the protocol approach proposed standard status (the first step in the Internet standards process) they have begun to stabilize and the list of features below is a pretty sure bet.

Version 3 of LDAP is compatible with version 2, but it expands the features of the protocol as explained in the following sections.

Information Model

LDAPv3 supports two extensions to the LDAP information model. *Attribute inheritance* allows an attribute to be derived from another attribute, called the parent attribute. Many attributes may be derived from a single parent. The derived attributes act like any other. But the parent attribute has some special properties. If a search or compare is performed on the parent attribute, that attribute and any of its derived attributes can match the query.

For example, LDAPv3 defines an attribute called name. The cn, sn, givenName, and several other name-oriented attributes are also defined, derived from the general name attribute. Clients can easily search all name-oriented attributes by using the name attribute. This is more than a useful shorthand for a search involving any of the known derived attributes. It allows clients to function without change even when new attributes they have never heard of before are derived from the name attribute.

Operational attributes are attributes that the directory maintains for its own purposes. While operational attributes are part of the entry and may be searched and retrieved like other attributes, they have some special properties. Operational attributes are only retrieved when named explicitly in a search request. They may be modifiable by users, like other attributes, or they may be maintained by the directory itself. Several useful features of LDAPv3 will likely be implemented using operational attributes.

For example, LDAPv3 will define two attributes called `modifiersName` and `modifiedTime` that may be automatically set by the LDAP server to reflect the time and DN that last modified an entry. There is also talk in the LDAPv3 community of defining an operational attribute called `modifyRight`. This attribute contains the access the requester has to various fields in the LDAP entry from which it was read. By reading this attribute, a client can determine which attributes of an entry it is allowed to change.

Schema

A known problem with LDAPv2 is that there is no way for a client to discover what schema elements (object classes and attributes) an LDAP server supports. LDAPv2 also is very rigid in its requirement that clients know and follow a well-defined set of schema rules, something not always appropriate for a given application.

Two new extensions to the way schema is handled in LDAP aimed at eliminating these drawbacks have been proposed. First, LDAPv3 may propose a new object class called `extensibleObject`. An entry that contains this special object class is allowed to contain any other attribute, regardless of other directory schema rules. This feature provides a convenient way to turn schema checking off, on a per-entry basis.

Second, LDAPv3 may provide a way for clients to discover the schema elements supported by an LDAP server. This support is provided through operational attributes in a special pseudo-entry called the root DSE. This entry is named with the NULL DN and can only be retrieved with a base object search. Values of the `attributes` attribute contain the definition of attributes supported by the server. Values of the `objectClasses` attribute contain the definition of object classes supported by the server. LDAPv3 servers may allow clients to modify these attributes, providing an online way to modify the LDAP schema rules.

Security

LDAPv3 will undoubtedly support important extensions to the rather weak authentication provided by LDAP version 2. LDAPv3 proposes an extensible authentication mechanism, based on SASL, the simple authentication and session layer. SASL is used by several other Internet protocols to provide authentication, including IMAP, POP, and NNTP.

The LDAP bind operation is being extended so that arbitrary credentials may be passed, authenticating client to server and server to client. Multi-step authentication methods are supported. In addition, LDAPv3 is officially sanctioned for use over SSL, providing additional lower-level security and privacy capabilities, as described in Chapter 13.

Internationalization

Among the most severe limitations with LDAP version 2 are its lack of support for non-ASCII character sets and non-English conventions for representing and presenting data. Another safe bet is that LDAPv3 will remove these limitations through the addition of three new features. First, textual data in LDAPv3 is carried in the UTF-8 character set instead of ASCII or T.61. UTF-8 is an encoding of the UNICODE universal character set in which the ASCII values 0 through 128 are preserved. This feature allows values in any character set to be represented.

Second, LDAPv3 will define a way for a client to select a preferred language. This selection will control how values supplied by the client are interpreted by the server, and the language and representation of data the server returns to the client.

Third, two new features of the search operation have been proposed in the LDAPv3 discussion. These features allow searches and search results to be customized based on different international conventions. Under the current proposal, search filters can be extended with arbitrary new matching rules. The new rules are identified by object identifiers. The search request in LDAPv3 can include a set of attributes and collation rules used to sort the results of the search. This feature allows entries to be sorted according to different national conventions.

Referrals

This feature is one of the most important additions to LDAPv3. As we discussed briefly in Chapter 3, in version 2 of LDAP, there is no way for a server to direct a client to other servers. An LDAPv2 server is required to answer the requests it receives or return an error. While both the University of Michigan and Netscape SDKs work around this limitation and support referrals in LDAPv2 through the use of a slightly kludgey protocol "back door," in LDAPv3, new protocol elements are being added to support referrals explicitly.

Search

Some more questionable features that may or may not end up in LDAPv3 include various extensions to the search operation. One LDAP version 3 proposal extends the search operation in a few simple ways, providing better extensibility and scalability. LDAPv3 allows the client to request that search results come back sorted. Multiple sort keys may be specified, along with different matching rules. Clients can also request extensible matching rules when searching.

In LDAP version 2, there is no way to separate search from retrieval. All entries matching a search come back to the client at once. If the client's search returns a lot of entries, this could take some time. The LDAPv3 search extension proposal introduces the concept of paged results from a search. Under this proposal an LDAPv3 client can request that the results of its search be sent back a page at a time, where the page size is specified by the client. Having retrieved the first page, the client can then retrieve other pages from the set of search results. There is no requirement that the pages retrieved be contiguous, allowing the client to window around within the result set.

The paged result feature is aimed at allowing the implementation of a "type down" interface, in which the user types the first letters of a desired name and is presented with a scrolling list of possible matches.

Extensibility

LDAP version 3 will undoubtedly include the ability to define extended operations. Using this feature, it's possible to extend the LDAP protocol without changing the protocol version. This feature is being used to enable at least one new feature in LDAPv3: support for dynamic directories. Dynamic directory information behaves like static information, but it is updated more frequently and must be refreshed by the client from time to time or the directory server will remove it.

The canonical example of such information is the IP address of a mobile user. When the user logs in, her IP address is registered in the directory. As long as the user is online and periodically refreshing the address, it remains in the directory. Otherwise, it is removed from the directory automatically.

Beyond LDAPv3

LDAP version 3 is designed to be extensible. If all goes well, these extensibility mechanisms can be used to add new features as they are required, and it will be a long time before another revision of the core protocol is needed. The possibilities for additional protocol features using the LDAPv3 extensibility mechanism are many.

One extension that has already been discussed is support for transactions. In LDAPv2, each update operation (add, delete, modify, or modify RDN) is automatic. Some applications may require a sequence of updates to be automatic. For example, suppose we want to change several entries in the directory at once. Either all the entries must be changed, or none of them should be changed.

By defining LDAPv3 extended operations for "begin transaction," "commit transaction," and "abort transaction," a client can wrap the sequence of operations it would like to be atomic. If some client or server failure occurs midway through the sequence of updates, all of the changes will be rolled back, leaving the directory in a consistent state.

New search operations can be defined by using the extensible matching rules provided by the LDAPv3 search operation. This is a powerful extensibility mechanism that can be used to provide all kinds of different searching mechanisms. Free-text search, nickname or spelling variation searches, sound-alike searches, or other more complicated searching algorithms can all be implemented using extensible matching rules, making this an important feature to get into the core of LDAPv3.

The Future of Directories

So far, the applications driving directories on the Internet are white pages and user and group management. In these applications, LDAP makes it possible to find users locally as easily as remotely. Users within an organization can be managed in a single, logically central location.

Close seconds to user and group management are user preference and server configuration storage. The former allows users to access their environment from anywhere on the network. The latter facilitates enterprise-wide server configuration and makes it easy both to bring up new services on a network and to change the configuration of a group of servers all at once.

As these applications of directory service and others become more widespread on the Internet and corporate intranets, LDAP will become as ubiquitous and second-nature to use as the DNS is today. Dynamic directory information will become more widespread as mobile computing (and therefore the need to dynamically change location and other information about users) becomes common.

Beyond static and dynamic directory information is the as yet untapped realm of *active* directory information. Imagine a directory attribute that does not merely hold static or dynamic information. Instead, it holds an active program or agent that will compute, retrieve, or otherwise create on the fly the information making up the attribute. Such attributes might be expressed in a cross-platform network-enabled language such as Java or JavaScript. While the applications of such technology are as yet unclear, the potential is exciting.

Better Living Through Directories

In summary, directories have a bright future on the Internet, and LDAP promises to make life easier for both users and application developers. From a central place to store and find information about yourself and other users, to a general configuration, preference, and management store for enterprise-wide administration, LDAP clearly has the potential to deliver on the promise of a distributed computing environment. LDAP provides the glue holding the elements of the Internet together into a cohesive whole.

Of course, integration with applications is the key to unlocking this potential. While this integration may not actually provide better living, it certainly will provide better computing, which, depending on your perspective, may amount to the same thing.

As you go forth into the world of LDAP programming, hopefully you will take with you some useful information learned in this book. As your experience increases and you learn more about LDAP, feel free to drop us a line with any suggestions you have for improving this book, or with any interesting LDAP experiences you have (good or bad). You can reach us on the Internet at the following addresses:

Tim Howes `<howes@netscape.com>`

Mark Smith `<mcs@netscape.com>`

LDAP Resources

This appendix provides pointers to many LDAP-related resources. These resources range from text documents to mailing lists to World Wide Web pages. Most of these resources are available on the Internet, so we provide an URL for them. Like all Internet resources, there is some chance that the location may change, so be sure to check the World Wide Web page for this book for the latest scoop. You can find it at `http://www.mcp.com/newriders/`.

General LDAP Resources

The University of Michigan LDAP Home Page

`http://www.umich.edu/~rsug/ldap/`

This is the first and still one of the best LDAP Web sites (this is actually the entry point to a whole series of pages). It includes pointers to many of the other resources that are listed in this appendix, and includes on-line documentation for the University of Michigan (U-M) LDAP SDK and other LDAP software. Since the authors left U-M, this site hasn't been updated as often as it used to be, but it is still one of the best sources of information on LDAP.

Critical Angle's LDAP World

`http://www.critical-angle.com/ldapworld/`

This site aims to "provide current information on the status of the LDAP specifications, availability of LDAP products, and deployment of LDAP-based directories" and does a very credible job. Includes a Frequently Asked Questions (FAQ) list, a survey of available LDAP implementations, and up-to-date information on version 3 of the LDAP protocol (LDAPv3). Maintained as a public service by Mark Wahl of Critical Angle, Inc.

X.500 & LDAP: Road Map & FAQ

`http://www-leland.stanford.edu/group/networking/directory/`
`x500ldapfaq.html`

This site offers a good overview that includes pointers to an impressive array of X.500 and LDAP-related documents. Maintained by Jeff Hodges of Stanford University.

LDAP Software and SDKs

The University of Michigan LDAP Package

```
ftp://terminator.rs.itd.umich.edu/ldap/
```

Distributed mainly in source form, this is the LDAP implementation on which many organizations, including Netscape, have based their LDAP products. Supports Windows 3.1, Windows 95/NT, Macintosh, and many UNIX platforms. Copyrighted but free, this code can be used to build non-commercial and commercial applications alike.

The Netscape LDAP SDK

```
http://developer.netscape.com/library/
```

This SDK supports Windows 3.1, Windows 95/NT, Macintosh, and all popular UNIX platforms. Available free of additional charge to members of the Netscape Developer Program (DevEdge), it is expected that the Netscape LDAP SDK will be bundled with their Directory Server product in the future as well.

Netscape Directory Server

```
http://home.netscape.com/comprod/server_central/
```

This is perhaps the best example of a commercial server that supports LDAP. Of course, we may be a bit biased, since we are part of the team that wrote it! Based on the University of Michigan SLAPD server with many bug fixes and enhancements, the Netscape Directory Server now contains many new features and tools to make administration of the server easier. The server runs on Windows NT and most popular UNIX platforms. It can be downloaded free of charge for customer "test drives."

Public Internet Mailing Lists

LDAP Discussion List

`ldap@umich.edu`

To join the list: `mailto:ldap-request@umich.edu`
List archive: `ftp://terminator.rs.itd.umich.edu/ldap/archive`

Started at and still maintained by the University of Michigan, this list was originally for people interested in the U-M LDAP implementation but has grown into a more general-purpose LDAP mailing list. At the time of this writing, the list volume is moderately low (5–10 messages per week).

IETF ASID List

`ietf-asid@umich.edu`

To join the list: `mailto:ietf-asid-request@umich.edu`
List archive: `ftp://terminator.rs.itd.umich.edu/ietf-asid/`

The Access and searching of Internet Directories working group of the Internet Engineering Task Force (IETF) is responsible for defining and progressing the LDAP standards. Like all IETF working groups, it is open to everyone without fee or prejudice. At the time of this writing, the list volume is fairly moderate (about 20 messages per week) but be warned that the volume spikes to very high levels when a hot issue is being discussed.

IETF IDS List

`ietf-ids@umich.edu`

To join the list: `mailto:ietf-ids-request@umich.edu`
List archive: `ftp://terminator.rs.itd.umich.edu/ietf-ids/`

The Integrated Directory Service working group is another IETF working group. IDS was chartered to "facilitate the integration and interoperability of current and future directories on the Internet." To accomplish this lofty goal, IDS works on directory service issues that are common to LDAP and other protocols such as WHOIS++. Examples of such issues include schema definition, legal and privacy issues, and tracking the status of directory pilot projects. Like all IETF working groups, this group is open to all who want to participate and have something to contribute. At the time of this writing, the list volume is fairly low (5–10 messages per week).

Technical Papers

The Lightweight Directory Access Protocol: X.500 Lite (CITI Tech Report 95-8)

```
ftp://terminator.rs.itd.umich.edu/ldap/papers/ldap.ps
```

```
http://www-leland.stanford.edu/group/networking/directory/doc/
ldap/ldap.html
```

Written by one of the authors (Tim), this paper provides a good introduction to LDAP and compares it with the X.500 family of protocols.

A Scalable, Deployable, Directory Service Framework for the Internet

```
http://info.isoc.org:80/HMP/PAPER/173/html/paper.html
```

Written by the authors and published as part of the INET '95 Conference Proceedings, this paper describes an experimental approach to solving the global Internet directory problem through the use of LDAP and the Domain Name System (DNS).

RFCs and Internet Drafts

Lightweight Directory Access Protocol (RFC-1777 and proposed revision)

```
ftp://ds.internic.net/rfc/rfc1777.txt
```

```
ftp://ftp.ietf.org/internet-drafts/draft-ietf-asid-ldapv2-
protocol-00.txt
```

This document defines version 2 of the Lightweight Directory Access Protocol itself. This is a fairly technical document that assumes some knowledge of the X.500 standards. It is an Internet standards track document.

String Representation of Standard Attribute Syntaxes (RFC-1778 and proposed revision)

```
ftp://ds.internic.net/rfc/rfc1778.txt
```

```
ftp://ftp.ietf.org/internet-drafts/draft-ietf-asid-ldapv2-
attributes-00.txt
```

A companion to RFC-1777, this document lists many attribute types supported in LDAP and shows how they are represented as text strings. It is an Internet standards track document.

A String Representation of Distinguished Names (RFC 1779)

```
ftp://ds.internic.net/rfc/rfc1778.txt
```

This RFC defines the format of DNs used within the LDAP protocol (and the LDAP SDKs discussed in this book). An Internet standards track document.

A String Representation of LDAP Search Filters (RFC 1960 and proposed update)

```
ftp://ds.internic.net/rfc/rfc1960.txt
```

```
ftp://ftp.ietf.org/internet-drafts/draft-ietf-asid-string-
filter-v2-00.txt
```

RFC 1960 contains the official definition of the LDAP search filter format used in the LDAP API. It is an Internet standards track document. The proposed revision updates the format to accommodate new features included in LDAPv3.

An LDAP URL Format (RFC 1959)

```
ftp://ds.internic.net/rfc/rfc1959.txt
```

This is the official definition of the LDAP URL format. It is an Internet standards track document.

The LDAP Application Program Interface (RFC 1823 and proposed revision)

```
ftp://ds.internic.net/rfc/rfc1823.txt
```

```
ftp://ftp.ietf.org//internet-drafts/draft-howes-ldap-api-
00.txt
```

RFC 1832 is an informational RFC (not on the standards track) that describes a subset of the University of Michigan LDAP API as it was defined in early 1995. The proposed revision takes into account recent changes made by Netscape and others and also includes some additional proposed API calls to support LDAPv3.

Connection-less Lightweight Directory Access Protocol (RFC 1798)

```
ftp://ds.internic.net/rfc/rfc1798.txt
```

This RFC defines a variation of LDAPv2 for use over connectionless transports such as UDP. It is an Internet standards track document.

Lightweight Directory Access Protocol (v3)

```
ftp://ftp.ietf.org//internet-drafts/draft-ietf-asid-ldapv3-
protocol-03.txt
```

This is the latest proposal for version 3 of the LDAP protocol. This document will eventually replace the LDAPv2 equivalent (RFC-1777 and its descendants). Beware that this document is currently being worked on at the time of this writing. Its name may well change (for example, the 3 could change to a 4).

LDAPv3: Standard and Pilot Attribute Definitions

```
ftp://ftp.ietf.org//internet-drafts/draft-ietf-asid-ldapv3-
attributes-03.txt
```

This document lists many attribute types supported in LDAPv3 and shows how they are represented as text strings. It will eventually replace the LDAPv2 equivalent (RFC-1778 and its descendants). Beware that this document is currently being worked on at the time of this writing. Its name may well change (for example, the 3 could change to a 4).

LDAPv3: UTF-8 String Representation of Distinguished Names

```
ftp://ftp.ietf.org//internet-drafts/draft-ietf-asid-ldapv3-dn-
00.txt
```

This document defines the string representation of DNs for LDAPv3. This document will eventually replace the LDAPv2 equivalent (RFC-1779 and its descendants).

LDAPv3: Extensions for Dynamic Directory Services

```
ftp://ftp.ietf.org//internet-drafts/draft-ietf-asid-ldapv3ext-
02.txt
```

This document describes a proposed extension for LDAPv3 that supports attributes whose values are valid only for brief periods of time such as while a user of an online service is actually connected to the service.

LDAPv3: Identifying Languages

```
ftp://ftp.ietf.org//internet-drafts/draft-ietf-asid-ldapv3-
lang.txt
```

This document describes how an indication of natural language can be associated with LDAP attributes and values, and how servers should interpret this langauage information. This feature is designed to support storage of LDAP directory information in languages other than U.S. English (for example, French, German, or Chinese).

X.500 and OSI-Related Resources

X.500 Directories Site at NEXOR

`http://web.nexor.co.uk/users/cjr/x500.html`

One-stop shopping for X.500 standards information, this page also contains pointers to directory service pilot activities, standards groups, and other useful information. Maintained by Colin Robins of NEXOR Ltd.

International Telecommunications Union Web Site

`http://www.itu.ch/`

This is the official source for all OSI standards documents, including the X.500 series of documents. Note that most documents are not freely available and you must pay a subscription fee to obtain access to them.

A Layman's Guide to a Subset of ASN.1, BER, and DER

`http://www.rsa.com/ftpdir/pub/pkcs/ascii/layman.asc`

This site provides a good introduction to a subset of OSI's Abstract Syntax Notation One (ASN.1), Basic Encoding Rules (BER), and Distinguished Encoding Rules (DER), which are the network encoding rules that LDAP uses. Published as part of RSA Data Security, Inc.'s Public-Key Cryptography Standards (PKCS).

LDAP API Reference

This appendix provides a summary of all the LDAP API functions and data structures discussed in this book. Most of the functions that are provided by the University of Michigan and Netscape LDAP Software Development Kits are listed here.

LDAP API Functions

ber_free()   See Chapter 9

Disposes of a BerElement structure.

Prototype:

```
void ber_free( BerElement *ber, int freebuf );
```

Parameters:

`BerElement *ber`: Pointer to a BerElement structure, as allocated by `ldap_get_first_attribute()` to track the attribute to return next.

`int freebuf`: A flag used to specify if a temporary buffer maintained within the BerElement should be freed. If you are using `ldap_first_attribute()` and `ldap_next_attribute()`, you will always pass zero for this parameter.

See Also:

`ldap_first_attribute()`, `ldap_next_attribute()`

ber_bvecfree()   See Chapter 9

Disposes of an array of pointers to struct berval structures.

Prototype:

```
void ber_bvecfree( struct berval **bvp );
```

Parameters:

`struct berval **bvp`: An array of pointers to struct berval structures, as returned by `ldap_get_values_len()`.

See Also:

`ldap_get_values_len()`

ldap_abandon()   See Chapter 9

Cancels an LDAP operation that has not yet completed.

Prototype:

```
int ldap_abandon( LDAP *ld, int msgid );
```

Return Value:

An LDAP error code.

Parameters:

LDAP *ld: An LDAP session handle.

int msgid: The message id of the operation to cancel (as returned by a call to one of the asynchronous LDAP operation functions).

ldap_add()   See Chapter 14

Initiates an LDAP add entry operation.

Prototype:

```
int ldap_add( LDAP *ld, char *entrydn, LDAPMod **attrs );
```

Return Value:

An LDAP message id or −1 if an error occurs.

Parameters:

LDAP *ld: An LDAP session handle.

char *entrydn: The name of the directory entry to create.

LDAPMod **attrs: This parameter specifies the attributes of the new directory entry named by the entrydn parameter. It is a NULL-terminated array of pointers to LDAPMod structures. Each LDAPMod structure describes one attribute of the new entry.

See Also:

ldap_add_s()

ldap_add_s()   See Chapter 14

Adds an entry to the directory.

Prototype:

int ldap_add_s(LDAP *ld, char *entrydn, LDAPMod **attrs);

Return Value:

An LDAP error code.

Parameters:

LDAP *ld: An LDAP session handle.

char *entrydn: The name of the directory entry to create.

LDAPMod **attrs: This parameter specifies the attributes of the new directory entry named by the entrydn parameter. It is a NULL-terminated array of pointers to LDAPMod structures. Each LDAPMod structure describes one attribute of the new entry.

See Also:

ldap_add()

ldap_bind()   See Chapter 13

Initiates an LDAP bind operation to identify, or authenticate, your application to the directory server using a Distinguished Name and some arbitrary credentials.

Prototype:

int ldap_bind(LDAP *ld, char *dn, char *creds, int method);

Returns:

An LDAP message id or −1 if an error occurs.

Parameters:

LDAP *ld: An LDAP session handle.

char *dn: Distinguished Name of the entry that is binding to the directory. Pass NULL or a zero-length string to perform an unauthenticated bind.

char *creds: A pointer to the authentication credentials. For simple password binds, this is a pointer to the password.

int method: Which authentication method to use. For simple password-based authentication, pass LDAP_AUTH_SIMPLE.

See Also:

ldap_bind_s(), ldap_result(), ldap_simple_bind(),
ldap_simple_bind_s(), ldap_set_rebind_proc()

ldap_bind_s()   See Chapter 13

Synchronously authenticates to the directory server using a Distinguished Name and some arbitrary credentials.

Prototype:

int ldap_bind_s(LDAP *ld, char *dn, char *passwd, int method);

Return Value:

An LDAP error code.

Parameters:

LDAP *ld: An LDAP session handle.

char *`dn`: The Distinguished Name of the entry that is binding to the directory. Pass `NULL` or a zero-length string to perform an unauthenticated bind.

char *`creds`: A pointer to the authentication credentials. For simple password binds, this is a pointer to the password.

int `method`: Which authentication method to use. For simple password-based authentication, pass `LDAP_AUTH_SIMPLE`.

See Also:

```
ldap_bind(), ldap_result(), ldap_simple_bind(),
ldap_simple_bind_s(), ldap_set_rebind_proc()
```

ldap_compare()   See Chapter 12

Initiates an LDAP operation to compare a value with an attribute value contained in an entry.

Prototype:

```
int ldap_compare( LDAP *ld, char *entrydn, char *type, char *value );
```

Return Value:

An LDAP message id or –1 if an error occurs.

Parameters:

LDAP *`ld`: An LDAP session handle.

char *`entrydn`: The name of the directory entry to perform the compare against.

char *`type`: The type portion of the attribute value assertion to test the entry for.

char *`value`: The value portion of the attribute value assertion to test the entry for.

See Also:

ldap_compare_s()

ldap_compare_s()   See Chapter 12

Compares a value with an attribute value contained in an entry.

Prototype:

```
int ldap_compare_s( LDAP *ld, char *entrydn, char *type, char
➥*value );
```

Return Value:

An LDAP error code.

Parameters:

LDAP *ld: An LDAP session handle.

char *entrydn: The name of the directory entry to perform the compare against.

char *type: The type portion of the attribute value assertion to test the entry for.

char *value: The value portion of the attribute value assertion to test the entry for.

See Also:

ldap_compare()

ldap_count_entries()   See Chapter 9

Determines the number of entries in an LDAP result message chain.

Prototype:

```
int ldap_count_entries( LDAP *ld, LDAPMessage *result );
```

Return Value:

The number of entries in the search result or –1 in case of error.

Parameters:

LDAP *ld: An LDAP session handle.

LDAPMessage *result: The search result, as returned by a successful call to ldap_search_s(), ldap_search_st(), or ldap_result().

See Also:

ldap_count_values(), ldap_count_values_len()

ldap_count_values()   See Chapter 9

Counts the number of values returned by ldap_get_values().

Prototype:

int ldap_count_values(char **values);

Return Value:

The number of values in the array.

Parameters:

char **values: The array of values.

See Also:

ldap_count_values_len(), ldap_get_values()

ldap_count_values_len()   See Chapter 9

Counts the number of values returned by ldap_get_values_len().

Prototype:

```
int ldap_count_values_len( struct berval **bvalues );
```

Return Value:

The number of values in the array.

Parameters:

`char **bvalues`: The array of values.

See Also:

`ldap_count_values ()`, `ldap_get_values_len()`

ldap_delete()   See Chapter 14

Initiates an LDAP delete entry operation.

Prototype:

```
int ldap_delete( LDAP *ld, char *entrydn );
```

Return Value:

An LDAP message id or –1 if an error occurs.

Parameters:

`LDAP *ld`: An LDAP session handle.

`char *entrydn`: The name of the directory entry to be removed.

See Also:

`ldap_delete_s()`

ldap_delete_s()   See Chapter 14

Deletes a directory entry.

Prototype:

```
int ldap_delete_s( LDAP *ld, char *entrydn );
```

Return Value:

An LDAP error code.

Parameters:

LDAP *ld: An LDAP session handle.

char *entrydn: The name of the directory entry to be removed.

See Also:

ldap_delete()

ldap_dn2ufn()   See Chapter 11

Converts a Distinguished Name (DN) into an easier-to-read form called a User Friendly Name (UFN).

Prototype:

```
char *ldap_dn2ufn( char *dn );
```

Return Value:

A pointer to a string that contains the UFN-form of a DN. If for some reason the DN cannot be converted, NULL is returned.

Parameters:

char *dn: An LDAP Distinguished Name.

See Also:

ldap_get_dn()

ldap_err2string()   See Chapter 8

Retrieves the error message string that corresponds to an LDAP error code.

Prototype:

```
char *ldap_err2string( int err );
```

Return Value:

A pointer to a static LDAP error string.

Parameters:

int *err*: An LDAP error code.

See Also:

ldap_perror(), ldap_get_lderrno(), ldap_result2error()

ldap_explode_dn()   See Chapter 11

Breaks a Distinguished Name (DN) up into its components.

Prototype:

```
char **ldap_explode_dn( char *dn, int notypes );
```

Return Value:

A pointer to a NULL-terminated array of character strings. If for some reason the DN cannot be broken up, NULL is returned.

Parameters:

char *dn: An LDAP Distinguished Name.

int *notypes*: A Boolean parameter that, if non-zero, causes the attribute type tags to be removed from the components returned.

See Also:

ldap_explode_rdn(), ldap_get_dn()

ldap_explode_rdn()   See Chapter 11

Breaks a Relative Distinguished Name (RDN) up into its components.

Prototype:

char **ldap_explode_rdn(char *rdn, int notypes);

Return Value:

A pointer to a NULL-terminated array of character strings. If the RDN cannot be broken up, NULL is returned.

Parameters:

char *rdn: An LDAP Relative Distinguished Name.

int notypes: A Boolean parameter that, if non-zero, causes the attribute type tags to be removed from the components returned.

See Also:

ldap_explode_dn(), ldap_get_dn()

ldap_first_attribute()   See Chapter 9

Returns the first attribute in an entry.

Prototype:

char *ldap_first_attribute(LDAP *ld, LDAPMessage *entry, BerElement ↪**ber);

Return Value:

A pointer to a copy of the first attribute or NULL if no attributes or an error occurs. This must be freed by calling ldap_memfree().

Parameters:

LDAP *ld*: An LDAP session handle.

LDAPMessage *entry*: The entry whose first attribute is to be returned. The entry must have been returned from a successful call to ldap_first_entry() or ldap_next_entry().

BerElement **ber*: A pointer to a pointer to an opaque data type that the ldap_first_attribute() and ldap_next_attribute() routines fill in and use to keep track of their position in the current entry.

See Also:

ldap_next_attribute(), ldap_first_entry(), ldap_next_entry()

ldap_first_entry()   See Chapter 9

Returns the first entry in a chain of results.

Prototype:

LDAPMessage *ldap_first_entry(LDAP *ld*, LDAPMessage *result*);

Return Value:

An LDAP entry handle or NULL if no entries or an error occurs.

Parameters:

LDAP *ld*: An LDAP session handle.

LDAPMessage *result*: The result of the search, obtained from a successful call to ldap_search_s(), ldap_search_st(), or ldap_result().

See Also:

ldap_next_entry(), ldap_search_s(), ldap_search_st, ldap_result()

ldap_free_urldesc()   See Chapter 15

Frees an URL description structure that was allocated by
ldap_url_parse().

Prototype:

void ldap_free_urldesc(LDAPURLDesc *ludp);

Parameter:

LDAPURLDesc *ludp: Pointer to an LDAP URL description structure.

See Also:

ldap_url_parse(), LDAPURLDesc

ldap_get_dn()   See Chapters 9 and 11

Retrieves the Distinguished Name of an entry.

Prototype:

char *ldap_get_dn(LDAP *ld, LDAPMessage *entry);

Return Value:

A pointer to the name of the entry or NULL if an error occurs. This must
be freed by calling ldap_memfree().

Parameters:

LDAP *ld: An LDAP session handle.

LDAPMessage *entry: The entry whose DN is to be returned. The entry
must have been returned from a successful call to ldap_first_entry()
or ldap_next_entry().

See Also:

```
ldap_first_entry(), ldap_next_entry()
```

ldap_getfilter_free() See Chapter 10

Frees resources allocated by `ldap_init_getfilter()`.

Prototype:

```
void ldap_getfilter_free( LDAPFilterDesc *fd );
```

Parameters:

`LDAPFilterDesc *fd`: A handle to an initialized *getfilter* configuration file, as returned from a successful call to `ldap_init_getfilter()`.

See Also:

```
ldap_init_getfilter()
```

ldap_getfirstfilter() See Chapter 10

Retrieves the first matching filter from a *getfilter* file.

Prototype:

```
LDAPFiltInfo *ldap_getfirstfilter( LDAPFilterDesc *fd, char *tag,
➥char *input );
```

Return Value:

A pointer to an `LDAPFiltInfo` structure containing information about the filter that was matched or `NULL` if no filters match the given input or an error occurs.

Parameters:

`LDAPFilterDesc *fd`: A handle to an initialized *getfilter* configuration file, as returned from a successful call to `ldap_init_getfilter()`.

char *`tag`: The tag at the head of the desired stanza within the filter configuration file. Tags are examined in the order in which they appear in the file to find a match.

char *`input`: String to match against the regular expressions in the *getfilter* file.

See Also:

`ldap_init_getfilter()`, `ldap_getnextfilter()`

ldap_getmsgid()   See Chapter 9

Extracts the message id from an LDAP result. Available in the Netscape SDK only.

Prototype:

`int ldap_getmsgid( LDAP *ld, LDAPMessage *result );`

Return Value:

The message id.

Parameters:

LDAP *`ld`: An LDAP session handle.

LDAPMessage *`result`: The result of the search, obtained from a successful call to `ldap_search_s()`, `ldap_search_st()`, or `ldap_result()`.

ldap_get_lderrno()   See Chapter 8

Retrieves information about the most recent LDAP error that occurred. Available in the Netscape SDK only.

Prototype:

`int ldap_get_lderrno( LDAP *ld, char **matched, char **msg );`

Return Value:

The LDAP error code returned by the most recent LDAP operation or API call.

Parameters:

LDAP *ld: An LDAP session handle.

char **matched: If a non-NULL pointer is passed, it will be set to point to a string that represents the portion of the Distinguished Name that was matched by the last LDAP operation.

char **msg: If a non-NULL pointer is passed, it will be set to point to the extra error message string that was returned by the server, if any.

See Also:

ldap_err2string(), ldap_perror(), ldap_result2error()

ldap_getnextfilter()   See Chapter 10

Retrieves the next matching filter from a *getfilter* file.

Prototype:

LDAPFiltInfo *ldap_getnextfilter(LDAPFilterDesc *fd);

Return Value:

The next matching filter string or NULL if no more filters are available or an error occurs.

Parameters:

LDAPFilterDesc *fd: A handle to an initialized *getfilter* configuration file, as returned from a successful call to ldap_init_getfilter().

See Also:

ldap_get_firstfilter(), ldap_init_getfilter()

ldap_get_option()   See Chapter 6

Retrieves the current setting of an LDAP session option. Available in the Netscape SDK only.

Prototype:

`int ldap_get_option( LDAP *ld, unsigned long option, void *out );`

Return Value:

Zero if successful, non-zero otherwise.

Parameters:

`LDAP *ld`: An LDAP session handle.

`unsigned long option`: The option to retrieve. One of the following constants:

```
LDAP_OPT_DEREF
LDAP_OPT_DESC
LDAP_OPT_IO_FN_PTRS
LDAP_OPT_REBIND_FN
LDAP_OPT_REBIND_ARG
LDAP_OPT_REFERRALS
LDAP_OPT_SIZELIMIT
LDAP_OPT_SSL
LDAP_OPT_THREAD_FN_PTRS
LDAP_OPT_TIMELIMIT
```

`void *out`: A pointer to the place to store the value of the retrieved option. The appropriate type to pass depends on what option is being retrieved.

See Also:

`ldap_set_option()`

ldap_get_values()   See Chapter 9

Retrieves a set of attribute values from an entry.

Prototype:

```
char **ldap_get_values( LDAP *ld, LDAPMessage *entry, char *attr );
```

Return Value:

A NULL-terminated array of character strings, or NULL if the attribute does not exist in the entry, the attribute contains no values, or some error occurred.

Parameters:

LDAP *ld: An LDAP session handle.

LDAPMessage *entry: The entry whose first attribute is to be returned. The entry must have been returned from a successful call to ldap_first_entry() or ldap_next_entry().

char *attr: The name of the attribute whose values are to be retrieved from the entry.

See Also:

```
ldap_get_values_len(), ldap_value_free()
```

ldap_get_values_len()   See Chapter 9

Retrieves a set of binary attribute values from an entry.

Prototype:

```
struct berval **ldap_get_values_len( LDAP *ld, LDAPMessage *entry,
⮕char *attr );
```

Return Value:

A `NULL`-terminated array of berval structures or `NULL` if the attribute does not exist in the entry, the attribute contains no values, or some error occurred.

Parameters:

`LDAP *ld`: An LDAP session handle.

`LDAPMessage *entry`: The entry whose first attribute is to be returned. The entry must have been returned from a successful call to `ldap_first_entry()` or `ldap_next_entry()`.

`char *attr`: The name of the attribute whose values are to be retrieved from the entry.

See Also:

`ldap_get_values()`, `ber_bvecfree()`

ldap_init()   See Chapter 6

Initializes the LDAP library and return a session handle for use in subsequent calls.

Prototype:

`LDAP *ldap_init( char *defhost, int defport );`

Return Value:

An LDAP session handle. If an error occurs, `NULL` is returned.

Parameters:

`char *defhost`: host name of the default LDAP server.

`int defport`: TCP port of the default LDAP server. Pass zero or `LDAP_PORT` to use the standard LDAP port of 389. If you are using the

Netscape SDK, you can pass `LDAPS_PORT` to indicate that the standard SSL port of 636 should be used.

See Also:

`ldap_open()`, `ldap_unbind()`

ldap_init_getfilter()   See Chapter 10

Reads a filter configuration file and initialize the *getfilter* system.

Prototype:

`LDAPFilterDesc *ldap_init_getfilter( char *filterfile );`

Return Value:

A handle to the initialized filter file or `NULL` if the file could not be read.

Parameter:

`char *filterfile`: The name of the *getfilter* configuration file to read.

See Also:

`ldap_init_getfilter_buf()`, `ldap_getfirstfilter()`, `ldap_getnextfilter()`

ldap_init_getfilter_buf()   See Chapter 10

Reads filter configuration information from an in-memory buffer.

Prototype:

`LDAPFilterDesc *ldap_init_getfilter_buf( char *buf, long buflen );`

Return Value:

A handle to the initialized filter file or `NULL` if the file could not be read.

Parameters:

char *buf: A pointer to memory that contains the contents of a *get-filter* configuration file or the equivalent.

long *buflen*: The length of *buf* in bytes.

See Also:

ldap_init_getfilter(), ldap_getfirstfilter(),
ldap_getnextfilter()

ldap_is_ldap_url()   See Chapter 15

Checks a string to see if it looks like an LDAP URL.

Prototype:

int ldap_is_ldap_url(char *url);

Return Value:

Non-zero if the *url* parameter looks like an LDAP URL; zero if not.

Parameters:

char *url: A string that may (or may not) be an LDAP URL.

See Also:

ldap_url_parse()

ldap_memfree()   See Chapter 9

Disposes of memory allocated by an LDAP API function.

Prototype:

void ldap_memfree(void *p);

Parameter:

void *p: Pointer to memory to be freed, as returned by LDAP API functions that return simple strings such as ldap_get_dn(), ldap_dn2ufn(), and others.

See Also:

ber_free(), ldap_msgfree(), ldap_value_free(), ldap_value_free(), ldap_getfilter_free(), ldap_free_urldesc()

ldap_msgfree()   See Chapter 9

Disposes of an LDAP result message.

Prototype:

int ldap_msgfree(LDAPMessage *result);

Return Value:

The type of the result message freed (see the description of the ldap_result() return value for a list of possible values).

Parameters:

LDAPMessage *result: The result of the search, obtained from a successful call to ldap_search_s(), ldap_search_st(), or ldap_result().

See Also:

ldap_result()

ldap_modify()   See Chapter 14

Initiates an operation to modify a directory entry.

Prototype:

int ldap_modify(LDAP *ld, char *entrydn, LDAPMod **mods);

Return Value:

An LDAP message id or –1 if an error occurs.

Parameters:

`LDAP *ld`: An LDAP session handle.

`char *entrydn`: The name of the directory entry whose contents are to be modified. The entry must exist in the directory already.

`LDAPMod **mods`: The modifications to make to the directory entry named by the *entrydn* parameter. It is a `NULL`-terminated array of pointers to `LDAPMod` structures. Each `LDAPMod` structure describes one sub-modification to make to the entry.

See Also:

`ldap_modify_s()`, `ldap_add_s()`, `ldap_modrdn2_s()`, `ldap_result()`

ldap_modify_s()   See Chapter 14

Modifies a directory entry.

Prototype:

`int ldap_modify_s( LDAP *ld, char *entrydn, LDAPMod **mods );`

Return Value:

An LDAP error code.

Parameters:

`LDAP *ld`: An LDAP session handle.

`char *entrydn`: The name of the directory entry whose contents are to be modified. The entry must exist in the directory already.

`LDAPMod **mods`: The modifications to make to the directory entry named by the *entrydn* parameter. It is a `NULL`-terminated array of pointers to `LDAPMod` structures. Each `LDAPMod` structure describes one sub-modification to make to the entry.

See Also:

`ldap_modify()`, `ldap_add_s()`, `ldap_modrdn2_s()`

ldap_modrdn2()   See Chapter 14

Initiates an LDAP operation to change the name of an entry.

Prototype:

`int ldap_modrdn2( LDAP *ld, char *entrydn, char *newrdn, int deleteoldrdn );`

Return Value:

An LDAP message id or −1 if an error occurs.

Parameters:

`LDAP *ld`: An LDAP session handle.

`char *entrydn`: The name of the directory entry to be renamed. This entry must be a leaf in the LDAP directory tree.

`char *newrdn`: The new name of the entry.

`int deleteoldrdn`: A Boolean flag that if non-zero indicates that the attribute values from the old name should be removed from the entry.

See Also:

`ldap_modrdn2_s()`, `ldap_result()`

ldap_modrdn2_s()   See Chapter 14

Changes the name of an entry.

Prototype:

```
int ldap_modrdn2_s( LDAP *ld, char *entrydn, char *newrdn, int
➥deleteoldrdn );
```

Return Value:

An LDAP error code.

Parameters:

`LDAP *ld`: An LDAP session handle.

`char *entrydn`: The name of the directory entry to be renamed. This entry must be a leaf in the LDAP directory tree.

`char *newrdn`: The new name of the entry.

`int deleteoldrdn`: A Boolean flag that if non-zero indicates that the attribute values from the old name should be removed from the entry.

See Also:

`ldap_modrdn2()`

ldap_next_attribute()   See Chapter 9

Returns the next attribute contained in an entry.

Prototype:

```
char *ldap_next_attribute(LDAP *ld, LDAPMessage *entry, BerElement
➥*ber );
```

Return Value:

A pointer to a copy of the first attribute or `NULL` if no attributes or an error occurs. This must be freed by calling `ldap_memfree()`.

Parameters:

`LDAP *ld`: An LDAP session handle.

LDAPMessage *entry: The entry whose next attribute is to be returned. The entry must have been returned from a successful call to ldap_first_entry() or ldap_next_entry().

BerElement **ber: A pointer to an opaque data type that was allocated by a previous call to ldap_first_attribute(). When you are done with this sequence of calls to ldap_first_attribute() and ldap_next_attribute(), this argument, if non-NULL, should be freed by calling ber_free() with a second argument of zero.

See Also:

ldap_next_attribute(), ldap_first_entry(), ldap_next_entry()

ldap_next_entry()   See Chapter 9

Returns the next entry in a chain of search results.

Prototype:

```
LDAPMessage *ldap_next_entry( LDAP *ld, LDAPMessage *result,
➥LDAPMessage *preventry );
```

Return Value:

An LDAP entry handle or NULL if there are no more entries or an error occurs.

Parameters:

LDAP *ld: An LDAP session handle.

LDAPMessage *result: The chain of results being stepped through, as returned from a successful call to ldap_search_s(), ldap_search_st(), or ldap_result().

LDAPMessage *preventry: This parameter is an entry returned from a previous successful call to ldap_first_entry() or ldap_next_entry(). The next entry in the chain will be returned.

See Also:

ldap_first_entry()

ldap_open()   See Chapter 6

Initializes the LDAP library, connect to a directory server, and return a session handle for use in subsequent calls.

Prototype:

int ldap_open(char *host, int port);

Return Value:

An LDAP session handle. If an error occurs, NULL is returned.

Parameters:

char *host: Host name of the LDAP server to connect to.

int port: TCP port of the LDAP server.

See Also:

ldap_init(), ldap_unbind()

ldap_perror()   See Chapter 8

Prints a message that corresponds to the most recent LDAP error that occurred.

Prototype:

void ldap_perror(LDAP *ld, char *s);

Parameters:

LDAP *ld: An LDAP session handle.

char *s: A message that is printed before the LDAP error message itself.

See Also:

ldap_err2string(), ldap_get_lderrno(), ldap_result2error()

ldap_result()   See Chapter 9

Retrieves the result of an operation initiated using an asynchronous LDAP call.

Prototype:

```
int ldap_result( LDAP *ld, int msgid, int all, struct timeval
➥*timeout, LDAPMessage **result );
```

Return Value:

−1 if an error occurs, or zero if a timeout occurs, or a positive number indicating the type of the message returned in the *result* parameter. The possible values (as defined in the ldap.h header file) are:

```
LDAP_RES_ADD
LDAP_RES_BIND
LDAP_RES_COMPARE
LDAP_RES_DELETE
LDAP_RES_MODIFY
LDAP_RES_MODRDN
LDAP_RES_SEARCH_ENTRY
LDAP_RES_SEARCH_RESULT
```

Parameters:

LDAP *ld: An LDAP session handle.

int *msgid*: The message id for which results are desired, as returned from a call to one of the asynchronous operation initiation routines. Pass the special value LDAP_RES_ANY to retrieve the next available result regardless of message id.

int *all*: A flag that determines whether search entries should be returned as they come in or not. Pass zero to receive entries as they arrive or a non-zero value to receive all of the entries in one result chain.

struct timeval *timeout*: Determines how long ldap_result() will wait for the requested result to arrive. Pass NULL to wait indefinitely, a pointer to a zeroed timeval structure for no delay, or a pointer to a timeval structure containing positive values to wait a specific number of seconds or microseconds.

LDAPMessage **result*: A pointer to an LDAPMessage pointer that is set if ldap_result() returns a positive number.

See Also:

ldap_msgfree(), ldap_result2error()

ldap_result2error()   See Chapter 8

Retrieves the error code that was returned in an LDAP operation result message.

Prototype:

int ldap_result2error(LDAP *ld*, LDAPMessage *res*, int *freeit*);

Return Value:

An LDAP error code.

Parameters:

LDAP *ld*: An LDAP session handle.

LDAPMessage *res*: An LDAP operation result, as returned by the ldap_result() function.

int *freeit*: A flag that, if non-zero, causes ldap_result2error() to free the memory occupied by the *res* parameter.

See Also:

ldap_err2string(), ldap_get_lderrno(), ldap_perror(), ldap_result()

ldap_search()   See Chapter 9

Initiates an LDAP search.

Prototype:

```
int ldap_search( LDAP *ld, char *base, int scope, char *filter, char
➥*attrs[], int attrsonly );
```

Return Value:

An LDAP message id or –1 if an error occurs.

Parameters:

LDAP *ld: An LDAP session handle.

char *base: The LDAP Distinguished Name used as the base object for the search operation.

int scope: The portion of the LDAP tree, relative to the base object, to search. It can have one of three possible values:

```
LDAP_SCOPE_BASE
LDAP_SCOPE_ONELEVEL
LDAP_SCOPE_SUBTREE
```

char *filter: An LDAP search filter.

char *attrs[]: A NULL-terminated array of character strings specifying the names of the attributes to be returned. Pass NULL to indicate that all available attributes should be returned.

int attrsonly: A flag that determines whether the values of the attributes are returned or not. Pass zero to retrieve both the attribute type and values or a non-zero value to retrieve the attribute types only.

See Also:

ldap_search_s(), ldap_search_st()

ldap_search_s()   See Chapter 9

Searches for directory entries.

Prototype:

```
int ldap_search_s( LDAP *ld, char *base, int scope, char *filter,
➥char *attrs[], int attrsonly, LDAPMessage **result );
```

Return Value:

An LDAP error code.

Parameters:

LDAP *ld: An LDAP session handle.

char *base: The LDAP Distinguished Name used as the base object for the search operation.

int scope: The portion of the LDAP tree, relative to the base object, to search. It can have one of three possible values:

```
LDAP_SCOPE_BASE
LDAP_SCOPE_ONELEVEL
LDAP_SCOPE_SUBTREE
```

char *filter: An LDAP search filter.

char *attrs[]: A NULL-terminated array of character strings specifying the names of the attributes to be returned. Pass NULL to indicate that all available attributes should be returned.

int attrsonly: A flag that determines whether the values of the attributes are returned or not. Pass zero to retrieve both the attribute type and values or a non-zero value to retrieve the attribute types only.

LDAPMessage **result: A pointer to an LDAPMessage * used to hold the result of a successful search.

See Also:
ldap_search(), ldap_search_s()

ldap_search_st()   See Chapter 9

Searches for directory entries, respecting a local timeout.

Prototype:
```
int ldap_search_st( LDAP *ld, char *base, int scope, char *filter,
➥char *attrs[], int attrsonly, LDAPMessage **result, struct timeval
➥*tv );
```

Return Value:
An LDAP error code.

Parameters:
LDAP *ld: An LDAP session handle.

char *base: The LDAP Distinguished Name used as the base object for the search operation.

int scope: The portion of the LDAP tree, relative to the base object, to search. It can have one of three possible values:

```
LDAP_SCOPE_BASE
LDAP_SCOPE_ONELEVEL
LDAP_SCOPE_SUBTREE
```

char *filter: An LDAP search filter.

char *attrs[]: A NULL-terminated array of character strings specifying the names of the attributes to be returned. Pass NULL to indicate that all available attributes should be returned.

int *attrsonly*: A flag that determines whether the values of the attributes are returned or not. Pass zero to retrieve both the attribute type and values or a non-zero value to retrieve the attribute types only.

LDAPMessage **result*: A pointer to an LDAPMessage * used to hold the result of a successful search.

struct timeval *tv*: A pointer to a timeval structure whose contents determine how long to wait for the search to complete.

See Also:

ldap_search(), ldap_search_s()

ldap_set_option()   See Chapter 6

Configures an LDAP session by changing session options. Available in the Netscape SDK only.

Prototype:

int ldap_set_option(LDAP *ld*, unsigned long *option*, void *in*);

Return Value:

If successful, zero is returned; non-zero otherwise.

Parameters:

LDAP *ld*: An LDAP session handle.

unsigned long *option*: The option to retrieve. One of the following constants:

```
LDAP_OPT_DEREF
LDAP_OPT_DESC
LDAP_OPT_IO_FN_PTRS
LDAP_OPT_REBIND_FN
LDAP_OPT_REBIND_ARG
LDAP_OPT_REFERRALS
```

```
LDAP_OPT_SIZELIMIT
LDAP_OPT_SSL
LDAP_OPT_THREAD_FN_PTRS
LDAP_OPT_TIMELIMIT
```

void *in: The new value for the option. The appropriate type to pass depends on what option is being set.

See Also:

ldap_get_option()

ldap_set_rebind_proc()   See Chapter 13

Installs an application-defined function that is called by the LDAP library when it needs to obtain authentication credentials.

Prototype (Netscape SDK):

```
int ldap_set_rebind_proc( LDAP *ld,
    (int (*rebindproc)( LDAP *ld, char **dnp, char **pwp,
        int *authmethodp, int freeit, void *arg )),
    void *arg );
```

Prototype (University of Michigan SDK):

```
int ldap_set_rebind_proc( LDAP *ld,
    (int (*rebindproc)( LDAP *ld, char **dnp, char **pwp,
        int *authmethodp, int freeit )));
```

Return Value:

An LDAP error code.

Parameters:

LDAP *ld: An LDAP session handle.

rebindproc: Rebind function to install.

void *arg: (Netscape SDK only) A parameter to be passed to the re-bind function.

See Also:

`ldap_bind()`, `ldap_get_option()`, `ldap_set_option()`, `rebindproc()`

ldap_simple_bind()   See Chapter 13

Initiates an LDAP bind operation to authenticate to the directory server using a Distinguished Name and password.

Prototype:

`int ldap_simple_bind( LDAP *ld, char *dn, char *passwd );`

Return Value:

An LDAP message id or –1 if an error occurs.

Parameters:

`LDAP *ld`: An LDAP session handle.

`char *dn`: The Distinguished Name of the entry that is binding to the directory. Pass NULL or a zero-length string to perform an unauthenticated bind.

`char *passwd`: The password associated with *dn*. If this is NULL or a zero-length string an unauthenticated bind is performed.

See Also:

`ldap_bind()`, `ldap_bind_s()`, `ldap_result()`, `ldap_simple_bind_s()`, `ldap_set_rebind_proc()`

ldap_simple_bind_s()   See Chapter 13

Synchronously authenticates to the directory server using a Distinguished Name and password.

Prototype:

```
int ldap_simple_bind_s( LDAP *ld, char *dn, char *passwd );
```

Return Value:

An LDAP error code.

Parameters:

LDAP *ld: An LDAP session handle.

char *dn: The Distinguished Name of the entry that is binding to the directory. Pass NULL or a zero-length string to perform an unauthenticated bind.

char *passwd: The password associated with *dn*. If this is NULL or a zero-length string an unauthenticated bind is performed.

See Also:

ldap_bind(), ldap_bind_s(), ldap_result(), ldap_simple_bind(), ldap_set_rebind_proc()

ldap_sort_entries()   See Chapter 11

Sorts a list of LDAP entries either by Distinguished Name or by an attribute value.

Prototype:

```
int ldap_sort_entries( LDAP *ld, LDAPMessage **chain, char *attr, int
➡(*cmp)( char *a, char *b ) );
```

Return Value:

Zero if all goes well; −1 if an error occurs.

Parameters:

LDAP *ld: An LDAP session handle.

`LDAPMessage **chain`: A pointer to the list of entries to be sorted.

`char *attr`: The name of the attribute whose values are used when sorting the entries. If NULL is passed, the Distinguished Names of the entries are used to reorder them.

`int (*cmp)( char *a, char *b )`: Pointer to a function that is used to compare two strings. This function is called just like the standard strcmp function, and should return zero if *a* and *b* are identical, a negative number if *a* is less than *b*, and a positive number if *b* is greater than *a*.

See Also:

`ldap_sort_values()`

ldap_sort_values()   See Chapter 11

Sorts an array of attribute values.

Prototype:

`int ldap_sort_values( LDAP *ld, char **vals, int (*cmp)( char **ap,`
➥`char **bp ) );`

Return Value:

Zero if all goes well; −1 if an error occurs.

Parameters:

`LDAP *ld`: An LDAP session handle.

`char **vals`: A NULL-terminated array of string values.

`int (*cmp)( char *ap, char *bp )`: Pointer to a function that is used to compare two strings. This function is called with two parameters that are pointers to pointers to two strings to be compared, not pointers to the strings themselves. The comparison function should return zero if *ap and *bp are identical, a negative number if *ap is less than *bp, and a positive number if *bp is greater than *ap.

See Also:

`ldap_sort_entries()`, `ldap_sort_strcasecmp()`

ldap_sort_strcasecmp() See Chapter 11

Performs an ASCII case-insensitive comparison of two strings.

Prototype:

`int ldap_sort_strcasecmp( char **ap, char **bp );`

Return Value:

An indication of the relative ordering of the two strings. If the string
*ap and *bp are identical, zero is returned. If *ap should come before
*bp, a negative number is returned. If *ap should come after *bp, a
positive number is returned.

Parameters:

`char **ap`: A pointer to a pointer to the first string to be compared.

`char **bp`: A pointer to a pointer to the second string to be compared.

See Also:

`ldap_sort_values()`

ldap_unbind() See Chapter 6

Disposes of an LDAP session, freeing all associated resources.

Prototype:

`int ldap_unbind( LDAP *ld );`

Return Value:

An LDAP error code.

Parameter:

LDAP *ld: An LDAP session handle.

See Also:

ldap_init(), ldap_open()

ldap_url_parse()   See Chapter 15

Breaks up an LDAP URL into its components.

Prototype:

int ldap_url_parse(char *url, LDAPURLDesc **ludpp);

Return Value:

If *url* is a valid LDAP URL and it was successfully parsed, zero is returned. If an error occurs, one of these constants is returned:

LDAP_URL_ERR_NOTLDAP	URL doesn't begin with ldap://
LDAP_URL_ERR_NODN	URL is missing the required base DN
LDAP_URL_ERR_BADSCOPE	URL scope string was invalid
LDAP_URL_ERR_MEM	memory allocation failed

Parameters:

char *url: An LDAP URL.

LDAPURLDesc **ludpp: A pointer to an LDAPURLDesc * structure pointer that, if this function returns zero, is set to a newly allocated URL description structure.

See Also:

ldap_free_urldesc(), LDAPURLDesc

ldap_url_search()   See Chapter 15

Initiates an asynchronous search of the LDAP directory based on the contents of an LDAP URL.

Prototype:

```
int ldap_url_search( LDAP *ld, char *url, int attrsonly );
```

Return Value:

An LDAP message id or −1 if an error occurs.

Parameters:

LDAP *ld: An LDAP session handle.

char *url: An LDAP URL.

int attrsonly: A flag that indicates whether both attribute types and values should be returned (zero) or types only should be returned (non-zero).

See Also:

ldap_url_parse(), ldap_url_search_s(), ldap_url_search_st()

ldap_url_search_s()   See Chapter 15

Synchronously searches the LDAP directory based on the contents of an LDAP URL.

Prototype:

```
int ldap_url_search_s( LDAP *ld, char *url, int attrsonly,
➥LDAPMessage **res );
```

Return Value:

An LDAP error code.

Parameters:

LDAP *ld: An LDAP session handle.

char *url: An LDAP URL.

int attrsonly: A flag that indicates whether both attribute types and values should be returned (zero) or types only should be returned (non-zero).

LDAPMessage **res: A pointer to an LDAPMessage * used to hold the result of a successful URL search.

See Also:

ldap_url_parse(), ldap_url_search(), ldap_url_search_st()

ldap_url_search_st()   See Chapter 15

Synchronously searches the LDAP directory based on the contents of an LDAP URL, respecting a local timeout.

Prototype:

int ldap_url_search_st(LDAP *ld, char *url, int attrsonly, struct
➡timeval *timeout, LDAPMessage **res);

Return Value:

An LDAP error code.

Parameters:

LDAP *ld: An LDAP session handle.

char *url: An LDAP URL.

int attrsonly: A flag that indicates whether both attribute types and values should be returned (zero) or types only should be returned (non-zero).

`struct timeval *timeout`: A pointer to a timeval structure.

`LDAPMessage **res`: A pointer to an LDAPMessage * used to hold the result of a successful URL search.

See Also:

`ldap_url_parse()`, `ldap_url_search()`, `ldap_url_search_s()`

ldap_value_free()   See Chapter 9

Frees memory allocated by a call to `ldap_get_values()`.

Prototype:

`void ldap_value_free( char **vals );`

Parameter:

`char **vals`: A pointer to a NULL-terminated array of string values.

See Also:

`ldap_get_values()`

ldap_value_free_len()   See Chapter 9

Frees memory allocated by a call to `ldap_get_values_len()`.

Prototype:

`void ldap_value_free_len( struct berval **bvals );`

Parameter:

`struct berval **bvals`: A pointer to a NULL-terminated array of berval structures.

See Also:

ldap_get_values_len()

Application-Defined Functions

rebindproc()   See Chapter 13

Application-defined function that is called by the LDAP library when it needs to obtain authentication credentials.

Prototype (Netscape SDK):

```
int rebindproc( LDAP *ld, char **dnp, char **pwp,
    int *authmethodp, int freeit, void *arg );
```

Prototype (University of Michigan SDK):

```
int rebindproc( LDAP *ld, char **dnp, char **pwp,
    int *authmethodp, int freeit );
```

Return Value:

An LDAP error code.

Parameters:

LDAP *ld: The LDAP session handle.

char **dnp: A pointer to the location where a pointer to the bind Distinguished Name should be stored.

char **pwp: A pointer to the location where a pointer to the bind password or other credentials should be stored.

int *authmethodp: A pointer to the location where the bind method should be stored. Set *authmethodp = LDAP_AUTH_SIMPLE for simple password authentication.

int *freeit*: If this parameter is zero, bind credentials are being requested and the *dnp*, *pwp*, and *authmethodp* pointers should be set. Otherwise, the rebind function is being called a second time to give you the opportunity to dispose of any memory or other resources that you used when returning the authentication credentials.

void *arg: (Netscape SDK only) The *arg* parameter that was passed to ldap_set_rebind_proc().

See Also:

ldap_set_rebind_proc()

Structures

struct berval   See Chapter 9

A structure used to represent values of arbitrary size and composition.

Definition:

```
struct berval {
    unsigned long    bv_len;
    char             *bv_val;
};
```

Fields:

unsigned long bv_len: The length of the data pointed to by the bv_val field.

char *bv_val: Pointer to the actual data.

See Also:

ldap_get_values_len(), ldap_value_free_len()

struct ldap_filt_info   See Chapter 10

An LDAP filter and its associated information.

Definition:

```
typedef struct ldap_filt_info {
    char                    *lfi_filter;
    char                    *lfi_desc;
    int                      lfi_scope;
    int                      lfi_isexact;
    struct ldap_filt_info    *lfi_next;
} LDAPFiltInfo;
```

Fields:

char *lfi_filter: An LDAP search filter that has been constructed from the filter pattern contained in the *getfilter* configuration file and the input parameter to ldap_getfirstfilter().

char *lfi_desc: The match description associated with the filter.

int lfi_scope: The search scope associated with the filter.

int lfi_isexact: A flag that indicates whether the filter contains any substring or approximate filter components. If zero, there are substring or approximate filter components; if non-zero there are only exact filter components.

struct ldap_filt_info *lfi_next: Used internally by the *getfilter* routines.

See Also:

ldap_getfirstfilter(), ldap_getnextfilter()

struct LDAPMod   See Chapter 14

A structure used to specify the changes to be made to an LDAP entry.

Definition:

```
typedef struct ldapmod {
    int     mod_op;
    char    *mod_type;
    union {
        char            **modv_strvals;
        struct berval   **modv_bvals;
    } mod_vals;
} LDAPMod;
#define mod_values      mod_vals.modv_strvals
#define mod_bvalues     mod_vals.modv_bvals
```

Fields:

`int mod_op`: The type of modification to perform. It contains one of these three values:

```
LDAP_MOD_ADD
LDAP_MOD_DELETE
LDAP_MOD_REPLACE
```

In addition, each of these values may be logically ANDed with the value `LDAP_MOD_BVALUES` to select the `mod_bvalues` rather than `mod_values` field.

`char *mod_type`: The attribute type to which the modification applies.

`char **mod_values`: A NULL-terminated array of attribute value strings to add, delete, or replace. Used if `LDAP_MOD_BVALUES` is not included in the mod_op field.

`struct berval **mod_bvalues`: A NULL-terminated array of binary attribute values to add, delete, or replace. Used if `LDAP_MOD_BVALUES` is included in the mod_op field.

See Also:

`ldap_modify()`, `ldap_modify_s()`

struct ldap_thread_fns   See Chapter 7

A structure to hold LDAP thread function pointers. Only used in the Netscape SDK.

Definition:

```
struct ldap_thread_fns {
    void    *(*ltf_mutex_alloc)( void );
    void     (*ltf_mutex_free)( void * );
    int      (*ltf_mutex_lock( void * );
    int      (*ltf_mutex_unlock)( void * );
    void     (*ltf_set_errno)( int );
    int      (*ltf_get_errno)( void );
    void     (*ltf_set_lderrno)( int, char *, char * );
    int      (*ltf_get_lderrno)( char **, char ** );
};
```

```
Fields:
```

void *(*ltf_mutex_alloc)(void): A function the LDAP library will call to allocate, initialize, and return a mutex.

void (*ltf_mutex_free)(void *): A function the LDAP library will call to free a mutex.

void (*ltf_mutex_lock)(void *): A function the LDAP library will call to lock a mutex.

void (*ltf_mutex_unlock)(void *): A function the LDAP library will call to unlock a mutex.

void (*ltf_set_errno)(int): A function that the LDAP library will call when it needs to set the value of errno.

int (*ltf_get_errno)(void): A function that the LDAP library will call when it needs to access the value of errno.

void (*ltf_set_lderrno)(int, char *, char *): A function that the LDAP library will call when it needs to set the value of the last LDAP error.

`int (*ltf_get_lderrno)( char **, char ** )`: A function that the LDAP library will call when it needs to access the value of the last LDAP error.

See Also:

`ldap_get_option(), ldap_set_option()`

struct LDAPURLDesc   See Chapter 15

A structure that holds the components of an LDAP URL.

Definition:

```
struct LDAPURLDesc {
    char        *lud_host;
    int         lud_port;
    char        *lud_dn;
    char        **lud_attrs;
    int         lud_scope;
    int         lud_filter;
};
```

Fields:

`char *lud_host`: The name of the LDAP directory server to contact. This may be NULL, in which case the application should choose a default directory server to use.

`int lud_port`: The TCP port of the directory server. If this value is zero, the default LDAP port should be used.

`char *lud_dn`: The Distinguished Name that was included in the URL.

`char **lud_attrs`: A NULL-terminated array of attributes to retrieve from the directory server. If this element is NULL, the URL did not contain a list of attributes.

`int lud_scope`: The search scope. It will be one of the following values:

```
LDAP_SCOPE_BASE
LDAP_SCOPE_ONELEVEL
LDAP_SCOPE_SUBTREE.
```

If no scope was included in the URL, this field is set to
`LDAP_SCOPE_BASE`.

`int lud_filter`: The LDAP search filter. If no filter was included in the
URL, this structure element will be set to the default filter of (`object-Class=*`).

See Also:

`ldap_free_urldesc(), ldap_url_parse()`

Lightweight Directory Access Protocol

Network Working Group   W. Yeong
Request for Comments: 1777 Performance Systems International
Obsoletes: 1487 T. Howes
Category: Standards Track University of Michigan
    S. Kille
    ISODE Consortium
    March 1995

Status of This Memo

This document specifies an Internet standards track protocol for the Internet community, and requests discussion and suggestions for improvements. Please refer to the current edition of the "Internet Official Protocol Standards" (STD 1) for the standardization state and status of this protocol. Distribution of this memo is unlimited.

Abstract

The protocol described in this document is designed to provide access to the X.500 Directory while not incurring the resource requirements of the Directory Access Protocol (DAP). This protocol is specifically targeted at simple management applications and browser applications that provide simple read/write interactive access to the X.500 Directory, and is intended to be a complement to the DAP itself.

Key aspects of LDAP are:

- Protocol elements are carried directly over TCP or other transport, bypassing much of the session/presentation overhead.

- Many protocol data elements are encoded as ordinary strings (for example, Distinguished Names).

- A lightweight BER encoding is used to encode all protocol elements.

1. History

The tremendous interest in X.500 [1, 2] technology in the Internet has led to efforts to reduce the high "cost of entry" associated with use of the technology, such as the Directory Assistance Service [3] and DIXIE [4]. While efforts such as these have met with success, they have been solutions based on particular implementations and as such have limited applicability. This document continues the efforts to define Directory protocol alternatives but departs from previous efforts in that it consciously avoids dependence on particular implementations.

2. Protocol Model

The general model adopted by this protocol is one of clients performing protocol operations against servers. In this model, this is accomplished by a client transmitting a protocol request describing the operation to be performed to a server, which is then responsible for performing the necessary operations on the Directory.

Upon completion of the necessary operations, the server returns a response containing any results or errors to the requesting client. In keeping with the goal of easing the costs associated with use of the Directory, it is an objective of this protocol to minimize the complexity of clients so as to facilitate widespread deployment of applications capable of utilizing the Directory.

Note that, although servers are required to return responses whenever such responses are defined in the protocol, there is no requirement for synchronous behavior on the part of either client or server implementations—requests and responses for multiple operations may be exchanged by clients and servers in any order, as long as clients eventually receive a response for every request that requires one.

Consistent with the model of servers performing protocol operations on behalf of clients, it is also to be noted that protocol servers are expected to handle referrals without resorting to the return of such referrals to the client. This protocol makes no provisions for the return of referrals to clients, as the model is one of servers ensuring the performance of all necessary operations in the Directory, with only final results or errors being returned by servers to clients.

Note that this protocol can be mapped to a strict subset of the directory abstract service, so it can be cleanly provided by the DAP.

3. Mapping onto Transport Services

This protocol is designed to run over connection-oriented, reliable transports, with all eight bits in an octet being significant in the data stream. Specifications for two underlying services are defined here, though others are also possible.

3.1. Transmission Control Protocol (TCP)

The LDAPMessage PDUs are mapped directly onto the TCP bytestream. Server implementations running over the TCP should provide a protocol listener on port 389.

3.2. Connection-Oriented Transport Service (COTS)

The connection is established. No special use of T-Connect is made. Each LDAPMessage PDU is mapped directly onto T-Data.

4. Elements of Protocol

For the purposes of protocol exchanges, all protocol operations are encapsulated in a common envelope, the LDAPMessage, which is defined as follows:

```
  LDAPMessage ::=
SEQUENCE {
  messageIDMessageID,
  protocolOp  CHOICE {
  bindRequest        BindRequest,
  bindResponse       BindResponse,
  unbindRequest      UnbindRequest,
  searchRequest      SearchRequest,
  searchResponse     SearchResponse,
  modifyRequest      ModifyRequest,
  modifyResponse     ModifyResponse,
  addRequest         AddRequest,
  addResponse        AddResponse,
  delRequest         DelRequest,
  delResponse        DelResponse,
  modifyRDNRequest   ModifyRDNRequest,
  modifyRDNResponse  ModifyRDNResponse,
  compareDNRequest   CompareRequest,
  compareDNResponse  CompareResponse,
  abandonRequest     AbandonRequest
  }
}
```

```
  MessageID ::= INTEGER (0 .. maxInt)
```

The function of the LDAPMessage is to provide an envelope containing common fields required in all protocol exchanges. At this time the only common field is a message ID, which is required to have a value different from the values of any other requests outstanding in the LDAP session of which this message is a part.

The message ID value must be echoed in all LDAPMessage envelopes encapsulting responses corresponding to the request contained in the LDAPMessage in which the message ID value was originally used.

In addition to the LDAPMessage defined previously, the following definitions are also used in defining protocol operations:

```
LDAPString ::= OCTET STRING
```

The LDAPString is a notational convenience to indicate that, although strings of LDAPString type encode as OCTET STRING types, the legal character set in such strings is limited to the IA5 character set.

```
LDAPDN ::= LDAPString

RelativeLDAPDN ::= LDAPString
```

An LDAPDN and a RelativeLDAPDN are respectively defined to be the representation of a Distinguished Name and a Relative Distinguished Name after encoding according to the specification in [5], such that

```
<distinguished-name> ::= <name>

<relative-distinguished-name> ::= <name-component>
```

where <name> and <name-component> are as defined in [5].

```
AttributeValueAssertion ::=
SEQUENCE {
  attributeType AttributeType,
  attributeValueAttributeValue
}
```

The AttributeValueAssertion type definition is similar to the one in the X.500 Directory standards.

```
AttributeType ::= LDAPString

AttributeValue ::= OCTET STRING
```

An AttributeType value takes on as its value the textual string associated with that AttributeType in the X.500 Directory standards. For example, the AttributeType "organizationName" with object identifier 2.5.4.10 is represented as an AttributeType in this protocol by the string "organizationName". In the event that a protocol implementation encounters an Attribute Type with which it cannot associate a textual string, an ASCII string encoding of the object identifier associated with the Attribute Type may be subsititued. For example, the organizationName AttributeType may be represented by the ASCII string "2.5.4.10" if a protocol implementation is unable to associate the string "organizationName" with it.

A field of type `AttributeValue` takes on as its value an octet string encoding of a Directory `AttributeValue` type. The definition of these string encodings for different Directory `AttributeValue` types may be found in companions to this document that define the encodings of various attribute syntaxes such as [6].

```
LDAPResult ::=
SEQUENCE {
 resultCode ENUMERATED {
  success (0),
  operationsError  (1),
  protocolError (2),
  timeLimitExceeded(3),
  sizeLimitExceeded(4),
  compareFalse  (5),
  compareTrue (6),
  authMethodNotSupported (7),
  strongAuthRequired  (8),
  noSuchAttribute  (16),
  undefinedAttributeType (17),
  inappropriateMatching  (18),
  constraintViolation (19),
  attributeOrValueExists (20),
  invalidAttributeSyntax (21),
  noSuchObject  (32),
  aliasProblem  (33),
  invalidDNSyntax  (34),
  isLeaf  (35),
  aliasDereferencingProblem (36),
  inappropriateAuthentication  (48),
  invalidCredentials  (49),
  insufficientAccessRights  (50),
  busy (51),
  unavailable (52),
```

```
  unwillingToPerform  (53),
  loopDetect (54),
  namingViolation  (64),
  objectClassViolation (65),
  notAllowedOnNonLeaf (66),
  notAllowedOnRDN  (67),
  entryAlreadyExists  (68),
  objectClassModsProhibited (69),
  other (80)
},
 matchedDN  LDAPDN,
 errorMessage  LDAPString
}
```

The LDAPResult is the construct used in this protocol to return success or failure indications from servers to clients. In response to various requests, servers will return responses containing fields of type LDAPResult to indicate the final status of a protocol operation request. The errorMessage field of this construct may, at the server's option, be used to return an ASCII string containing a textual, human-readable error diagnostic. As this error diagnostic is not standardized, implementations should not rely on the values returned. If the server chooses not to return a textual diagnostic, the errorMessage field of the LDAPResult type should contain a zero-length string.

For resultCodes of noSuchObject, aliasProblem, invalidDNSyntax, isLeaf, and aliasDereferencingProblem, the matchedDN field is set to the name of the lowest entry (object or alias) in the DIT that was matched and is a truncated form of the name provided or, if an alias has been dereferenced, of the resulting name. The matchedDN field should be set to NULL DN (a zero-length string) in all other cases.

4.1. Bind Operation

The function of the Bind Operation is to initiate a protocol session between a client and a server, and to allow the authentication of the client to the server. The Bind Operation must be the first operation request received by a server from a client in a protocol session.

The Bind Request is defined as follows:

```
BindRequest ::=
[APPLICATION 0] SEQUENCE {
 versionINTEGER (1 .. 127),
 nameLDAPDN,
 authentication CHOICE {
simple  [0] OCTET STRING,
krbv42LDAP [1] OCTET STRING,
krbv42DSA  [2] OCTET STRING
 }
}
```

Parameters of the Bind Request are:

- version: A version number indicating the version of the protocol to be used in this protocol session. This document describes version 2 of the LDAP protocol. Note that there is no version negotiation, and the client should just set this parameter to the version it desires.

- name: The name of the Directory object that the client wishes to bind as. This field may take on a null value (a zero-length string) for the purposes of anonymous binds.

- authentication: Information used to authenticate the name, if any, provided in the Bind Request. The simple authentication option provides minimal authentication facilities, with the contents of the authentication field consisting only of a cleartext password. This option should also be used when unauthenticated or anonymous binds are to be performed, with the field containing a zero-length string in such cases. Kerberos version 4 [7] authentication to the LDAP server and the DSA is accomplished by using the krbv42LDAP and krbv42DSA authentication options, respectively. Note that though they are referred to as separate entities here, there is no requirement these two entities be distinct (that is, a DSA could speak to LDAP directly). Two separate authentication options are provided to support all implementations. Each octet string should contain the kerberos ticket (for example, as returned by krb_mk_req()) for the appropriate service. The suggested service name for authentication to the LDAP server is "ldapserver". The suggested service name for authentication to the DSA is "x500dsa". In both cases, the suggested instance name for the service is the name of the host on which the service is running. Of course, the actual service names and instances will depend on what is entered in the local kerberos principal database.

The Bind Operation requires a response, the Bind Response, which I defined as:

```
BindResponse ::= [APPLICATION 1] LDAPResult
```

A Bind Response consists simply of an indication from the server of the status of the client's request for the initiation of a protocol session.

Upon receipt of a Bind Request, a protocol server will authenticate the requesting client if necessary, and attempt to set up a protocol session with that client. The server will then return a Bind Response to the client indicating the status of the session setup request.

4.2.   Unbind Operation

The function of the Unbind Operation is to terminate a protocol session. The Unbind Operation is defined as follows:

```
UnbindRequest ::= [APPLICATION 2] NULL
```

The Unbind Operation has no response defined. Upon transmission of an UnbindRequest, a protocol client may assume that the protocol session is terminated. Upon receipt of an UnbindRequest, a protocol server may assume that the requesting client has terminated the session and that all outstanding requests may be discarded.

4.3.   Search Operation

The Search Operation allows a client to request that a search be performed on its behalf by a server. The Search Request is defined as follows:

```
    SearchRequest ::=
[APPLICATION 3] SEQUENCE {
 baseObject LDAPDN,
 scopeENUMERATED {
  baseObject(0),
  singleLevel (1),
  wholeSubtree (2)
},
 derefAliases  ENUMERATED {
 neverDerefAliases  (0),
 derefInSearching(1),
 derefFindingBaseObj(2),
 derefAlways  (3)
  },
 sizeLimit  INTEGER (0 .. maxInt),
 timeLimit  INTEGER (0 .. maxInt),
 attrsOnly  BOOLEAN,
 filter  Filter,
 attributes SEQUENCE OF AttributeType
  }

  Filter ::=
CHOICE {
 and [0] SET OF Filter,
 or  [1] SET OF Filter,
 not [2] Filter,
 equalityMatch [3] AttributeValueAssertion,
 substrings [4] SubstringFilter,
 greaterOrEqual  [5] AttributeValueAssertion,
 lessOrEqual  [6] AttributeValueAssertion,
 present [7] AttributeType,
 approxMatch  [8] AttributeValueAssertion
 }

  SubstringFilter
SEQUENCE {
typeAttributeType,
 SEQUENCE OF CHOICE {
  initial  [0] LDAPString,
  any [1] LDAPString,
  final [2] LDAPString
 }
}
```

Parameters of the Search Request are:

- `baseObject`: An LDAPDN that is the base object entry relative to which the search is to be performed.

- `scope`: An indicator of the scope of the search to be performed. The semantics of the possible values of this field are identical to the semantics of the scope field in the Directory Search Operation.

- `derefAliases`: An indicator as to how alias objects should be handled in searching. The semantics of the possible values of this field are, in order of increasing value:

    - `neverDerefAliases`: Does not dereference aliases in searching or in locating the base object of the search;

    - `derefInSearching`: Dereferences aliases in subordinates of the base object in searching, but not in locating the base object of the search;

    - `derefFindingBaseObject`: Dereferences aliases in locating the base object of the search, but not when searching subordinates of the base object;

    - `derefAlways`: Dereferences aliases both in searching and in locating the base object of the search.

- `sizelimit`: A sizelimit that restricts the maximum number of entries to be returned as a result of the search. A value of 0 in this field indicates that no sizelimit restrictions are in effect for the search.

- `timelimit`: A timelimit that restricts the maximum time (in seconds) allowed for a search. A value of 0 in this field indicates that no timelimit restrictions are in effect for the search.

- `attrsOnly`: An indicator as to whether search results should contain both attribute types and values, or just attribute types. Setting this field to TRUE causes only attribute types (no values) to be returned. Setting this field to FALSE causes both attribute types and values to be returned.

- filter: A filter that defines the conditions that must be fulfilled in order for the search to match a given entry.

- attributes: A list of the attributes from each entry found as a result of the search to be returned. An empty list signifies that all attributes from each entry found in the search are to be returned.

The results of the search attempted by the server upon receipt of a Search Request are returned in Search Responses, defined as follows:

```
   Search Response ::=
CHOICE {
  entry [APPLICATION 4] SEQUENCE {
objectName  LDAPDN,
 attributes  SEQUENCE OF SEQUENCE {
AttributeType,
SET OF AttributeValue
 }
 },
 resultCode  [APPLICATION 5] LDAPResult
 }
```

Upon receipt of a Search Request, a server will perform the necessary search of the DIT. The server will return to the client a sequence of responses comprised of:

- Zero or more Search Responses each consisting of an entry found during the search

- A single Search Response containing an indication of success, or detailing any errors that have occurred

Each entry returned will contain all attributes, complete with associated values if necessary, as specified in the "attributes" field of the Search Request.

Note that an X.500 "list" operation can be emulated by a one-level LDAP search operation with a filter checking for the existence of the objectClass attribute, and that an X.500 "read" operation can be emulated by a base object LDAP search operation with the same filter.

4.4.   Modify Operation

The Modify Operation allows a client to request that a modification of the DIB be performed on its behalf by a server. The Modify Request is defined as follows:

```
ModifyRequest ::=
 [APPLICATION 6] SEQUENCE {
objectLDAPDN,
modificationSEQUENCE OF SEQUENCE {
  operationENUMERATED {
 add (0),
 delete (1),
 replace(2)
  },
  modificationSEQUENCE {
  type AttributeType,
  values  SET OF
AttributeValue
  }
}
 }
```

Parameters of the Modify Request are:

- object: The object to be modified. The value of this field should name the object to be modified after all aliases have been dereferenced. The server will not perform any alias dereferencing in determining the object to be modified.

- A list of modifications to be performed on the entry to be modified. The entire list of entry modifications should be performed in the order they are listed, as a single atomic operation. While individual modifications may violate the Directory schema, the resulting entry after the entire list of modifications is performed must conform to the requirements of the Directory schema. The values that may be taken on by the "operation" field in each modification construct have the following semantics respectively:

  - add: Adds values listed to the given attribute, creating the attribute if necessary;

delete: Deletes values listed from the given attribute, removing the entire attribute if no values are listed, or if all current values of the attribute are listed for deletion;

replace: Replaces existing values of the given attribute with the new values listed, creating the attribute if necessary.

The result of the modify attempted by the server upon receipt of a Modify Request is returned in a Modify Response, defined as follows:

```
ModifyResponse ::= [APPLICATION 7] LDAPResult
```

Upon receipt of a Modify Request, a server will perform the necessary modifications to the DIB.

The server will return to the client a single Modify Response indicating either the successful completion of the DIB modification, or the reason that the modification failed. Note that due to the requirement for atomicity in applying the list of modifications in the Modify Request, the client may expect that no modifications of the DIB have been performed if the Modify Response received indicates any sort of error, and that all requested modifications have been performed if the Modify Response indicates successful completion of the Modify Operation.

4.5. Add Operation

The Add Operation allows a client to request the addition of an entry into the Directory. The Add Request is defined as follows:

```
  AddRequest ::=
[APPLICATION 8] SEQUENCE {
  entry LDAPDN,
  attrs SEQUENCE OF SEQUENCE {
 type AttributeType,
 values  SET OF AttributeValue
  }
}
```

Parameters of the Add Request are:

- entry: The Distinguished Name of the entry to be added. Note that all components of the name except for the last RDN component must exist for the add to succeed.

- attrs: The list of attributes that make up the content of the entry being added.

The result of the add attempted by the server upon receipt of an Add Request is returned in the Add Response, defined as follows:

```
AddResponse ::= [APPLICATION 9] LDAPResult
```

Upon receipt of an Add Request, a server will attempt to perform the add requested. The result of the add attempt will be returned to the client in the Add Response.

4.6.   Delete Operation

The Delete Operation allows a client to request the removal of an entry from the Directory. The Delete Request is defined as follows:

```
DelRequest ::= [APPLICATION 10] LDAPDN
```

The Delete Request consists only of the Distinguished Name of the entry to be deleted. The result of the delete attempted by the server upon receipt of a Delete Request is returned in the Delete Response, defined as follows:

```
DelResponse ::= [APPLICATION 11] LDAPResult
```

Upon receipt of a Delete Request, a server will attempt to perform the entry removal requested. The result of the delete attempt will be returned to the client in the Delete Response. Note that only leaf objects may be deleted with this operation.

4.7.   Modify RDN Operation

The Modify RDN Operation allows a client to change the last component of the name of an entry in the Directory. The Modify RDN Request is defined as follows:

```
ModifyRDNRequest ::=
[APPLICATION 12] SEQUENCE {
  entry LDAPDN,
  newrdnRelativeLDAPDN,
  deleteoldrdnBOOLEAN
}
```

Parameters of the Modify RDN Request are:

- entry: The name of the entry to be changed.

- newrdn: The RDN that will form the last component of the new name.

- deleteoldrdn: A Boolean parameter that controls whether the old RDN attribute values should be retained as attributes of the entry or deleted from the entry.

The result of the name change attempted by the server upon receipt of a Modify RDN Request is returned in the Modify RDN Response, defined as follows:

```
ModifyRDNResponse ::= [APPLICATION 13] LDAPResult
```

Upon receipt of a Modify RDN Request, a server will attempt to perform the name change. The result of the name change attempt will be returned to the client in the Modify RDN Response. The attributes that make up the old RDN are deleted from the entry, or kept, depending on the setting of the deleteoldrdn parameter.

4.8. Compare Operation

The Compare Operation allows a client to compare an assertion provided with an entry in the Directory. The Compare Request is defined as follows:

```
CompareRequest ::=
[APPLICATION 14] SEQUENCE {
  entry LDAPDN,
  avaAttributeValueAssertion
}
```

Parameters of the Compare Request are:

- entry: The name of the entry to be compared with.

- ava: The assertion with which the entry is to be compared.

The result of the compare attempted by the server upon receipt of a Compare Request is returned in the Compare Response, defined as follows:

```
CompareResponse ::= [APPLICATION 15] LDAPResult
```

Upon receipt of a Compare Request, a server will attempt to perform the requested comparison. The result of the comparison will be returned to the client in the Compare Response. Note that errors and the result of the comparison are all returned in the same construct.

4.9.   Abandon Operation

The function of the Abandon Operation is to allow a client to request that the server abandon an outstanding operation. The Abandon Request is defined as follows:

```
AbandonRequest ::= [APPLICATION 16] MessageID
```

There is no response defined in the Abandon Operation. Upon transmission of an Abandon Operation, a client may expect that the operation identified by the Message ID in the Abandon Request has been abandoned. In the event that a server receives an Abandon Request on a Search Operation in the midst of transmitting responses to that search, that server should cease transmitting responses to the abandoned search immediately.

5.   Protocol Element Encodings

The protocol elements of LDAP are encoded for exchange using the Basic Encoding Rules (BER) [12] of ASN.1 [11]. However, due to the high overhead involved in using certain elements of the BER, the following additional restrictions are placed on BER-encodings of LDAP protocol elements:

1. Only the definite form of length encoding will be used.

2. Bitstrings and octet strings and all character string types will be encoded in the primitive form only.

6. Security Considerations

This version of the protocol provides facilities only for simple authentication using a cleartext password, and for kerberos version 4 authentication. Future versions of LDAP will likely include support for other authentication methods.

7. Bibliography

[1] The Directory: Overview of Concepts, Models and Service. CCITT Recommendation X.500, 1988.

[2] Information Processing Systems—Open Systems Interconnection— The Directory: Overview of Concepts, Models and Service. ISO/IEC JTC 1/SC21; International Standard 9594-1, 1988

[3] Rose, M., "Directory Assistance Service," RFC 1202, Performance Systems International, Inc., February 1991.

[4] Howes, T., Smith, M., and B. Beecher, "DIXIE Protocol Specification," RFC 1249, University of Michigan, August 1991.

[5] Kille, S., "A String Representation of Distinguished Names," RFC 1779, ISODE Consortium, March 1995.

[6] Howes, T., Kille, S., Yeong, W., and C. Robbins, "Lightweight Directory Access Protocol," RFC 1488, University of Michigan, ISODE Consortium, Performance Systems International, NeXor Ltd., July 1993.

[7] Kerberos Authentication and Authorization System. S.P. Miller, B.C. Neuman, J.I. Schiller, J.H. Saltzer; MIT Project Athena Documentation Section E.2.1, December 1987.

[8] The Directory: Models. CCITT Recommendation X.501 ISO/ IEC JTC 1/SC21; International Standard 9594-2, 1988.

[10] The Directory: Abstract Service Definition. CCITT Recommendation X.511, ISO/IEC JTC 1/SC21; International Standard 9594-3, 1988.

[11] Specification of Abstract Syntax Notation One (ASN.1). CCITT Recommendation X.208, 1988.

[12] Specification of Basic Encoding Rules for Abstract Syntax Notation One (ASN.1). CCITT Recommendation X.209, 1988.

8. Authors' Addresses

Wengyik Yeong
PSI Inc.
510 Huntmar Park Drive
Herndon, VA 22070
USA

Phone: +1 703-450-8001
E-mail: yeongw@psilink.com

Tim Howes
University of Michigan
ITD Research Systems
535 W William St.
Ann Arbor, MI 48103-4943
USA

Phone: +1 313-747-4454
E-mail:tim@umich.edu

Steve Kille
ISODE Consortium
PO Box 505
London
SW11 1DX
UK

Phone: +44-71-223-4062
E-mail: S.Kille@isode.com

A String Representation of
Standard Attribute Syntaxes

Network Working Group   T. Howes
Request for Comments: 1778   University of Michigan
Obsoletes: 1488   S. Kille
Category: Standards Track   ISODE Consortium
         W. Yeong
         Performance Systems International
         C. Robbins
         NeXor Ltd.
         March 1995

Status of This Memo

Abstract

The Lightweight Directory Access Protocol (LDAP) [9] requires that the contents of AttributeValue fields in protocol elements be octet strings. This document defines the requirements that must be satisfied by encoding rules used to render X.500 Directory attribute syntaxes into a form suitable for use in the LDAP, then goes on to define the encoding rules for the standard set of attribute syntaxes defined in [1,2] and [3].

1. Attribute Syntax Encoding Requirements

This section defines general requirements for lightweight directory protocol attribute syntax encodings. All documents defining attribute syntax encodings for use by the lightweight directory protocols are expected to conform to these requirements.

The encoding rules defined for a given attribute syntax must produce octet strings. To the greatest extent possible, encoded octet strings should be usable in their native encoded form for display purposes. In particular, encoding rules for attribute syntaxes defining non-binary values should produce strings that can be displayed with little or no translation by clients implementing the lightweight directory protocols.

2. Standard Attribute Syntax Encodings

For the purposes of defining the encoding rules for the standard attribute syntaxes, the following auxiliary BNF definitions will be used:

```
<a> ::= 'a' | 'b' | 'c' | 'd' | 'e' | 'f' | 'g' | 'h' | 'i' |
'j' | 'k' | 'l' | 'm' | 'n' | 'o' | 'p' | 'q' | 'r' |
's' | 't' | 'u' | 'v' | 'w' | 'x' | 'y' | 'z' | 'A' |
'B' | 'C' | 'D' | 'E' | 'F' | 'G' | 'H' | 'I' | 'J' |
'K' | 'L' | 'M' | 'N' | 'O' | 'P' | 'Q' | 'R' | 'S' |
'T' | 'U' | 'V' | 'W' | 'X' | 'Y' | 'Z'
<d> ::= '0' | '1' | '2' | '3' | '4' | '5' | '6' | '7' | '8' | '9'
<hex-digit> ::= <d> | 'a' | 'b' | 'c' | 'd' | 'e' | 'f' |
'A' | 'B' | 'C' | 'D' | 'E' | 'F'
<k> ::= <a> | <d> | '-'
<p> ::= <a> | <d> | '''  | '(' | ')' | '+' | ',' | '-' | '.' |
'/' | ':' | '?' | ' '
<CRLF> ::= The ASCII newline character with hexadecimal value 0x0A
<letterstring> ::= <a> | <a> <letterstring>
<numericstring> ::= <d> | <d> <numericstring>
<keystring> ::= <a> | <a> <anhstring>
<anhstring> ::= <k> | <k> <anhstring>
```

```
<printablestring> ::= <p> | <p> <printablestring>
<space> ::= ' ' | ' ' <space>
```

2.1. Undefined

Values of type Undefined are encoded as if they were values of type Octet String, with the string value being the BER-encoded version of the value.

2.2. caseIgnoreStringSyntax

A string of type caseIgnoreStringSyntax is encoded as the string value itself.

2.3. caseExactStringSyntax

The encoding of a string of type caseExactStringSyntax is the string value itself.

2.4. printableStringSyntax

The encoding of a string of type printableStringSyntax is the string value itself.

2.5. numericStringSyntax

The encoding of a string of type numericStringSyntax is the string value itself.

2.6. octetStringSyntax

The encoding of a string of type octetStringSyntax is the string value itself.

2.7. caseIgnoreIA5String

The encoding of a string of type caseIgnoreIA5String is the string value itself.

2.8. iA5StringSyntax

The encoding of a string of type iA5StringSyntax is the string value itself.

2.9. t61StringSyntax

The encoding of a string of type t61StringSyntax is the string value itself.

2.10. caseIgnoreListSyntax

Values of type caseIgnoreListSyntax are encoded according to the following BNF:

```
<caseignorelist> ::= <caseignorestring> |
<caseignorestring> '$' <caseignorelist>
<caseignorestring> ::= a string encoded according to the rules for
➥Case Ignore String as above.
```

2.11. caseExactListSyntax

Values of type caseExactListSyntax are encoded according to the following BNF:

```
<caseexactlist> ::= <caseexactstring> |
<caseexactstring> '$' <caseexactlist>

<caseexactstring> ::= a string encoded according to the rules for
➥Case Exact String as above.
```

2.12. distinguishedNameSyntax

Values of type distinguishedNameSyntax are encoded to have the representation defined in [5].

2.13.   booleanSyntax

Values of type `booleanSyntax` are encoded according to the following BNF:

```
<boolean> ::= "TRUE" | "FALSE"
```

Boolean values have an encoding of `"TRUE"` if they are logically true, and have an encoding of `"FALSE"` otherwise.

2.14.   integerSyntax

Values of type `integerSyntax` are encoded as the decimal representation of their values, with each decimal digit represented by its character equivalent.

2.15.   objectIdentifierSyntax

Values of type `objectIdentifierSyntax` are encoded according to the following BNF:

```
<oid> ::= <descr> | <descr> '.' <numericoid> | <numericoid>
<descr> ::= <keystring>
<numericoid> ::= <numericstring> | <numericstring> '.' <numericoid>
```

In the preceding BNF, `<descr>` is the syntactic representation of an object descriptor. When encoding values of type `objectIdentifierSyntax`, the first encoding option should be used in preference to the second, which should be used in preference to the third wherever possible. That is, in encoding object identifiers, object descriptors (where assigned and known by the implementation) should be used in preference to numeric oids to the greatest extent possible. For example, in encoding the object identifier representing an `organizationName`, the descriptor "organizationName" is preferable to "ds.4.10", which is in turn preferable to the string "2.5.4.10".

2.16. telephoneNumberSyntax

Values of type `telephoneNumberSyntax` are encoded as if they were Printable String types.

2.17. telexNumberSyntax

Values of type `telexNumberSyntax` are encoded according to the following BNF:

```
<telex-number> ::= <actual-number> '$' <country> '$' <answerback>
<actual-number> ::= <printablestring>
<country> ::= <printablestring>
<answerback> ::= <printablestring>
```

In the preceding, `<actual-number>` is the syntactic representation of the number portion of the TELEX number being encoded, `<country>` is the TELEX country code, and `<answerback>` is the answerback code of a TELEX terminal.

2.18. teletexTerminalIdentifier

Values of type `teletexTerminalIdentifier` are encoded according to the following BNF:

```
<teletex-id> ::= <printablestring>  0*('$' <ttx-parm>)
<ttx-param> ::= <ttx-key> ':' <ttx-value>
<ttx-key> ::= 'graphic' | 'control' | 'misc' | 'page' | 'private'
<ttx-value> ::= <octetstring>
```

In the preceding, the first `<printablestring>` is the encoding of the first portion of the teletex terminal identifier to be encoded, and the subsequent 0 or more `<printablestrings>` are subsequent portions of the teletex terminal identifier.

2.19. facsimileTelephoneNumber

Values of type `facsimileTelephoneNumber` are encoded according to the following BNF:

```
<fax-number> ::= <printablestring> [ '$' <faxparameters> ]
<faxparameters> ::= <faxparm> | <faxparm> '$' <faxparameters>
<faxparm> ::= 'twoDimensional' | 'fineResolution' | 'unlimitedLength' |
  'b4Length' | 'a3Width' | 'b4Width' | 'uncompressed'
```

In the preceding, the first <printablestring> is the actual fax number, and the <faxparm> tokens represent fax parameters.

2.20.   presentationAddress

Values of type presentationAddress are encoded to have the representation described in [6].

2.21.   uTCTimeSyntax

Values of type uTCTimeSyntax are encoded as if they were Printable Strings with the strings containing a UTCTime value.

2.22.   Guide (searchGuide)

Values of type Guide, such as values of the searchGuide attribute, are encoded according to the following BNF:

```
<guide-value> ::= [ <object-class> '#' ] <criteria>
<object-class> ::= an encoded value of type objectIdentifierSyntax
<criteria> ::= <criteria-item> | <criteria-set> | '!' <criteria>
<criteria-set> ::= [ '(' ] <criteria> '&' <criteria-set> [ ')' ] |
  [ '(' ] <criteria> '|' <criteria-set> [ ')' ]
<criteria-item> ::= [ '(' ] <attributetype> '$' <match-type> [ ')' ]
<match-type> ::= "EQ" | "SUBSTR" | "GE" | "LE" | "APPROX"
```

2.23.   PostalAddress

Values of type PostalAddress are encoded according to the following BNF:

```
<postal-address> ::= <t61string> | <t61string> '$' <postal-address>
```

In the preceding, each <t61string> component of a postal address value is encoded as a value of type t61StringSyntax.

2.24. userPasswordSyntax

Values of type userPasswordSyntax are encoded as if they were of type octetStringSyntax.

2.25. userCertificate

Values of type userCertificate are encoded according to the following BNF:

```
<certificate> ::= <version> '#' <serial> '#' <signature-algorithm-
➥id>
'#' <issuer> '#' <validity> '#' <subject>
'#' <public-key-info> '#' <encrypted-sign-value>
  <version> ::= <integervalue>
  <serial> ::= <integervalue>
  <signature-algorithm-id> ::= <algorithm-id>
  <issuer> ::= an encoded Distinguished Name
  <validity> ::= <not-before-time> '#' <not-after-time>
  <not-before-time> ::= <utc-time>
  <not-after-time> ::= <utc-time>
  <algorithm-parameters> ::=  <null> | <integervalue> |
'{ASN}' <hex-string>
  <subject> ::= an encoded Distinguished Name
  <public-key-info> ::= <algorithm-id> '#' <encrypted-sign-value>
  <encrypted-sign-value> ::= <hex-string> | <hex-string> '-' <d>
  <algorithm-id> ::= <oid> '#' <algorithm-parameters>
<utc-time> ::= an encoded UTCTime value
  <hex-string> ::= <hex-digit> | <hex-digit> <hex-string>
```

2.26. CA Certificate

Values of type cACertificate are encoded as if the values were of type userCertificate.

2.27.   authorityRevocationList

Values of type `authorityRevocationList` are encoded according to the following BNF:

```
<certificate-list> ::= <signature-algorithm-id> '#' <issuer> '#'
↪<utc-time>
[ '#' <revoked-certificates> ]
'#' <signature-algorithm-id>
'#' <encrypted-sign-value>
<revoked-certificates> ::= 1*( '#' <revoked-certificate> )
<signature-algorithm-id> '#' <encrypted-sign-value>
<revoked-certificate> ::= <signature-algorithm-id> '#' <issuer> '#'
<serial> '#' <utc-time>
```

The syntactic components `<signature-algorithm-id>`, `<issuer>`, `<encrypted-sign-value>`, `<utc-time>`, `<subject>`, and `<serial>` have the same definitions as in the BNF for the `userCertificate` attribute syntax.

2.28.   certificateRevocationList

Values of type `certificateRevocationList` are encoded as if the values were of type `authorityRevocationList`.

2.29.   crossCertificatePair

Values of type `crossCertificatePair` are encoded according to the following BNF:

```
<certificate-pair> ::= <forward> '#' <reverse>
| <forward>
| <reverse>
<forward> ::= 'forward:' <certificate>
<reverse> ::= 'reverse:' <certificate>
```

The syntactic component `<certificate>` has the same definition as in the BNF for the `userCertificate` attribute syntax.

2.30. deliveryMethod

Values of type `deliveryMethod` are encoded according to the following BNF:

```
<delivery-value> ::= <pdm> | <pdm> '$' <delivery-value>
<pdm> ::= 'any' | 'mhs' | 'physical' | 'telex' | 'teletex' |
'g3fax' | 'g4fax' | 'ia5' | 'videotex' | 'telephone'
```

2.31. otherMailboxSyntax

Values of the type `otherMailboxSyntax` are encoded according to the following BNF:

```
<otherMailbox> ::= <mailbox-type> '$' <mailbox>
<mailbox-type> ::= an encoded Printable String
<mailbox> ::= an encoded IA5 String
```

In the preceding, `<mailbox-type>` represents the type of mail system in which the mailbox resides, for example "Internet" or "MCIMail"; and `<mailbox>` is the actual mailbox in the mail system defined by `<mailbox-type>`.

2.32. mailPreferenceOption

Values of type `mailPreferenceOption` are encoded according to the following BNF:

```
<mail-preference> ::= "NO-LISTS" | "ANY-LIST" | "PROFESSIONAL-
➡LISTS"
```

2.33. MHS OR Address

Values of type `MHS OR Address` are encoded as strings, according to the format defined in [10].

2.34.   Distribution List Submit Permission

Values of type `DLSubmitPermission` are encoded as strings, according to the following BNF:

```
<dlsubmit-perm> ::= <dlgroup_label> ':' <dlgroup-value>
| <dl-label> ':' <dl-value>
<dlgroup-label> ::= 'group_member'
<dlgroup-value> ::= <name>
<name> ::= an encoded Distinguished Name
<dl-label> ::= 'individual' | 'dl_member' | 'pattern'
<dl-value> ::= <orname>
<orname> ::= <address> '#' <dn>
|  <address>
<address> ::= <add-label> ':' <oraddress>
<dn> ::= <dn-label> ':' <name>
<add-label> = 'X400'
<dn-label> = 'X500'
```

where <oraddress> is as defined in RFC 1327.

2.35.   Photo

Values of type `Photo` are encoded as if they were octet strings containing JPEG images in the JPEG File Interchange Format (JFIF), as described in [8].

2.36.   Fax

Values of type `Fax` are encoded as if they were octet strings containing Group 3 Fax images as defined in [7].

3.   Security Considerations

Security issues are not discussed in this memo.

4. Acknowledgments

Many of the attribute syntax encodings defined in this document are adapted from those used in the QUIPU X.500 implementation. The contributions of the authors of the QUIPU implementation in the specification of the QUIPU syntaxes [4] are gratefully acknowledged.

5. Bibliography

[1] The Directory: Selected Attribute Syntaxes. CCITT, Recommendation X.520.

[2] Information Processing Systems—Open Systems Interconnection—The Directory: Selected Attribute Syntaxes.

[3] Barker, P., and S. Kille, "The COSINE and Internet X.500 Schema," RFC 1274, University College London, November 1991.

[4] The ISO Development Environment: User's Manual — Volume 5: QUIPU. Colin Robbins, Stephen E. Kille.

[5] Kille, S., "A String Representation of Distinguished Names," RFC 1779, ISODE Consortium, March 1995.

[6] Kille, S., "A String Representation for Presentation Addresses," RFC 1278, University College London, November 1991.

[7] Terminal Equipment and Protocols for Telematic Services—Standardization of Group 3 facsimile apparatus for document transmission. CCITT, Recommendation T.4.

[8] JPEG File Interchange Format (Version 1.02). Eric Hamilton, C- Cube Microsystems, Milpitas, CA, September 1, 1992.

[9] Yeong, W., Howes, T., and S. Kille, "Lightweight Directory Access Protocol," RFC 1777, Performance Systems International, University of Michigan, ISODE Consortium, March 1995.

[10] Alvestrand, H., Kille, S., Miles, R., Rose, M., and S. Thompson, "Mapping between X.400 and RFC-822 Message Bodies," RFC 1495,

SINTEF DELAB, ISODE Consortium, Soft*Switch, Inc., Dover Beach Consulting, Inc., Soft*Switch, Inc., August 1993.

6. Authors' Addresses

Tim Howes
University of Michigan
ITD Research Systems
535 W William St.
Ann Arbor, MI 48103-4943
USA

Phone: +1 313 747-4454
E-mail: tim@umich.edu

Steve Kille
ISODE Consortium
PO Box 505
London
SW11 1DX
UK

Phone: +44-71-223-4062
E-mail: S.Kille@isode.com

Wengyik Yeong
PSI Inc.
510 Huntmar Park Drive
Herndon, VA 22070
USA

Phone: +1 703-450-8001
E-mail: yeongw@psilink.com

Colin Robbins
NeXor Ltd
University Park
Nottingham
NG7 2RD
UK

A String Representation of Distinguished Names

Network Working Group   S. Kille
Request for Comments: 1779   ISODE Consortium
Obsoletes: 1485   March 1995
Category: Standards Track

Status of This Memo

This document specifies an Internet standards track protocol for the Internet community, and requests discussion and suggestions for improvements. Please refer to the current edition of the "Internet Official Protocol Standards" (STD 1) for the standardization state and status of this protocol. Distribution of this memo is unlimited.

Abstract

The OSI Directory uses distinguished names as the primary keys to entries in the directory. Distinguished names are encoded in ASN.1. When a distinguished name is communicated between two users not using a directory protocol (for example, in a mail message), there is a need to have a user-oriented string representation of distinguished name. This specification defines a string format for representing names, which is designed to give a clean representation of commonly used names, while being able to represent any distinguished name.

1. Why a Notation Is Needed

Many OSI applications make use of Distinguished Names (DN) as defined in the OSI Directory, commonly known as X.500 [1]. This specification assumes familiarity with X.500, and the concept of Distinguished Name. It is important to have a common format to be able to unambiguously represent a distinguished name. This might be done to represent a directory name on a business card or in an e-mail message. There is a need for a format to support human-to-human communication, which must be string-based (not ASN.1) and user-oriented. This notation is targeted toward a general user-oriented system, and in particular to represent the names of humans. Other syntaxes may be more appropriate for other uses of the directory. For example, the OSF Syntax may be more appropriate for some system-oriented uses. (The OSF Syntax uses "/" as a separator, and forms names in a manner intended to resemble Unix file names.)

2. A Notation for Distinguished Name

2.1. Goals

The following goals are laid out:

- To provide an unambiguous representation of a distinguished name

- To be an intuitive format for the majority of names

- To be fully general, and able to represent any distinguished name

- To be amenable to a number of different layouts to achieve an attractive representation

- To give a clear representation of the contents of the distinguished name

2.2.   Informal Definition

This notation is designed to be convenient for common forms of name. Some examples are given. The author's directory distinguished name would be written as follows:

```
CN=Steve Kille,
O=ISODE Consortium, C=GB
```

This may be folded, perhaps to display in multi-column format. For example:

```
CN=Steve Kille,
O=ISODE Consortium,
C=GB
```

Another name might be:

```
CN=Christian Huitema, O=INRIA, C=FR
```

Semicolon (;) may be used as an alternate separator. The separators may be mixed, but this usage is discouraged.

```
CN=Christian Huitema; O=INRIA; C=FR
```

In running text, this would be written as <CN=Christian Huitema; O=INRIA; C=FR>. Another example shows how different attribute types are handled:

```
CN=James Hacker,
L=Basingstoke,
O=Widget Inc,
C=GB
```

Here is an example of a multi-valued Relative Distinguished Name, where the namespace is flat within an organization, and department is used to disambiguate certain names:

```
OU=Sales + CN=J. Smith, O=Widget Inc., C=US
```

The final examples show both methods of quoting a comma in an Organization name:

```
CN=L. Eagle, O="Sue, Grabbit and Runn", C=GB
CN=L. Eagle, O=Sue\, Grabbit and Runn, C=GB
```

2.3. Formal Definition

A formal definition can now be given. This BNF uses the grammar defined in RFC 822, with the terminals enclosed in <> [2]. This definition is in an abstract character set, and so may be written in any character set supporting the explicitly defined special characters. The quoting mechanism is used for the following cases:

- Strings containing ",", "+", "=" or """ , <CR>, "<", ">", "#", or ";".

- Strings with leading or trailing spaces

- Strings containing consecutive spaces

There is an escape mechanism from the normal user-oriented form, so that this syntax may be used to print any valid distinguished name. This is ugly. It is expected to be used only in pathological cases. There are two parts to this mechanism:

1. Attributes types are represented in a (big-endian) dotted notation (for example, OID.2.6.53).

2. Attribute values are represented in hexadecimal (for example, #0A56CF). Each pair of hex digits defines an octet, which is the ASN.1 Basic Encoding Rules value of the Attribute Value.

The keyword specification is optional in the BNF, but mandatory for this specification. This is so that the same BNF may be used for the related specification on User Friendly Naming [5]. When this specification is followed, the attribute type keywords must always be present.

A list of valid keywords for well-known attribute types used in naming is given in Table 1. Keywords may contain spaces, but shall not have leading or trailing spaces. This is a list of keywords that must be supported. These are chosen because they appear in common forms of name, and can do so in a place that does not correspond to the default schema used. A register of valid keywords is maintained by the IANA.

```
<name> ::= <name-component> ( <spaced-separator> )
        | <name-component> <spaced-separator> <name>

  <spaced-separator> ::= <optional-space>
                    <separator>
                    <optional-space>

  <separator> ::=  ","  |  ";"

  <optional-space> ::= ( <CR> ) *( " " )

  <name-component> ::= <attribute>
        | <attribute> <optional-space> "+"
          <optional-space> <name-component>

  <attribute> ::= <string>
        | <key> <optional-space> "=" <optional-space> <string>

  <key> ::= 1*( <keychar> ) | "OID." <oid> | "oid." <oid>
  <keychar> ::= letters, numbers, and space

  <oid> ::= <digitstring> | <digitstring> "." <oid>
  <digitstring> ::= 1*<digit>
  <digit> ::= digits 0-9

  <string> ::= *( <stringchar> | <pair> )
        | '"' *( <stringchar> | <special> | <pair> ) '"'
        | "#" <hex>


  <special> ::= "," | "=" | <CR> | "+" | "<" |  ">"
          | "#" | ";"

  <pair> ::= "\" ( <special> | "\" | '"')
  <stringchar> ::= any character except <special> or "\" or '"'


  <hex> ::= 2*<hexchar>
  <hexchar> ::= 0-9, a-f, A-F
```

Table E.1

Standardized Keywords	
Key	Attribute (X.520 keys)
CN	CommonName
L	LocalityName
ST	StateOrProvinceName
O	OrganizationName
OU	OrganizationalUnitName
C	CountryName
STREET	StreetAddress

Only string type attributes are considered, but other attribute syntaxes could be supported locally (for example, by use of the syntaxes defined in [3].) It is assumed that the interface will translate from the supplied string into an appropriate Directory String encoding. The "+" notation is used to specify multi-component RDNs. In this case, the types for attributes in the RDN must be explicit.

The name is presented/input in a little-endian order (most significant component last). When an address is written in a context where there is a need to delimit the entire address (for example, in free text), it is recommended that the delimiters <> are used. The terminator > is a special in the notation to facilitate this delimitation.

3. Examples

This section gives a few examples of distinguished names written using this notation:

```
CN=Marshall T. Rose, O=Dover Beach Consulting, L=Santa Clara,
➥ST=California, C=US

CN=FTAM Service, CN=Bells, OU=Computer Science, O=University College
➥London, C=GB
```

```
CN=Markus Kuhn, O=University of Erlangen, C=DE

CN=Steve Kille, O=ISODE Consortium, C=GB

CN=Steve Kille, O = ISODE Consortium, C=GB

CN=Steve Kille, O=ISODE Consortium, C=GB
```

4. Acknowledgments

This work was based on research work done at University College London [4], and evolved by the IETF OSI-DS WG. Input for this version of the document was received from: Allan Cargille (University of Wisconsin); John Dale (COS); Philip Gladstone (Onsett); John Hawthorne (US Air Force); Roland Hedberg (University of Umea); Kipp Hickman (Mosaic Communications Corp.); Markus Kuhn (University of Erlangen); Elisabeth Roudier (E3X); Mark Wahl (ISODE Consortium).

5. References

[1] The Directory—overview of concepts, models and services, 1993. CCITT X.500 Series Recommendations.

[2] Crocker, D., "Standard of the Format of ARPA-Internet Text Messages," STD 11, RFC 822, University of Delaware, August 1982.

[3] Yeong, W., Howes, T., and S. Kille, "Lightweight Directory Access Protocol," RFC 1777, Performance Systems International, University of Michigan, ISODE Consortium, March 1995.

[4] S.E. Kille. Using the OSI directory to achieve user-friendly naming. Research Note RN/20/29, Department of Computer Science, University College London, February 1990.

[5] Kille, S., "Using the OSI Directory to Achieve User Friendly Naming," RFC 1781, ISODE Consortium, March 1995.

6. Security Considerations

Security issues are not discussed in this memo.

7. Author's Address

Steve Kille
ISODE Consortium
The Dome
The Square
Richmond, Surrey
TW9 1DT
England

Phone: +44-181-332-9091
E-mail: S.Kille@ISODE.COM

DN: CN=Steve Kille, O=ISODE Consortium, C=GB

UFN: S. Kille, ISODE Consortium, GB

An LDAP URL Format

Network Working Group   T. Howes
Request for Comments: 1959   M. Smith
Category: Standards Track   University of Michigan
June 1996

Status of This Memo

This document specifies an Internet standards track protocol for the Internet community, and requests discussion and suggestions for improvements. Please refer to the current edition of the "Internet Official Protocol Standards" (STD 1) for the standardization state and status of this protocol. Distribution of this memo is unlimited.

1.   Abstract

LDAP is the Lightweight Directory Access Protocol, defined in [1] and [2]. This document describes a format for an LDAP Uniform Resource Locator that will allow Internet clients to have direct access to the LDAP protocol. While LDAP currently is used only as a front end to the X.500 directory, the URL format described here is general enough to handle the case of stand-alone LDAP servers (that is, LDAP servers not back-ended by X.500).

2. URL Definition

An LDAP URL begins with the protocol prefix "ldap" and is defined by the following grammar.

```
<ldapurl> ::= "ldap://" [ <hostport> ] "/" <dn> [ "?" <at
➥tributes>
                       [ "?" <scope> "?" <filter> ] ]
<hostport> ::= <hostname> [ ":" <portnumber> ]
<dn> ::= a string as defined in RFC 1485
<attributes> ::= NULL | <attributelist>
<attributelist> ::= <attributetype>
                       | <attributetype> [ "," <attributelist> ]
<attributetype> ::= a string as defined in RFC 1777
<scope> ::= "base" | "one" | "sub"
<filter> ::= a string as defined in RFC 1558
```

The ldap prefix indicates an entry or entries residing in the LDAP server running on the given <hostname> at the given <portnumber>. The default port is TCP port 389. The <dn> is an LDAP Distinguished Name using the string format described in [1], with any URL-illegal characters (for example, spaces) escaped using the % method described in RFC 1738.

The <attributes> construct is used to indicate which attributes should be returned from the entry or entries. Individual <attributetype> names are as defined for AttributeType in RFC 1777. If the <attributes> part is omitted, all attributes of the entry or entries should be returned.

The <scope> construct is used to specify the scope of the search to perform in the given LDAP server. The allowable scopes are "base" for a base object search, "one" for a one-level search, or "sub" for a subtree search. If <scope> is omitted, a scope of "base" is assumed.

The <filter> is used to specify the search filter to apply to entries within the specified scope during the search. It has the format specified in [4], with any URL-illegal characters escaped using the % method described in RFC 1738. If <filter> is omitted, a filter of "(objectClass=*)" is assumed.

Note that if the entry resides in the X.500 namespace, it should be reachable from any LDAP server that is providing front-end access to the X.500 directory. If the <hostport> part of the URL is missing, the URL can be resolved by contacting any X.500-back-ended LDAP server.

3. Examples

The following are some example LDAP URLs using the format defined previously. An LDAP URL referring to the University of Michigan entry, available from any X.500-capable LDAP server:

```
ldap:///o=University%20of%20Michigan,c=US
```

An LDAP URL referring to the University of Michigan entry in a particular LDAP server:

```
ldap://ldap.itd.umich.edu/o=University%20of%20Michigan,c=US
```

This URL corresponds to a base object search of the "o=University of Michigan, c=US" entry using a filter of (objectclass=*), requesting all attributes.

An LDAP URL referring to only the postalAddress attribute of the University of Michigan entry:

```
ldap://ldap.itd.umich.edu/o=University%20of%20Michigan,c=US?
postalAddress
```

The corresponding LDAP search operation is the same as in the previous example, except that only the postalAddress attribute is requested.

An LDAP URL referring to the set of entries found by querying any X.500-capable LDAP server and doing a subtree search of the University of Michigan for any entry with a common name of "Babs Jensen," retrieving all attributes:

```
ldap:///o=University%20of%20Michigan,c=US??sub?(cn=Babs%20Jensen)
```

An LDAP URL referring to all children of the c=GB entry:

```
ldap://ldap.itd.umich.edu/c=GB?objectClass?one
```

The objectClass attribute is requested to be returned along with the entries.

4. Security Considerations

The LDAP URL format does not provide a way to specify credentials to use when resolving the URL. Therefore, it is expected that such requests will be unauthenticated. The security implications of resolving an LDAP URL are the same as those of resolving any LDAP query. See the RFC 1777 for more details.

5. Prototype Implementation Availability

There is a prototype implementation of the specification defined in this document available. It is an extension to the libwww client library, provided in both source and binary forms. Also included are binary versions of the Mosaic WWW client for various platforms. See the following URL for more details:

```
ftp://terminator.rs.itd.umich.edu/ldap/url/
```

6. Bibliography

[1] Kille, S., "A String Representation of Distinguished Names," RFC 1779, March 1995.

[2] Yeong, W., Howes, T., and S. Kille, "Lightweight Directory Access Protocol," RFC 1777, March 1995.

[3] Howes, R., Kille, S., Yeong, W., and C. Robbins, "The String Representation of Standard Attribute Syntaxes," RFC 1778, March 1995.

[4] Howes, T., "A String Representation of LDAP Search Filters," RFC 1558, December 1993.

[5] Berners-Lee, T., Masinter, L., and M. McCahill, "Uniform Resource Locators (URL)," RFC 1738, December 1994.

7.   Acknowledgments

This material is based upon work supported by the National Science Foundation under Grant No. NCR-9416667.

8.   Authors' Addresses

Tim Howes
University of Michigan
ITD Research Systems
535 W William St.
Ann Arbor, MI 48103-4943
USA

Phone: +1 313 747-4454
E-mail: tim@umich.edu

Mark Smith
University of Michigan
ITD Research Systems
535 W William St.
Ann Arbor, MI 48103-4943
USA

Phone: +1 313 764-2277
E-mail: mcs@umich.edu

A String Representation of LDAP Search Filters

Network Working Group   T. Howes

Request for Comments: 1960
University of Michigan
Obsoletes: 1558
June 1996

Category: Standards Track

Status of This Memo

This document specifies an Internet standards track protocol for the Internet community, and requests discussion and suggestions for improvements. Please refer to the current edition of the "Internet Official Protocol Standards" (STD 1) for the standardization state and status of this protocol. Distribution of this memo is unlimited.

1.   Abstract

The Lightweight Directory Access Protocol (LDAP) [1] defines a network representation of a search filter transmitted to an LDAP server. Some applications may find it useful to have a common way of representing these search filters in a human-readable form. This document defines a human-readable string format for representing LDAP search filters.

2.   LDAP Search Filter Definition

An LDAP search filter is defined in [1] as follows:

```
Filter ::= CHOICE {
        and                 [0] SET OF Filter,
        or                  [1] SET OF Filter,
        not                 [2] Filter,
        equalityMatch       [3] AttributeValueAssertion,
        substrings          [4] SubstringFilter,
        greaterOrEqual      [5] AttributeValueAssertion,
        lessOrEqual         [6] AttributeValueAssertion,
        present             [7] AttributeType,
        approxMatch         [8] AttributeValueAssertion
}

SubstringFilter ::= SEQUENCE {
        type    AttributeType,
        SEQUENCE OF CHOICE {
                initial     [0] LDAPString,
                any         [1] LDAPString,
                final       [2] LDAPString
        }
}
AttributeValueAssertion ::= SEQUENCE {
        attributeType   AttributeType,
        attributeValue  AttributeValue
}

AttributeType ::= LDAPString

AttributeValue ::= OCTET STRING

LDAPString ::= OCTET STRING
```

where the preceding LDAPString is limited to the IA5 character set. The AttributeType is a string representation of the attribute type name and is defined in [1]. The AttributeValue OCTET STRING has the form defined in [2]. The Filter is encoded for transmission over a network using the Basic Encoding Rules defined in [3], with simplifications described in [1].

3.   String Search Filter Definition

The string representation of an LDAP search filter is defined by the following grammar. It uses a prefix format.

```
<filter> ::= '(' <filtercomp> ')'
<filtercomp> ::= <and> | <or> | <not> | <item>
<and> ::= '&' <filterlist>
<or> ::= '|' <filterlist>
<not> ::= '!' <filter>
<filterlist> ::= <filter> | <filter> <filterlist>
<item> ::= <simple> | <present> | <substring>
<simple> ::= <attr> <filtertype> <value>
<filtertype> ::= <equal> | <approx> | <greater> | <less>
<equal> ::= '='
<approx> ::= '~='
<greater> ::= '>='
<less> ::= '<='
<present> ::= <attr> '=*'
<substring> ::= <attr> '=' <initial> <any> <final>
<initial> ::= NULL | <value>
<any> ::= '*' <starval>
<starval> ::= NULL | <value> '*' <starval>
<final> ::= NULL | <value>
```

<attr> is a string representing an AttributeType, and has the format defined in [1]. <value> is a string representing an AttributeValue, or part of one, and has the form defined in [2]. If a <value> must contain one of the characters '*' or '(' or ')', these characters should be escaped by preceding them with the backslash '\' character.

Note that although both the <substring> and <present> productions can produce the 'attr=*' construct, this construct is used only to denote a presence filter.

4.   Examples

This section gives a few examples of search filters written using this notation.

```
(cn=Babs Jensen)
(!(cn=Tim Howes))
(&(objectClass=Person)(|(sn=Jensen)(cn=Babs J*)))
(o=univ*of*mich*)
```

5. Security Considerations

Security considerations are not discussed in this memo.

6. Bibliography

[1] Yeong, W., Howes, T., and S. Kille, "Lightweight Directory Access Protocol," RFC 1777, March 1995.

[2] Howes, R., Kille, S., Yeong, W., and C. Robbins, "The String Representation of Standard Attribute Syntaxes," RFC 1778, March 1995.

[3] Specification of Basic Encoding Rules for Abstract Syntax Notation One (ASN.1). CCITT Recommendation X.209, 1988.

7. Author's Address

Tim Howes
University of Michigan
ITD Research Systems
535 W William St.
Ann Arbor, MI 48103-4943
USA

Phone: +1 313 747-4454
E-mail: tim@umich.edu

Index

MACMILLAN COMPUTER PUBLISHING USA

A V I A C O M   C O M P A N Y

Technical

Support:

If you need assistance with the information in this book,
please access the Knowledge Base on our Web site at
http://www.superlibrary.com/general/support. Our most
Frequently Asked Questions are answered there. If you do not
find the answer to your questions on our Web site, you may
contact Macmillan Technical Support **(317) 581-3833** or e-mail
us at **support@mcp.com**.